THE
Jacksonian Promise

The American Moment

Stanley I. Kutler
SERIES EDITOR

THE
Jacksonian Promise

AMERICA, 1815–1840

DANIEL FELLER

The Johns Hopkins University Press

BALTIMORE AND LONDON

© 1995 The Johns Hopkins University Press
All rights reserved. Published 1995
Printed in the United States of America on acid-free paper
04 03 02 01 00 99 98 97 96 95   5 4 3 2 1

The Johns Hopkins University Press
2715 North Charles Street
Baltimore, Maryland 21218-4319
The Johns Hopkins Press Ltd., London

ISBN 0-8018-5167-X
ISBN 0-8018-5168-8 (pbk)

Library of Congress Cataloging-in-Publication Data and a list of books in the
American Moment series will be found at the end of this book.
A catalog record for this book is available from
the British Library.

for Claudia
the better angel of my nature

Contents

	Series Editor's Foreword	ix
	Preface	xi
One	The Year of Jubilee	1
Two	The Spirit of Improvement	14
Three	The Law of Enterprise	33
Four	The Statecraft of Progress	53
Five	The Realm of Reason	76
Six	The Kingdom of Christ	95
Seven	The Republic of Labor	118
Eight	The Elevation of Character	138
Nine	The Politics of Democracy	160
Ten	Descent into Discord	185
	Bibliographical Essay	205
	Index	219

Series Editor's Foreword

About forty years after American independence, significant change occurred in America. At one time, historians labeled it "the era of the common man," and we celebrated a purported democratization of mind, manners, and morals. We then focused on political developments, including the growth of parties and mass participation in the political process. We also spoke of popular leadership and the notion of the leader as tribune, whether as president of the nation or as governor of a state. Later, we described the period as a powerful expression of "republicanism," one marked by a deep-rooted anxiety for the safety and survival of the nation. Still later, we discovered a market revolution and the commercialization of just about everything in American life. The notion of the self-sufficient yeoman farmer vanished into legend and the United States emerged into a market-oriented, totally capitalistic society. With that, of course, came the inevitable stress on the darker legacy of slavery, racism, commercialism, and the destruction of community. All these ideas have some validity and are useful for explaining the phenomenon we always have called "Jacksonianism."

Daniel Feller is acutely aware of these conflicting and complementary views. From them, he has ventured a strikingly fresh synthesis of the period beginning with the end of the War of 1812—a second war for independence—and 1840—a moment when the centrifugal forces long tearing at the nation's fabric began to spin out of control. As he notes, it now is fashionable to see the Age of Jackson as the beginnings of what went wrong in America, an attempt often laced with pessimism over the present state of American society.

Feller wisely avoids such a presentist trap. Instead, he has immersed himself in what members of Jacksonian society themselves thought about new and different circumstances, and how these might affect their lives in the future. They recognized, as Feller notes, "an onrush of concrete, novel, exciting (and sometimes perturbing) events." Above all, they had almost a limitless faith in their ability to shape their future, and not be captive to some anonymous, inexorable forces. Accordingly, innovation and experimentation marked the period as Americans developed their factory system, expanded their transportation infrastructure with canals and the new railroads, and pursued a program of social improvement that included the prohibition of alcohol, religious "revivals," and common schools.

The belief in the promise of America was the "Jacksonian promise," as well. Despite a constant assault of pessimism and despair, that optimism—that faith in the "American dream"—pervaded society. While the Jacksonian period ended amid a growing sense of sectional conflict and division, the Jacksonian optimism, notions of progress, and above all, an unbounded belief in individual and societal capacities, offer perhaps the most revealing and enduring legacy of all.

STANLEY I. KUTLER
THE UNIVERSITY OF WISCONSIN

Preface

In this book I undertake to offer a fresh look at American life from 1815 to 1840. Americans in these years, I will argue, believed themselves uniquely blessed by providence and destined for some special purpose. Yet they disagreed over what that purpose was and how to achieve it. Their disagreements gave rise to thriving debate about how to organize their future. Competing visions of a better society spurred citizens to articulate new ideas, organize new institutions, and pursue new goals. In arenas of law and politics, business and labor, social and racial relations, religion and reform, and school and family, Americans contended over what the United States stood for and where it should go.

To the reader of history the Age of Jackson presents the curious spectacle of an era in search of a theme. Jacksonian historians see this period as the seedbed of modern America. In these years, they say, appeared the distinctive features that have marked our society ever since.

But scholarly concord ends there. As ideas of what constitutes modern America have shifted over time, historians' themes have shifted as well. Some writers traced the western influence in Jacksonian culture and politics. Others spied the rise of democracy and the "common man," or the first flowering of a lasting penchant for experiment and reform. Still others saw the formative stage in an ongoing class struggle between progressive labor and conservative business.

Despite their disagreements, most of these historians celebrated the Age of Jackson as the birth of something good. Today's investigators paint in darker shades. They point to the entrenchment of inequality, the sundering of old ties of community and tradition, and the depredation of minorities as the era's most salient and ominous developments. Even environmental destruction gets worked in. One new study ends with Jacksonian America's sorry legacy of "ravaged land." *

Andrew Jackson himself is no help in untangling this jungle of perspectives. Everyone sees him as the era's central figure. No one agrees why. Jackson is nearly unique in having a period of American history named for him. Yet historians who concur on his importance still fight over what he means. Compared to such icons as George Washington or Abraham Lincoln or Franklin Roosevelt, Jackson provides his age with a fractured, prismatic unity. His discordant images point off in different directions instead of toward a clarifying center.

Historians argue whether Andrew Jackson championed or challenged the major trends of his day. He has been cast as liberal and conservative, reformist and reactionary, the representative of modernizing entrepreneurs and of tradition-clinging agriculturists, the spokesman of plain pioneers and opulent planters and factory wage-hands. Historians invoke Jackson to symbolize class conflict and classlessness, equality and inequality, the depth of American political contention and its essential emptiness, the rise of the common man and the repression of women, Indians, and blacks. A myriad of seeming contradictions, Jackson offers enough puzzles and paradoxes to keep the wheels of controversy forever turning.

Though dispute still rages around Jackson, recently something of a consensus has formed concerning his era. Historians have found a common theme, or at least a common tone. They describe Jacksonian Americans as steeped in foreboding over their future. Where historians once traced moods of confidence and exuberance, today's scholarship uncovers uncertainty and insecurity. Rereading Jacksonian discourse, historians no longer see citizens fired by faith in the progress of liberty and equality. Instead they see them enmeshed in fears of conspiracy and corruption. It now appears that Jacksonian Americans did more worrying than glorying over their experiment in self-government.

Going further, some historians link fears about the fate of the republic to deepening anxieties over social and economic change. The latest Jacksonian scholarship groups innovations in transportation, manufacturing, business methods, and work discipline together under the rubric of the "market revolution." Its effect upon the citizens appears to have been mainly negative. Changes that we once believed had brightened Ameri-

---

* Quotations in this preface come from Charles Sellers, *The Market Revolution* (1991), a brilliant synthesis and epitome of recent Jacksonian scholarship.

cans' outlook and broadened their choices now seem to have sown only destruction and disorientation.

The picture that emerges from this re-evaluation of Jacksonian Americans is revealing—as revealing, perhaps, of our time as of theirs. The era still seems the seedbed of modern America, but in a new way—as the point at which things went decisively wrong. Where historians once spied the flowering of America's promise, they now see the start of its descent. Calamity looms everywhere: in the ejection of the Indians, the subordination of women, the harnessing of proud farmers and tradespeople to a distant and faceless market. The quality of life deteriorates as its tempo accelerates. Rootlessness and dependency spread. Simplicity drowns in complexity; family, fraternity, and community unravel. The 1820s, when these trends supposedly gathered irreversible force, become the "gloomy twenties," a "dismal decade."

Gloomy and dismal things happened in the 1820s, as in all decades. The Jacksonian years, like any others, produced hardship and heartbreak, and left unrighted wrongs and postponed reckonings. But none of this justifies intruding our own doubts and despairs upon a people who could not even imagine, much less share, them. Recent historians replace naive celebrations of national "progress" with a superficially sophisticated but equally narrow pessimism over all it produced. Perhaps circumstances today warrant pessimism. But reading the past in light of our disappointment with the present does not help us to understand Americans of a century and a half ago.

This book aims for a different approach. I am less interested in judging the consequences of Jacksonian events than in comprehending their causes. Those causes lay partly in external circumstance, yet also, even especially, in the purposes and expectations of Americans themselves. For in this era, perhaps more than at any other time in our history, citizens believed in their ability to mold and direct their own destiny and that of the world.

In pursuing this thesis I offer a treatment of Jacksonian America that is thematic rather than comprehensive. I have focused more on ideas and actions than on conditions and structures, and more on what was new and distinctive than old and familiar. I am less concerned with describing the routine of people's lives than with apprehending their ideas about the future. If I am correct in my understanding of them, this emphasis mirrors their own.

In short, I have tried to tell the story in terms that the people who lived it would have understood. To further that purpose, I make no reference in the text to historians or historiography. I also avoid some common generalizing terms, including *industrialization, modernization, capitalism,* and *market revolution.* None of these phrases were then in use. Nor could they have been, for they imply a mechanistic inevitability and a knowledge of consequences yet unknown. Only in hindsight, and through the light of theoretical schemes developed years later, does the opening of the Lowell mills or the building of the Erie Canal mark a stage in something called industrialization or modernization or the emergence of capitalism.

Among other hazards, tendentious history invites muddling chronology and dragging things in before their time. Accounts of broad historical processes commonly encompass half a century and more. Because of this, and perhaps also because of the absence of obvious breakpoints within the era, Jacksonian scholars are often unusually careless with chronology and hence with causality. Studies of social, cultural, and political movements rove freely in search of motives and causes, drawing evidence from late in the period to explain things that happened years before. Only a presumption of stasis can justify such technique. Yet the United States in these decades was arguably changing as fast as at any time in its history. America in 1840 was vastly different from what it had been twenty years earlier.

To understand Jacksonian Americans, we must put aside our knowledge of how their story turned out, along with the conceptual crutches we lean on to organize that knowledge. We must try to see the age as they saw it, with fresh, unjaded eyes. Americans of the Jacksonian era felt change everywhere, in every part of their lives. What they perceived, however, was not an inexorable process grinding toward a fixed result, but an onrush of concrete, novel, exciting (and sometimes perturbing) events. How those events would cohere, and what they would lead to in the end, no one knew. But one thing everyone assumed: human energies, not mere abstract forces, were at work. Americans understood history as something wrought by human hands. That understanding gave them faith in their capacity to shape themselves, their society, and their world. They may have been wrong. But that was what they believed, and to slight that conviction is to render them, their actions, and their era inexplicable.

I owe thanks to Stanley Kutler and Henry Tom for offering this opportunity; to Howard Rabinowitz, Johanna Shields, and especially Lawrence Kohl for their close reading and frank criticism of the manuscript; and to those colleagues in the Society for Historians of the Early American Republic (SHEAR) who have endured my monologues on Jacksonian America. My deepest debt, as always, is to Dick Sewell.

THE
Jacksonian Promise

The Year of Jubilee

And ye shall hallow the fiftieth year, and proclaim liberty
throughout all the land unto all the inhabitants thereof.
—Leviticus 25:10

In 1826 the United States of America marked its fiftieth year of independence. For citizens across the country it was an occasion to rejoice but also to reflect, to look forward as well as back, to assess where the country had been and where it might be going.

A Visitor

The anniversary commemoration began nearly two years early. On August 15, 1824, the ship *Cadmus* from France anchored off New York. The Marquis de Lafayette, hero of the Revolution and now its only surviving general, was returning to America as the guest of the United States Congress and President James Monroe. Arriving on a Sunday, Lafayette tarried on Staten Island with Vice President Daniel Tompkins while a welcome was prepared. The next day he was escorted across the bay by a steamboat flotilla and stepped ashore in New York City to the cheers of fifty thousand ecstatic citizens. Greeters included dignitaries, aged comrades-in-arms, and "six or seven hundred American youths, the future conservators of his fame," with whom the general shook hands. At a loss to describe the affecting scene, news reports could give only "a faint outline of the proceedings of a day which shines proudly in the annals of our country—proceedings which were more brilliant than any that have ever been witnessed in America, and which will rarely, if ever, be equalled."

This was only the beginning. After four days of honor and ceremony in New York, "the Nation's Guest" proceeded to Boston. There he toured old battle sites, attended commencement at Harvard College, and visited with former president John Adams, now old and feeble. Then it was back to New York for a gala at Castle Garden, of which the *New York Evening Post* boasted, "we hazard nothing in saying it was the most magnificent fete under cover in the world, . . . a festival that realizes all that we read of in the Persian tales or Arabian Nights, which dazzled the eye and bewildered the imagination."

After a trip up the Hudson to Albany, Lafayette departed southward for Philadelphia, Baltimore, and Washington. A companion called his reception on "the happy shores of freedom" the "greatest spectacle the world ever saw." Bonfires and artillery salutes hailed his passage. Town after town embraced the aged hero with cheering crowds, mounted escorts, torchlight parades, musical performances, militia reviews, veterans' reunions, Masonic receptions, ceremonial banquets, and illuminations. In Philadelphia the welcoming procession included two brigades of infantry, companies of cavalry and artillery, and two thousand tradesmen—cordwainers, weavers, ropemakers, shipbuilders, coopers, butchers, cartmen, and mechanics of all sorts. The cavalcade entered the city under a huge arch designed to evoke the glory and splendor of ancient Rome.

Continuing into Virginia, Lafayette stopped at Mount Vernon to pay his respects at George Washington's tomb, and at Yorktown to commemorate the Revolution's final victory. He stayed ten days with former president Thomas Jefferson at Monticello and four more with Jefferson's neighbor and successor, James Madison. Back in Washington for the winter, Congress gave Lafayette a formal reception, then honored him with an unprecedented gift of $200,000 and a township (36 square miles, or 23,040 acres) of wilderness land in Florida Territory.

In February 1825 Lafayette and his entourage left the capital to tour through the Carolinas, Georgia, and Alabama to New Orleans, then up the Mississippi to St. Louis. In Nashville he lunched with another warrior legend, General Andrew Jackson, hero of the Battle of New Orleans in the War of 1812. In Lexington Lafayette stopped at the home of Speaker of the House of Representatives Henry Clay. Passing quickly through Cincinnati and Pittsburgh, and across New York state on part of the new Erie Canal, Lafayette reached Boston on June 15.

Two days later, on the fiftieth anniversary of the battle of Bunker Hill, Lafayette laid the cornerstone of a monument on the field. Witnesses called the ceremony "unequalled in magnificence by any thing of the kind that had been seen in New England." A procession seven thousand strong composed of dignitaries, troops, Revolutionary veterans, the Masonic fraternity in full regalia, and a host of societies bearing badges and banners marched to the site, followed by masses of onlookers. Daniel Webster, Massachusetts congressman and president of the Bunker Hill Monument Association, gave the oration. Addressing a crowd estimated at forty thousand, "as great a multitude as was ever perhaps assembled within the sound of a human voice," Webster hailed the American Revolution as "that prodigy of modern times, at once the wonder and the blessing of the world," whose example pointed the way to "human freedom and human happiness."

After Bunker Hill Lafayette again circled New England, spent Independence Day in New York, and finally returned to Washington, where he stayed with the new president, John Quincy Adams. In September 1825, after a great state dinner and an emotional farewell, he boarded the new American frigate *Brandywine* (named for a Revolutionary battle where he took a slight wound) and sailed for home.

The Jubilee Celebration

Ceremonies of American nationality climaxed on July 4, 1826, fiftieth anniversary of the Declaration of Independence. On that Day of Jubilee, citizens drank toasts and heard speeches and fired salutes throughout the land. And on the same day, John Adams and Thomas Jefferson, founding fathers whose lives and legacies had shaped the country's history for half a century, died quietly at their respective homes in Massachusetts and Virginia.

Americans took their deaths as good news. In patriotic eyes the passing of independence's twin apostles on the Declaration's anniversary day was an auspicious omen, not a fearsome one. John Quincy Adams, son of the late John and now himself president of the United States, thought the strange coincidence a "visible and palpable" sign of divine favor. In a eulogy at Faneuil Hall in Boston Daniel Webster explained. The loss of such illustrious statesmen, severing nearly the last link to Revolutionary memory, would have left "an immense void" at any other time. Yet this day made the deaths providential. The old men's work was done. The half-century point marked a fitting moment to pass the torch to the next generation. From here on, the legacy of liberty was "ours to enjoy, ours to preserve, ours to transmit." On the day after Jubilee the Revolution's children were left to find their own glory in the future.

Americans in 1826 saw themselves standing between a receding heroic past and a wonderful future just beginning to unfold. The effusive welcome for Lafayette that ushered in the Jubilee renewed their reverence for the Revolution. His return to old battlefields and reunion with old comrades brought the country's fabled origins alive, made them seem real and immediate. The novelist James Fenimore Cooper, one of the welcoming committee at Lafayette's first arrival in New York, remarked that to most of those present,

his form must have worn the air of some image drawn from the pages of history. Half a century had carried nearly all of his contemporary actors of the Revolution into the great abyss of time, and he now stood, like an imposing column that had been reared to commemorate deeds and principles that a whole people had been taught to reverence.

Lafayette's tour reminded Americans who had grown up since independence how young the country really was. Every president was still alive in 1825 to greet him save one, and that one was represented in the person of his namesake, Lafayette's son and traveling companion George Washington Lafayette.

Beginning with Lafayette's tour, the festival of Jubilee wore on for nearly two years. Still the revelers never grew tired. Americans could not stop cheering the Revolution, for their gratitude for its accomplishment knew no end. Yet their patriotic celebrations looked forward as well as back. Welcoming Lafayette to the House of Representatives in Washington, Speaker Henry Clay invited him to contemplate the changes *since* independence— "the forests felled, the cities built, the mountains leveled, the canals cut, the highways constructed, the progress of the arts, the advancement of learning, and the increase of population." At Bunker Hill Webster projected progress into the future: "Let our age be the age of improvement. . . . Let us develop the resources of our land, call forth its powers, build up its institutions, promote all its great interests, and see whether we also, in our day and generation, may not perform something to be remembered." Gracing the table at a New York banquet for Lafayette was a seventy-five-foot replica of the state's mammoth Erie Canal, now nearly completed after eight years of building, and already hailed as the engineering marvel of the world.

This was the true, and wholly deliberate, meaning of the Jubilee. It offered a chance not only to revel in old glories but to hail the greater glory of an unbounded future. In Americans' eyes the greatness of the Revolution was not only in what it had done, but in what it would enable them to do. It had freed them to pursue a destiny brighter than any in history. The next age of humanity, Webster predicted in his eulogy to Adams and Jefferson, would be "distinguished by free representative governments, by entire religious liberty, by improved systems of national intercourse, by a newly awakened and an unconquerable spirit of free inquiry, and by a diffusion of knowledge through the community, such as has been before altogether unknown and unheard of." In all of these, Americans would lead. "In America," said Webster, "a new era commences in human affairs."

Lafayette's pilgrimage across the country marked the nation's advance even as it hallowed its history. At every town his hosts displayed items of local manufacture, proof of American ingenuity and skill. Lafayette saw landmarks of civic and cultural progress—colleges, academies, museums, Masonic temples, theaters, statehouses, city halls, waterworks, asylums, hospitals, deaf and dumb schools, almshouses, orphanages, penitentiaries, historical and philosophical and literary and agricultural societies— all sprung up since he had left the country forty years before. At Troy, New York, a town "arisen as if by enchantment" during the years of Lafayette's absence, the students of Emma Hart Willard's Female Seminary, America's first higher school for girls, serenaded him. Traveling by the new modes of canal and steamboat, Lafayette criss-crossed the country with an ease and speed unthinkable a few years before. He even experienced that characteristic American mishap, a steamboat wreck. Touching all twenty-four states, Lafayette saw every place from Cincinnati, so new and impressive he thought it "the eighth wonder of the world," to a Carolina backwoods clearing, which he was told would soon be a thriving town. In solemn ritual he laid the foundations for a new generation of public works—the Bunker Hill monument in Boston, a college in Vermont, a library in Brooklyn.

The adulation that Americans showered on Lafayette mirrored their excitement over their own achievements and prospects. As they praised him, they praised themselves. From Carolina to New England, patriotic orators strained for superlatives to capture American greatness. Already, proclaimed Hugh Swinton Legaré in Charleston on Independence Day in 1823, Americans had "outstripped every competitor" in the "race of moral improvement" and carried human institutions to "a higher pitch of perfection than ever warmed the dreams of enthusiasm or the speculations of the theorist." Nothing could make

a nobler and more interesting subject of contemplation and discourse, than the causes which led to the foundation of this mighty empire—than the wonderful and almost incredible history of what it has since done and is already grown to—than the scene of unmingled prosperity and happiness that is opening and spreading all around us—than the prospect as dazzling as it is vast, that lies before us.

These sentiments were not fashioned just for civic occasions. They surfaced in conversation, letters, and literature, in private musings as well as public speeches. In his journal the young schoolteacher Ralph Waldo Emerson vented his contempt for "the ruinous & enslaved institutions" of Europe. The perpetuation of American government, thought Emerson, "will be matter of deep congratulation to the human race; for the Utopian dreams which visionaries have pursued and sages exploded, will find their beautiful theories rivalled & outdone by the reality, which it has pleased God to bestow upon United America." The United States began a new epoch in history. "For centuries back the progress of human affairs has appeared to indicate some better era; & finally when all events were prepared God has opened a new theatre for this ultimate trial."

Emerson believed "the free institutions which prevail here & here alone have attracted to this country the eyes of the world." Even the most cosmopolitan Americans concurred. After the Jubilee James Fenimore Cooper departed for Europe, where he stayed some time with his newfound friend Lafayette. Encouraged by the general, in 1828 he published *Notions of the Americans*. Disguised as a fictional traveler's narrative, *Notions* was an extended panegyric on American customs and institutions, designed to combat foreign misconceptions and prejudices. Like Emerson, Cooper celebrated America's promise even more than its past: "here, though the brief retrospect be so creditable it absolutely sinks into insignificance compared with the mighty future." Americans were already "the freest and the happiest, as they will shortly be, in my poor opinion, the wealthiest and most powerful nation of the globe, let other people like the prediction as they may."

Some Europeans did not, in truth, like it much. Curious travelers flocked to the United States in the 1820s, and many of them gagged at what one (Adam Hodgson) called "the inflated ideas and extravagant anticipations which many Americans indulge, when contemplating the future destinies of their infant country." Frances Trollope, an acerbic Englishwoman who arrived in 1827, found Americans' self-obsession repellent. Querying citizens of different states, she noticed

some points certainly on which they all agree—namely, that the American government is the best in the world. That America has produced the greatest men that ever existed. That all the nations of the earth look upon them with a mixture of wonder and envy and that in time they will all follow their great example and have a president. This, or something like it, I heard everywhere.

Unable to reconcile this nationalism with the fierce regional prejudice she also observed, Trollope gave up and confessed, "I do not understand the American people." Later observers and historians have echoed her puzzlement. Americans' patriotic pufferies seem so incessant and overblown that it is tempting to doubt their sincerity—to dismiss them as mere wind, or to probe beneath their surface for some deep-seated insecurity they must have been contrived to mask.

The truth is simpler. The exuberance was real. On their country's fiftieth birthday Americans saw themselves standing on the threshhold of a new and better world.

America As a New World

Since they first learned of its existence, Europeans had reposed dreams of a different future upon American soil. In their eyes it was a new world, where anything was possible. Here humanity could shed the errors and follies of the past and start over. Plans for English settlement in America featured novel forms of religious and social organization. Though colonists brought with them language and culture, none came merely to replicate the world they had left behind. Some emigrants dreamed of finding utopia, or of building a city on a hill. All, in one way or another, sought a better life.

The Revolution reinforced Americans' feeling of distinctiveness and recharged their sense of pioneering in the worldwide march of progress. It not only secured independence, but inaugurated a republican government like no other then on earth. By grounding political legitimacy in the expressed will of "the people," the Revolution also triggered a broad ideological assault on all forms of hierarchy and superiority. Strengthened by American society's lack of hereditary distinctions and orders, the principle of equal rights challenged exclusivity and privilege in politics, religion, and commerce. Every artificial distinction, every vestige of "aristocracy," came under attack.

Disdaining to hold society in place by rank and repression, Americans placed their faith in the beneficent workings of enlightened self-interest. In their thinking liberty became the key to individual achievement and social advance. Here, with a vast new field to work on, people might at last reach their true potential. Released from the shackles of old-world tyranny and oppression, free for the first time to pursue their own happiness, Americans could break through the historic limits on human aspiration to reach new, unlimited heights.

Equality and opportunity gave hope of transforming human nature. On his way to volunteer for Revolutionary service, the young Lafayette wrote his wife that "the welfare of America is intimately connected with the happiness of all mankind; she will become the respectable and safe asylum of virtue, integrity, tolerance, equality, and a peaceful liberty." Another Frenchman, J. Hector St. John de Crèvecoeur, observed in the American "a new man, who acts upon new principles; he must therefore entertain new ideas and form new opinions." In America Crèvecoeur saw none of the distinctions that doomed the masses everywhere to poverty and dependence. Here were no great lords, no monopoly of land or capital, "no aristocratical families, no courts, no kings, no bishops. . . . Here man is free as he ought to be." "New laws, a new mode of living, a new social system" regenerated the broken refugees of Europe. "Here they are become men."

Not republican government alone, nor individual liberty, nor the vastness of American resources, but the combination of all these blessings—a combination so stunning that everyone thought it providential—seemed to mark the United States for some special future. "We have it in our power to begin the world over again," announced Thomas Paine in *Common Sense* in 1776. "The birth-day of a new world is at hand." The Great Seal of the United States proclaimed a *novus ordo seclorum,* a "new order of the ages."

In some ways, experience after independence fulfilled this hope. Population and wealth increased as the new country added states and acquired territory. Still, the ordeal of nation-making in a hostile world tended to submerge dreams of transcendent destiny. For forty years after the Revolution the United States was wracked by spasms internal and external. Domestic controversy and foreign crisis cleaved the country's leaders into opposing Federalists and Republicans. Some came to despair of the republic's special mission and to question its survival. Republican Thomas Jefferson's election as president in 1800 marked, in defeated Federalists' eyes, the failure of America's experiment in popular government. But more Americans saw it as did Jefferson himself, as renewed proof of the people's virtue and the country's promise. "We can no longer say there is nothing new under the sun," exulted Jefferson. "For this whole chapter in the history of man is new. The great extent of our Republic is new. Its sparse habitation is new. The mighty wave of public opinion which has rolled over it is new."

By the 1820s the obstacles that stood between Americans and their dreams seemed at last to have been cleared. Napoleon was overthrown and the European world at peace. The United States had vindicated its rights and honor against Great Britain, survived without injury the War of 1812, and weathered the wrenching adjustment to a peacetime economy brought on by the depression of 1819. Party strife had precipitously, and people hoped permanently, collapsed. Foreign wars of revolution and conquest, domestic divisions of Federalist and Republican, the uncertainty and danger of a world in upheaval, all now seemed safely past.

Never since the Revolution had the future seemed so inviting. In 1823 *Niles' Weekly Register,* the great national news compendium, listed the circumstances that ensured Americans "the greatest possible sum of human happiness." They numbered fully eighteen, but could be summarized in three: an open continent with untapped resources; an "active, industrious, energetic, enterprising and ingenious" population; and of course a republican government, "the most free and liberal that ever existed." The potential that had captivated revolutionaries was now becoming real. New modes of transportation and manufacture promised a material abundance and an ease of communication hitherto unthinkable. The millions of western acres awaiting settlement, the admission of six new states to the Union between 1816 and 1821, and the acquisition of Florida and extension of American territory to the Pacific in 1819 all held promise of what Hezekiah Niles called "boundless prosperity and happiness."

The United States was beginning to act on the world stage as well. As Daniel Webster pointed out at Bunker Hill, the wave of revolutions in Latin America and the struggle for independence in Greece seemed to herald that remaking of the world in America's image foretold by patriots a half-century before. Americans were now secure enough in nationhood that they could debate whether to aid the cause of European republicanism by assistance or example. Closer to home, they could challenge the great powers directly. In his annual message of December 1823, President James Monroe warned off European nations from further colonization or conquest in the Americas. Lafayette, a lover of liberty everywhere, called this pronouncement "the best little bit of paper that God had ever permitted any man to give to the World."

Looking around, Americans saw themselves endowed with material and moral riches no people had ever enjoyed—the best government on earth, sustained by a virtuous and intelligent citizenry; an inexhaustible store of land and resources; and a population keen to develop them. Truly, it seemed, America had been blessed with illimitable prospects. What should Americans make of them?

Options and Choices

Even as they sang their Jubilee, citizens began to argue this question. The debate took many forms. In politics, it shattered the fragile nonpartisanship achieved under the administration of President James Monroe. In Washington over the winter of 1824–25, Lafayette witnessed the denouement of the closest presidential election since 1800. Andrew Jackson, hero of New Orleans, led the four-man field. But the House of Representatives spurned him and chose John Quincy Adams, runner-up in the popular and electoral vote. The election foreshadowed a new competitive politics that would offer, and require, real choices in personalities, policies, and philosophies. Adams, surveying American history and prospects in his inaugural address, found cause for "grateful exultation" at past success and "cheering hope" for domestic harmony in a world at peace. Yet his own disputed ascension to the presidency shattered that hope. When Adams announced a bold program of "moral, political, intellectual improvement" and challenged Congress to enact it, an opposition converged around Jackson.

Outside politics, other choices beckoned. "The spirit of improvement is abroad upon the earth," Adams proclaimed, and so most Americans believed. But their enthusiasm masked divergent, even contradictory, ideas of just what improvement meant. Some of the most urgent debate emerged around questions of economy, family, and religion.

In November 1824, just as Lafayette returned from Virginia to spend the winter in Washington, another distinguished foreigner arrived in town. Unlike some Britons, Robert Owen of New Lanark, Scotland, did not come to scoff at Americans' aspirations. He came because he shared them. He was on his way to Indiana to purchase a town site and inaugurate "a new system of society." On February 25, 1825, in an address in the Capitol building in Washington, Owen announced his mission. From his community of New Harmony he promised nothing less than an immediate revolution in human affairs, one that would substitute "universal charity, benevolence, and kindness" for "universal discord, confusion, and suffering." With one "mighty deed" he would work a change "greater than all the changes which have hitherto occured in the affairs of mankind." Defects in education, economy, and social relations would vanish. "Old things shall pass away, and all shall become new, and beautiful, and delightful, bringing unnumbered and unlimited blessings to every one."

This promise of instant utopia might seem a crackpot's dream. But Robert Owen was an industrialist and philanthropist of international renown, and people took him seriously. By the time he reached Washington, a core of the country's leading scientists and educators had already agreed to join his Indiana venture. The audience at Owen's Capitol address included President James Monroe, president-elect Adams, members of the cabinet, Supreme Court justices, senators, and congressmen. Many returned to hear another three-hour discourse two weeks later, among them John Quincy Adams, who on his third day as president of the United States did not lack for other pressing things to do.

Robert Owen commanded a close hearing because in the United States in 1825, his hope of "an immediate, and almost instantaneous, revolution in the minds and manners of the society" did not seem fantastic. Many Americans shared his faith in human perfectibility and his belief that here and now were the place and time to begin remaking the world. What in Europe might seem visionary zealotry struck Americans as highly plausible.

The particulars of Owen's scheme, once they emerged, were another matter. In Washington he divulged few specifics. But at New Harmony he unveiled the full scope of his reform notions. There, on the Jubilee day of American independence in 1826, Owen offered "A Declaration of Mental Independence" from the "TRINITY *of the most monstrous evils that could be combined to inflict mental and physical evil*" upon the whole human race —namely, "PRIVATE, OR INDIVIDUAL PROPERTY—ABSURD AND IRRATIONAL SYSTEMS OF RELIGION," and a repressive marriage relationship grounded on both.

Owen's plans entranced Frances Wright, a young Scotswoman on her second visit to the United States. Wright's first trip, five years previous, had inspired her to write *Views of Society and Manners in America*, an homage to this country where "man might awake to the full knowledge and full exercise of his powers." Wright's praise was so effusive that even Fenimore Cooper termed her book "nauseous flattery." But it recommended her to the philosopher Jeremy Bentham in England. He in turn introduced her to Lafayette in France. On their first meeting Wright and Lafayette talked long into the night, and "the main subject of our discourse was America." They soon drew as close as father and daughter—or, rumor had it, as lovers. When Lafayette came to the United States in 1824, Wright followed. She was in the gallery with him when the House of Representatives made

John Quincy Adams president in February 1825. Later that month she attended the first of Robert Owen's Washington addresses. Owen's call fired Wright's own leaning toward radical social change. Soon she enlisted in his cause.

America's exhilirating potential inspired people like Owen and Wright to dream of reconstructing human relations along new and daring lines. Here, where society lay still unencrusted by age-old accumulations of tradition and authority, one could contemplate wiping out imbalances of wealth, remodeling sexual and familial relations, and throwing off the dead weight of Christian dogma.

But most Americans' dreams, while equally heady, ran in other directions. Attacks on private property, marriage, and religion—the very foundations of civil society—repelled far more citizens than they attracted. Equally committed to human improvement, defenders of these institutions saw them as vehicles, not obstacles. They sought to energize them, not destroy them.

Even as Robert Owen spoke, a thousand schemes of progress were forming. Entrepreneurs conceived a new world of abundance built on precisely the competitive and individualistic economic arrangements that Owen hoped to supplant. Teachers and thinkers enshrined the traditional family, with its separation of tasks for men and women, as the key to elevating human character. And Christian evangelists swept the country, reviving old faiths and planting new ones, offering religious routes to personal redemption and societal regeneration.

The Jubilee years thus witnessed an eruption of debate over the direction of American society. As the cordial welcome for Robert Owen showed, Americans were willing to hear and consider almost anything. Discussion flourished in a host of forums. Mill owners and artisans grappled over principles of economic organization and relations of capital and labor. Philanthropists and plain citizens hatched schemes of elevation and uplift. Systems of progress vied for the support of statesmen and voters, while creeds without number competed for converts.

Everywhere choices lay in the offing. At the Jubilee citizens reaffirmed their faith in America as a repository for humanity's fondest hopes. The chance still lay, as Paine had said in 1776, to "begin the world over again." That sense of possibility inspired optimism and exuberance. It also imparted an earnest and even terrible urgency. Decision would produce losers as well as winners. It would secure some ends only by foreclosing others. And while nothing seemed beyond Americans' grasp, everyone sensed that this opportunity might not last. Options would not always remain so open. Wrong paths, once taken, might never be retraced. Chances missed might never be recalled. Americans saw themselves at a prophetic moment in history, with the fate of the country and even the world resting in their hands.

Americans at the Jubilee felt it in their power to determine their future. What choices they made, and what results followed, these pages will show.

The Spirit of Improvement

The March of Man! how slow his dull career
In Eastern Climes! how swift and splendid here!
Tis Freedom's force that works the wondrous odds
Freedom the friend of man, the bane of kings and gods.
        —Joel Barlow, c. 1800

In the predawn darkness of Independence Day, July 4, 1817, a group of men with digging tools assembled in the village of Utica, New York. Early-rising spectators gathered around them. As the sun rose, one of the men stepped forward and addressed the crowd, promising that "unborn millions" would benefit from the task about to begin. Then another man sank his shovel into the ground, "and the laborers, amidst the acclamations of the people and the discharges of artillery, commenced the mighty work." Construction of New York's grand waterway from the Hudson River to the Great Lakes, the Erie Canal, had begun.

In the early United States, transportation projects, known as "internal improvements," inspired a peculiar rapture among citizens who dreamed of national greatness. In 1815 the country's eight million people lay scattered along a thousand miles of seacoast from Maine to Georgia and inland across the Appalachians and up the Mississippi. Within this vast domain, communication was fitful and precarious. News traveled slowly, passengers more slowly still, and freight often not at all, unless it was worth enough to bear the high cost of wagon haulage or could use a water route to avoid the rough and difficult roads.

Better transport would at once integrate the nation's economy, promote the exchange of goods and information, and throw open for development millions of acres of western land. With this stimulus, road and canal promoters expected the country's untapped agricultural and mineral resources to yield a material abundance beyond any ever imagined. They looked for political and social rewards as well. Swift communication would foster patriotism, promote literature and the arts, and inspire refinement in intellect and morals. A Virginia legislative committee in 1815 declared internal improvements "an important auxiliary, if not a necessary ingredient of political liberty" itself. "They tend to diffuse more equally the knowledge which experience acquires, and the leisure which wealth alone can purchase; they strengthen the cords of social union, and quicken [a] generous feeling of patriotism."

This promise of endless advance waited only to be set in motion. One early canal publicist foresaw in the western interior "a great republican community. . . . Yes, in this noble race of citizens, we see the cradle of liberty, laws, and the arts,—we see the hallowed light of our liberal institutions beaming in its native purity, blended with the mild lustre of virtue, magnanimity and intelligence." Gouverneur Morris of New York boasted in 1800 that "the proudest empire in Europe is but a bauble compared to what America *will* be, *must* be, in the course of two centuries, perhaps of one."

But before these dreams could be realized, some practical questions intervened. What kinds of improvements should be built, and where? Who would construct and operate them? Were such works feasible in a new country, short on capital, labor, and engineering skill? The Erie Canal provided some answers.

The Erie Canal

Even before the Revolution, the cleft in the Appalachian wall carved by the Mohawk and Hudson rivers in northern New York caught the eye of those eager to exploit the future trade of the great West. In 1724 Cadwallader Colden, surveyor of New York colony, noted the possibility of an inland water route to the Great Lakes. After the Revolution promoters spread the idea, and in 1792 the New York state legislature authorized a private company to begin work. Lacking funds, expertise, materials, and men, this venture built only a few miles of canal.

Canal enthusiasts, who included landowners and speculators, town promoters, New York City merchants, and politicians, turned to state and federal authorities for help. In 1808 Albert Gallatin, secretary of the Treasury under President Thomas Jefferson, included the New York project in his plan for a national transportation system. Gallatin envisioned several thousand miles of improvements: canals along the coast and around the falls of rivers, river-and-road routes across the mountains, a turnpike from Maine to Georgia. Gallatin reasoned that only the central government could afford such a program, and that "no other single operation, within the power of Government, can more effectually tend to strengthen and perpetuate that Union which secures external independence, domestic peace, and internal liberty." He reckoned the cost for the whole network at $20 million over ten years.

This estimate proved far too optimistic, but it hardly mattered. Congress was hindered by debt, distracted by foreign crisis, and deterred by the doubts of leading statesmen, including President Jefferson and his successor James Madison, about the legitimacy of federal spending on internal improvement. Gallatin's majestic report lay on the table.

New York forged ahead alone. The legislature sponsored a series of route surveys and then, after a hiatus during the War of 1812, authorized construction of the Erie in a grand Canal Law of April 1817. "It remains," said De Witt Clinton, chief canal promoter and soon to be governor of New York, "for a free state to create a new era in history, and to erect a work more stupendous, more magnificent, and more beneficial than has hitherto been achieved by the human race."

The simple opening ceremony at Utica three months later thus followed years of speculating, surveying, publicizing, and politicking. Still, for all its preparation, the Erie Canal was an audacious undertaking. Its projected length of 353 miles was ten times longer than any existing American canal and three times the country's entire canal mileage in 1817. Designed for horse-drawn barges, the Erie would measure 40 feet wide and 4 feet deep, ascending via 77 locks from the Hudson River at Albany to Lake Erie. Though some long stretches were level, the canal would have to bridge rivers and streams, pierce through a rocky ridge several miles thick, and at one point climb a nearly vertical 60-foot slope. Parts of the route, including its western terminus, were still unlocated when digging began.

The countryside the canal would pass through was thinly populated, some of it nearly wilderness. The projected cost was several times larger than New York state's entire annual budget. No one knew for certain where or whether the money could be obtained. Neither the men who drew the plans nor those who would supervise the work had formal training as engineers or experience at building canals.

The only comparable works known in America, the great canals of

Europe, were much shorter than the Erie, traversed a more settled landscape, and could draw upon ample private funds or the resources of national governments. Some Americans viewed the Erie with incredulity. Thomas Jefferson thought it "little short of madness," a hundred years premature. New York City editor Mordecai Noah called it a "monument of weakness and folly." In the face of such doubts, the decision to go ahead affirmed an untested faith in American ingenuity and American destiny.

The faith was justified. In three years the canal's easy central section was finished, and tolls on its traffic already exceeded interest on the money the state had borrowed to finance construction. Engineers and contractors learned on the job, devising new inventions to speed the work: an improved wheelbarrow, a tree-felling machine, a cement that would harden underwater. Taking on more difficult tasks as the canal stretched west and east, they became adept at burrowing through rock, constructing locks, and erecting gigantic stone aqueducts, some more than a thousand feet long.

The canal's completion in 1825 drove New Yorkers to a delirium of self-congratulation. In Rochester, a city suddenly sprung to prominence at the canal's juncture with the Genesee River, the *Telegraph* proclaimed: "The Work is finished! Our brightest, highest hopes, are all consummated. Let the shouts of triumph be heard from Erie to the Atlantic, and from the Atlantic resound back to Erie. Let the air itself be made vocal with our paeans of exultation and gratitude."

On October 26, 1825, while a chain of cannon boomed the news all the way to New York City and back, a flotilla led by the canal boat *Seneca Chief,* bearing Governor Clinton and other dignitaries, entered the waterway at Lake Erie. Hailed at every village along the way, it arrived precisely a week later at Albany on the Hudson. From there the fleet, now accompanied by a steamboat escort, proceeded downriver to New York City, where citizens staged a celebration to outshine even the previous year's welcome for Lafayette. Committees representing every occupation and constituency in the city laid plans for a "Grand Aquatic Display," a "Grand Procession through the City," and an "Exhibition of Artificial Fire Works."

In the words of an official report, the spectacle presented "One Entire Whole, surpassing in novelty, magnificence, and grandeur, any exhibition which is recorded in history." Circled by canal boats, steamboats, pilot boats, warships, revenue cutters, and barges, Clinton poured a keg of Erie water into the Atlantic, invoking "the God of the Heavens and the Earth" to "smile most propitiously on this work, and render it subservient to the best interests of the human race." As the boats returned to shore, they were met by fourteen shouted toasts, among them:

The great event which we this day celebrate—it is a proud monument of the genius and patriotism of a free people.

The State of New York, unaided and alone, has achieved a work which will cover her with imperishable glory.

The Fourth of July seventeen hundred and seventy-six, and the Fourth of July eighteen hundred and seventeen. Two great eras. The first gave birth to all that is wonderful and moral in war; the other has produced a stupendous effort of the arts of peace.

In the parade that followed, fifty-nine groups with banners and decorated carts made up a line of march a mile long, beginning with "Horsemen, with trumpets," and continuing through farmers and gardeners, cordwainers, furriers, hatters, chair makers, upholsterers, tin-plate workers, the medical society, the bar, and "Strangers of Distinction."

Completion of the Erie sparked rejoicing almost without reservation. In 1825 Americans were not yet inured to technological advance and its consequences. Improvement and invention were still new and exciting. The changes they brought seemed nearly miraculous. Canals opened up such vast opportunities that Americans groped for words to describe them. Celebrants hailed the Erie as insuring "to us a reward for industry, to our posterity an antidote for idleness; to the future inhabitants, the fertile lands of the West; the incalculable blessings of law, religion, morality and virtue; the legitimate offspring of knowledge and industry."

Sensitive to foreign jibes at American backwardness, New Yorkers crowed "that THEY HAVE BUILT THE LONGEST CANAL IN THE WORLD IN THE LEAST TIME, WITH THE LEAST EXPERIENCE, FOR THE LEAST MONEY, AND TO THE GREATEST PUBLIC BENEFIT." In patriots' eyes the canal proved the purity of American political institutions. Such a work could only have been "achieved by the spirit and perseverance of Republican Freemen." Europeans touted their superior civilization, but "where is there a work of their hands which will compare in grandeur and utility with the great Western canal?" Euphoric editors hailed the Erie as "next to the establishment of American Independence, . . . the greatest achievement of the age." The aged Jefferson, happy to be proven wrong, traced the result to Americans' "moral superiority."

In practical results the canal surpassed expectations. Travel time across New York state shrank from weeks to days. Land values rose as settlers flooded into the interior. The cost of carrying flour, grain, foodstuffs, and lumber to New York City plummeted, raising profits for producers while lowering prices for consumers. Westbound traffic brought manufactured goods and thousands of emigrants to upstate New York and the shores of Lake Erie. Slashing freight rates as much as 90 percent, the canal did more than quicken and cheapen exchange. It created it, opening markets where none existed before and showering the fruits of commerce on everyone within its reach.

Canal Fever

An engineering, financial, and commercial triumph, the Erie inspired faith in canals and in state enterprise. Other states rushed to copy its success. Already Virginia, North Carolina, South Carolina, and Georgia were pursuing internal improvement programs that blended public and private resources. West of the mountains, Ohio was the first to stir. Fronting Lake Erie on one side and the Ohio River on the other, Ohio straddled the divide between the Great Lakes and Mississippi River drainage systems. By bridging the summit with canals, Ohio could extend the Erie route across the state, completing an interior passageway all the way from New York City to New Orleans.

In 1818 Governor Ethan Allen Brown began agitating for a cross-state canal. The legislature authorized surveys in 1822 and construction three years later. At a ceremony on Independence Day, 1825, at the Licking Summit, east of Columbus near the center of the state, New York's visiting governor De Witt Clinton turned the first shovelful of earth on the 308-mile Ohio Canal.

This venture was in some ways even more ambitious than the Erie, for Ohio was a young community just emerging from the frontier, with half New York's population and only a fraction of its wealth. John C. Calhoun of South Carolina thought it "almost a miracle that a State in its infancy should undertake, and successfully execute so great a work, and it may be cited as one of the strongest proofs of the admirable effects of our political institutions in giving a high degree of intelligence and enterprize." But the Erie had shown the feasibility of mammoth canals and trained a cadre of engineers and contractors who now fanned out to design and build similar works throughout the union. Evangelists of progress spread the canal gospel, spurring initiative and fanning expectations. "A great spirit of improvement prevails in our country," observed Boston merchant Lewis Tappan in 1825 to his brother Benjamin, an Ohio canal commissioner.

Never, I suppose, was so much mind at work, and never was matter in such agitation. . . . Long may we continue in the full career of improvement; may our children excel us in usefulness, and be able to look back on the present time as we do on years past with astonishment at the strides we have made & the changes we have noticed.

On July 4, 1825, the same day as the Ohio commencement, Connecticut governor Oliver Wolcott broke ground for a canal into western Massachusetts. Another was already being built inland from Rhode Island. New York soon began a series of lateral feeders to expand the completed Erie into a statewide network. The governor of Georgia proposed a state canal system, while Chief Justice John Marshall of the United States Supreme Court and former president James Monroe pressed for progress on Virginia's James River route to the Appalachians. Congress joined in the enthusiasm, pledging federal funds for selected projects. In 1830 a compiler counted more than thirty canals "finished or well advanced" and another ninety contemplated or under way, for a grand total of more than ten thousand miles.

Completion of the Erie spurred activity in Philadelphia and Baltimore. Philadelphia was New York City's rival for national preeminence in population and finance. Philadelphia and Baltimore were also the eastern depots for the over-mountain turnpike trade to Pittsburgh and the Ohio valley. This trade was mainly in westbound manufactured goods, while interior farm and forest products were floated down the western rivers to New Orleans. But now the New York–Ohio connection threatened to siphon off the whole future commerce of the West, in both directions, to New York City.

Philadelphia and Baltimore were both closer to the Ohio than was New York, and canals from either city could operate longer through the winter, when the Erie was closed by ice. But they would also have to climb over Appalachian ridges two thousand feet high or else tunnel right through them. There was little time to ponder these alternatives. Under the frantic urgings of Philadelphia and Pittsburgh businessmen, Pennsylvania authorized the first stages of a cross-state waterway in 1826. Work began, of course, on the Fourth of July. Not until five years later did the state abandon the idea of running a canal through the mountains. It settled instead for a thirty-six-mile "portage railway" at the summit, where stationary steam engines raised and lowered disassembled boat sections to the canal at either end. Even with this compromise, the completed Pennsylvania Mainline Canal in 1834 was longer than the Erie, had twice as much lockage, and cost nearly twice as much to build.

Like New Yorkers, Marylanders and Virginians had eyed a Potomac River route to the West since before the Revolution. A company headed by George Washington did some digging in the 1790s. In 1825 Maryland authorized the Chesapeake and Ohio Canal. As this project would pass through three states (Maryland, Virginia, and Pennsylvania) and the federal District of Columbia, it was to be built by a private stock company, but with expected state and federal help.

United States engineers surveyed the route. The state of Maryland, the national Congress, and the city of Washington pledged funds; and on July 4, 1828, with ceremony appropriate to the occasion, President John Quincy Adams turned the first earth. A large crowd listened politely as the president proclaimed America to be "the empire of learning and the arts" and the canal itself to be "a conquest over physical nature, such as has never yet been achieved by man." But they really came alive when he sank his spade into the ground and struck a root. After three or four ineffectual thrusts, the usually reserved Adams "threw off my coat, and, resuming the spade, raised a shovelful of the earth," provoking "loud and unanimous cheering, which continued for some time."

On this same Independence Day, just forty miles away in Baltimore, what one report called "the most splendid civic procession, perhaps, ever exhibited in America" was taking place. Fifty thousand spectators cheered as troops, dignitaries, musical bands, fraternal societies, school groups, and uniformed contingents from thirty-four trades with horse-drawn floats and tableaux marched to a field two miles from town. There, ninety-year-old Charles Carroll of Carrollton, last surviving signer of the Declaration of Independence, laid the foundation stone of yet another "GREAT ROAD" to unite east and west.

This ceremony, eleven years to the day from the one in Utica that launched the Erie Canal, ushered in yet another chapter in American transportation. The Baltimore and Ohio, unlike the New York or Pennsylvania works, was a private project, though state and local governments helped finance it. What is more, it was no canal, but a railroad.

Like the projectors of the Erie a decade before, the Baltimore businessmen who organized the venture were stepping into the unknown. No general-purpose railway existed in the United States. In Britain, where dozens of short roads were built or in progress by 1828, the relative merits of propulsion by horses, steam locomotives, or stationary engines were still being debated. So were track and roadbed design and even the very nature of the enterprise: Should it be, like a turnpike or canal, a highway open to public use, or a route reserved for the company's own cars?

Refusing to wait for answers to these questions, the Baltimoreans began without quite knowing what they were building. Work progressed slowly but steadily as technical and financial problems were resolved. In 1852, twenty-four years later, the Baltimore and Ohio Railroad reached the Ohio River at Wheeling, Virginia (now West Virginia). Meanwhile, its twin, the Chesapeake and Ohio Canal, crept up the Potomac and finally stalled with its western terminus at Cumberland, Maryland, still short of the mountains. Even while canals were entering their heyday in the 1820s, their successors had already appeared. In the end railroads would vanquish canals.

Of course no one knew this in 1828, and what is most remarkable is not the different fate of these two ventures but the grand expectations that underlay both of them. The impulse that spurred Marylanders to begin two gigantic projects on the same day—one an imitative canal, the other a daringly experimental railroad—reflected a nationwide surge of energy. The spirit of improvement propelled an accelerating cycle of innovation, emulation, and rivalry. States, communities, and citizens competed to seize the fruits of progress. Civic pride fused with hope of gain to drive forward invention and experiment. A half-century after the Declaration of Independence, internal improvements were finally realizing the hopes of the Founding Fathers. Quickening the flow of people, goods, and ideas throughout the country, they cemented the Union by collapsing distances and widening horizons.

The Steamboat

The capital requirements of great canals and railroads demanded public subsidies or outright state control. Other innovations in transport, less monumental but just as important, relied more on diffused private energies. Foremost among them was the river steamboat.

British and American inventors had been working to harness steam power for propulsion on land and water since the 1780s. In the United States John Fitch and James Rumsey produced early steam vessels, and in 1805 Oliver Evans placed a steam engine in a boat, mounted it on wheels, and drove it through the streets of Philadelphia to the Schuylkill River. Two years later Robert Fulton's *North River* (better known as the *Cler-*

mont) performed its famous trial on the Hudson, steaming from New York City to Albany and back in five days. In 1811 the first western steamboat, built in Pittsburgh, ventured down the Ohio and Mississippi rivers to New Orleans.

By the War of 1812 boats built by Fulton and John Stevens were in regular use around New York and Philadelphia, and the practicability of steam craft was clear. But primitive design and workmanship, scarce capital, and legal battles over patents and franchise rights still hampered their spread. After the war these barriers fell away, and steamboats multiplied on coastal and inland waterways. Improvement in engines and hulls made boats bigger, faster, and more reliable. Thomas Gibbons in New York and Henry Miller Shreve in Louisiana broke the Fulton legal monopoly on steam navigation, clearing the way for competition. In 1815 Shreve's *Enterprise* made the first upriver voyage from New Orleans to Pittsburgh. By 1825 eighty steamboats plied western waters. Ten years more, and steam tonnage on the Ohio and Mississippi topped that of the Atlantic coast, and nearly equaled that of the whole British empire.

Eastern steamboats shuttled passengers along sheltered coastal routes, leaving longer, more dangerous open-water voyages to sailing craft. No longer subject to vagaries of wind and tide, steam vessels offered travelers speed, economy, and comfort. But the real impact was felt in the West. There, on the long rivers, steamboats carried freight as well as passengers, inaugurating a new era in inland commerce.

Before the steamboat, over-mountain settlers had floated their products on flatboats down the Mississippi and its tributaries to New Orleans. Though inexpensive, the trip was slow and risky. At its end the boats were broken up for lumber. Most of the crews walked back. Upriver transport was by keelboats and barges, laboriously poled and dragged against the current. By keelboat from New Orleans to Louisville, 1,350 miles by river, took three or four months; continuing to Pittsburgh, 600 miles further up the Ohio, added another month or more.

Few items were worth the expense of upriver haulage or wagon carriage over the mountains from Philadelphia or Baltimore. Inland residents paid dearly for outside goods or managed without them. High transport costs encouraged local manufacturing by shielding Pittsburgh glass and iron and Kentucky hemp and textiles from competition. Still, the drawbacks of distance far outweighed the benefits. The transmontane West boomed briefly after the War of 1812. But isolation impeded its growth, discouraging emigration and frustrating enterprise. The depression of 1819 brought an end to prosperity, heightening westerners' discomfiture and their resentment of what they perceived as the rest of the nation's indifference and neglect.

To communities alive with hopes of greatness but chagrined at their stalled progress, the steamboat appeared as an angel of deliverance. Yet steamboats, like canals and railroads, did not just appear on the landscape. Adapting them to western conditions required mechanical ingenuity, entrepreneurial energy, and government aid. To run on shallow and variable streams, boat builders devised high-topped, flat-bottomed vessels that could operate on amazingly light drafts. Congress sponsored surveys of the Ohio and Mississippi channels and appropriated funds to clear them of snags (submerged tree-trunks that ripped hulls), sandbars, and other obstructions. The federally subsidized Louisville and Portland Canal, begun in 1825 and opened five years later, bypassed the hazardous falls of the Ohio, permitting regular through-traffic from New Orleans to Cincinnati and Pittsburgh. In its first year the canal logged more than four hundred passages.

Travel times shrank as improvements made steam navigation swifter and more reliable. In 1817 Henry Shreve's twenty-five-day upriver run from New Orleans to Louisville was considered a fast passage. But in 1819 this record was cut to fourteen days, in 1824 to eleven days, and two years later to eight. "If any one had said this was possible . . . thirty years ago," mused Hezekiah Niles, "we should have been ready to send him to a mad-house."

Steamboat arrivals, like canal and railroad inaugurations, occasioned rejoicing that merged patriotism with local boosting. "Their appearance would create a great excitement along the banks, and at the towns and villages their arrival and landing were great occasions," one participant recalled. "The citizens turned out, and civic ceremonies were observed." Cannon boomed and crowds cheered each new steamer "as if there never had been and never would be another."

Even as steamboats multiplied on the main stems of the Ohio-Mississippi system, keelboats continued to operate on their upper reaches and shallow tributaries, and even on the big rivers in times of low water. Flatboats, slow but cheap, still floated some bulk goods downstream, the crews now returning by steamboat instead of on foot. Steam did not wholly banish muscle power from western rivers. But it reawakened visions of accelerating development and gave new reign to prophecies of western greatness. Noting a new record passage upstream, Niles' Weekly Register pondered "what a progress is this against the currents of the rivers of the west—what a field does it present to the speculative mind, disposed to anticipate the future condition of things!"

In the West it was hard to tell speculative from practical minds, or dreams from expectations, for today's fancy might be tomorrow's reality. In 1828 a Cincinnatian observed that "the steam engine in five years has enabled us to anticipate a state of things, which in the ordinary course of events, it would have required a century to produce." With faraway markets suddenly brought to their door, riverine westerners bent their energies to industry and commerce. Boat building flourished along the Ohio. Pittsburgh nurtured its iron foundries and glassworks, Cincinnati its processing of pork and grain. Steamboats linked St. Louis merchants to the lead mines of the upper Mississippi and the fur trade of the upper Missouri.

Town Promotion

By bringing communities closer together, steamboats gave new spark to urban rivalries and new impetus to the old penchant for town promotion. Canal and river towns strove to improve their advantage in the battle for population and trade, while off-water rivals sought to neutralize it. Both spewed forth plans for connecting roads, canals, and river improvements. Civic boosters waged a war of words. Cincinnati was the "Queen City," Pittsburgh the "Iron City." Both claimed the title of "Western Emporium." Stranded by the steamboat, Lexington, Kentucky, settled for cultural distinction as "Athens of the West," "capital of Science and Letters." At every likely spot planners conjured up another mighty city, destined to be a future metropolis—depot of trade, hive of manufacturing, seat of government, citadel of learning and the arts!

At Buffalo, New York, western terminus of the Erie Canal, the Englishwoman Frances Trollope observed that

all the buildings have the appearance of having been run up in a hurry, though every thing has an air of great pretension. . . . Every body tells you there, as in all their other new-born towns, and every body believes, that their improvement, and their progression, are more rapid, more wonderful, than the earth ever before witnessed.

Trollope bridled at such conceit, yet even she acknowledged "the people of America to be the most enterprising in the world," and marveled at the "boldness and energy" of their public works and the "inconceivable rapidity" with which their cities rose from the forest.

Westerners laughed at their own exaggerations. A Missouri newspaper advertised the community of Ne Plus Ultra. Strategically located astride the routes from Washington to China and from Mexico to the North Pole, this great city was "destined to be the capital of the western empire, or perhaps the world." A visiting New Englander enjoyed the satire. Yet contemplating "the astonishing change, which the last ten years have introduced over the whole face of the United States," the inexhaustible richness of western resources, and "the guardian genius, Liberty, hovering over the country," he could not help thinking that somewhere in the interior would appear a real Ne Plus Ultra. Four years later, speculators laid out the village of Chicago at the mouth of a projected canal into Lake Michigan. Most sites billed as future great cities settled in the end for the modest prosperity of a county seat or market town. Some, like Hygeia, Kentucky, across the Ohio River from Cincinnati, existed only in the elaborate plans and excited hopes of their sponsors.

The antics of western town promoters and the more dignified, though hardly less eager, competition among established cities like Louisville, Pittsburgh, and Cincinnati found reflection also in the port cities of the East. Thirst for civic distinction and commercial advantage led merchants and shippers to regularize and expedite seaborne commerce. Here, as in canal-building, New Yorkers took the lead. In January 1818 a New York City firm inaugurated the first scheduled transatlantic packet service. In seven years the original four ships plying the route grew to twenty-eight.

Playing off the natural advantages of the harbor—its central location, ample shelter, deep channel, and close access to the sea—New York merchants in the decade after 1815 corralled the largest share of the burgeoning coastal and overseas trade. By 1830 New York handled a quarter of the country's exports and fully half its imports. Carolina and Georgia cotton and Chesapeake tobacco brought around by sea, along with flour from the Erie Canal, cleared for foreign ports via New York, while the city's jobbers and commission merchants distributed British textiles and other goods to customers throughout the nation. New York soared past its rivals to become, at the Jubilee, the undisputed "great commercial emporium of America" and one of the busiest ports in the world.

American Manufactures

Whether by canal, rail, steam, or sail, advances in transport at once built upon and encouraged experiment in techniques of building and fabricating. Canal builders developed new methods and tools of surveying, excavating, and stone laying. The use of steam for inland navigation spawned new ideas in naval architecture and engine design. Meanwhile, in dozens of workshops scattered up the coast from Baltimore to Boston, mechanics and in-

ventors devised ways to speed the production of everything from guns and
clocks to cloth and newspapers. In manufacturing, as in transportation,
the spirit of improvement was afoot.

For long after independence the United States had trailed Great Britain
in industrial achievement. American artisans, less practiced than European
craftsmen, generally worked with clumsier tools and inferior materials.
Capital shortages thwarted the occasional effort to organize production
on a large scale, or to exploit an isolated technological advance. In textile
manufacturing, a leading industry by the end of the eighteenth century,
American imitators struggled to match British success in mechanizing basic
processes.

Still the United States presented a promising field for industry despite,
and even in part because of, its lag in experience and skill. The scarcity
and high cost of American labor offered incentive as well as impediment
to manufacturing enterprise. Resources of iron, coal, building materials,
waterpower, and especially wood were cheap and plentiful. Cultural and
commercial ties across the Atlantic offered access to British expertise, while
a prosperous, expanding farm economy ensured a home market. If American mechanics were less specialized than Europeans, they were also more
versatile. The flexibility of a youthful society invited experiment. No craft
guilds or entrenched social orders put up resistance to change.

Born of these conditions and of Americans' fascination with things
new and better, the urge to tinker and invent was deeply ingrained in the
national character. Alexander Hamilton in 1791 noted "a remark often
to be met with—namely that there is, in the genius of the people of this
country, a peculiar aptitude for mechanic improvements." That aptitude
showed in the early experiments with steam power and in the adulation
given to Benjamin Franklin, who became the first American cultural hero
by exemplifying the penchant for novelty and efficiency.

Americans' willingness to try new things encouraged the efforts of native
wizards like Eli Whitney, a Yankee who invented the cotton gin in 1793 and
later made muskets with interchangeable parts, and Oliver Evans, trained
as a wheelwright, who devised a fully automated flour mill in 1785, built
the first commercial high-pressure steam engine in 1801, and wrote a series
of manuals for young mechanics and engineers. American opportunity also
lured enterprising immigrants like Benjamin Henry Latrobe, architect and
engineer, and Samuel Slater, an English textile manager who arrived in 1789
and, with backing from Rhode Island merchants, established the country's
first mechanized cotton spinning mill.

Statesmen and civic leaders of the young republic championed manufacturing, sometimes for their own profit, but also as a patriotic service, a way to promote national self-reliance in peace and self-sufficiency in war, expand the home market for farm goods, and create useful work for the poor and for idle women and children. Invoking all these aims, Treasury secretary Alexander Hamilton and his assistant Tench Coxe in 1791 urged government support for manufacturing and collaborated in founding the Society for Establishing Useful Manufactures.

Hamilton's proposals for federal subsidy died amid the emerging factionalism that produced the Federalist and Jeffersonian Republican parties. But stripped of its entanglement with government policy, the enthusiasm for invention and improvement knew no political bounds. Jefferson, his occasional outbursts against cities and manufacturing notwithstanding, was an avid tinkerer who ran nail and textile works on his plantation, encouraged new mechanical discoveries, and designed several ingenious time- and labor-saving devices. Joel Barlow, Jeffersonian diplomat and poet, sponsored Robert Fulton's work on steamboats and submarines. Tom Paine, radical pamphleteer, designed smokeless candles and iron arch bridges. All these men avowed civic and patriotic motives for their work. All regarded material advance as the natural fruit of American republicanism and proof of the country's virtue and promise.

Like the first efforts to build canals, early attempts at large-scale production in the United States foundered for lack of managerial and mechanical skill, capital, and incentive. Manufacturing might be patriotic, but overseas trade brought greater rewards. But the War of 1812 renewed interest in domestic industry. In retirement, Thomas Jefferson abandoned his last reservations. Admitting that "experience has taught me that manufactures are now as necessary to our independence as to our comfort," he concluded in 1816 that "we must now place the manufacturer by the side of the agriculturist."

The postwar resumption of British imports and the depression of 1819 dealt setbacks to nascent American producers. But by the mid-1820s industrial establishments were spreading across the countryside. Cotton and woolen spinning mills, driven by waterpower and for the most part still small and family owned, dotted streams and rivers across the northeast and Ohio valley. A thriving small-arms industry grew up along the Connecticut River, anchored by the federal armory at Springfield, Massachusetts. In Philadelphia and New York and Pittsburgh, ironworks, foundries, and machine shops produced tools and engines to power the new factories and steamboats.

Experiment yielded a growing tide of designs and devices. As the German visitor Friedrich List observed, "anything new is quickly introduced here, and all the latest inventions. There is no clinging to old ways, the moment an American hears the word 'invention' he pricks up his ears." In the 1820s the federal government doubled its annual issuance of patents. The most important developments were in machine tools—lathes, planes, milling machines and other wood- and metalworking devices fashioned by master mechanics, an inquisitive group that traveled widely and exchanged technical information freely on both sides of the Atlantic.

Together, improvements in transport and manufacture wrought a change in communications unrivaled since the printing press. In the 1820s entrepreneurs installed new technologies, both invented and imported, to mechanize the laborious work of paper-making. Steam presses, introduced in the early 1830s, multiplied printing speed twenty-five times. The output of publications soared as costs tumbled. Books and newspapers, religious and agricultural and literary journals, pamphlets and tracts of every description clattered off the presses. The Erie and other canals became conduits of ideas, carrying information and opinion back and forth across the country. Five thousand new post offices opened between 1819 and 1832, twelve hundred in the Jubilee year alone.

In 1811 Francis Cabot Lowell, a Boston merchant visiting in England, observed the new machinery for weaving cotton cloth in Manchester. Back in the United States he designed a power loom with the help of a master mechanic. Recruiting capital from fellow merchants, Lowell secured a charter from the Massachusetts legislature for the Boston Manufacturing Company. The company's new mill at Waltham thrived, and in 1822 the merchant group, latterly known as the Boston Associates, purchased land and waterpower rights at a nearly vacant site on the Merrimack River, north of Boston. There they erected a factory village from scratch, complete with mills, domiciles, and public buildings. In 1823 the first spindle turned, and three years later the newborn community became an incorporated city, named Lowell.

The Boston Associates negated the British textile industry's half-century head start in one huge leap. Lavishly financed, employing the latest machinery (including some wholly new devices as well as an improved version of the pirated power loom), and for the first time combining all the operations of production under a single roof, the Waltham and Lowell mills could compete with any textile manufacturer in the world. In the difficult years after the War of 1812, while British producers flooded the American market with cheap goods and small domestic firms failed by the dozens, crying for federal tariff protection as they went down, Waltham earned steady dividends averaging nearly 20 percent.

Implications of Improvement

In 1825 a Massachusetts minister named Timothy Flint returned home from a ten years' sojourn in the Mississippi valley. Passing through the Pawtucket textile district in Rhode Island, site of Samuel Slater's first small spinning mill a generation earlier, he inquired about the huge buildings he saw in the distance. Flint wondered if New England "had at last invented a new worship, and that these buildings were the temples. And so in truth I found it, the worship of the golden shrine," filled not with Christian devotees but with "mechanicians and manufacturers." At the peaceful old hamlet of East Chelmsford, now being reborn as Lowell, Flint was startled by the roar of construction blasts, the giant factory buildings going up in rows, the crash of machinery, "the noise, confusion, and clatter, of an incipient babble."

Like other Americans, Flint marveled at the changes he saw. Crossing the turbulent Mohawk River on an Erie Canal aqueduct, a "river in the air," he indulged a "feeling of sublimity," a conviction that nothing was "impossible to the union of intellectual and physical power." Yet Flint's enthusiasm was tempered with doubt. Our country "is great already," he acknowledged—"and may it be happy. What will it be in half a century to come?" Excited by progress, Flint also worried about the morals of children growing up in cotton mills, about the spread of "extravagance and luxury," about where "this rage for travelling, this manufacturing and money-getting impulse, and the new modes of reasoning and acting" would lead.

He was not the only one wondering. In Indiana young Robert Dale Owen, son of the philanthropist, having seen the misery of British factory life firsthand, also questioned.

Shall we proceed as at present on the road to wealth and prosperity, *with the certainty before us*, that so soon as we have over-supplied all our wants and all the wants of our neighbors, we shall begin to starve? not from famine or failure of crops, or loss of property; no, *only because we have too much of every thing*. *Must* abundance lead to want? prosperity to adversity? riches to poverty? plenty to starvation?

Hezekiah Niles, editor of the influential *Weekly Register*, gloried in the march of improvement and yearned to see American industry surpass even

Great Britain's. Yet looking at recent advances that "may be literally said to overcome the laws of nature, time, and space," even Niles could not help asking, "in astonishment, where is the end of all this, whereat shall we stop? . . . In contemplating the increase of labor-saving machinery and ease of transportation, may it not be feared that these things will be carried too far?" Niles thought another half-century of accelerating change might eliminate the need to work altogether, producing idleness and "a common degeneracy."

In the end he decided it was not worth worrying about. "It would not be wise to make ourselves miserable, because, in the improvement of our own condition, it is possible that posterity may have too much of the good things of this life!" But it was revealing that even this indefatigable enthusiast for progress could voice such qualms. And while the problem of superabundance could be safely left for later generations to handle, other questions could not.

At the Jubilee year, the new Erie Canal and Lowell mills signified the country's vigor in transportation and manufacturing. Surpassing anything in old Europe, they fulfilled the founding generation's hope of American leadership in the march of humanity. But they also brought thoughtful observers suddenly face to face with the full implications and consequences of progress. New means of travel and communication bypassed old towns while raising new cities, and disrupted familiar ways of living even as they introduced new goods and ideas. Factory production heralded a growing material abundance. But the din and dirt of the workplace belied arcadian visions of new-world tranquility, while the gulf between employers' luxury and employees' drudgery seemed to imperil America's treasured exemption from European class divisions and social strife.

A burgeoning economy raised questions along with opportunities. How could the unbridled and inevitably unequal acquisition of wealth, and of the power that came with it, be reconciled with Americans' cherished equality? Now that the fruits of improvement were multiplying beyond all precedent, who would ensure their fair distribution—who, indeed, would define what was fair? And in a society equally dedicated to democratic decision-making, the rule of law, the rights of private property, and the rewards of enterprise—precepts which, as Americans were now beginning to discover, sometimes crossed one another—how were such questions to be resolved?

The broader question facing citizens at the Jubilee was not if they would cling to tradition or accept a changing future. America had always been the land of promise, of belief in a better tomorrow. Few doubted that the country's best years lay ahead. What they had to decide was not whether to welcome progress, but what content and meaning to assign to it.

As new horizons opened for future growth, the options for its direction also widened. A dizzying variety of plans appeared for reaching what everyone believed was America's special destiny. After a half-century of deferred hopes, suddenly, and finally, all things were possible. From the high vantage point of the Jubilee, Americans could see pots of gold shining at the end of a dozen different rainbows. Which one should they strike for? Debate was soon stirring.

CHAPTER Three

The Law of Enterprise

Commerce is universally acknowledged to be both the
parent and the offspring of liberty.
                                   —James Fenimore Cooper, 1828

While the rush of improvement raised hopes of material and moral betterment, it also placed novel demands and responsibilities upon local, state,
and national governments, and posed new questions for judges, juries, and
legislators. In their effort to fit old law and custom to new circumstance,
Americans confronted some of the implications and dilemmas of progress
for the first time.

Changing Rules of Commerce

Americans in the early nineteenth century did not need to invent rationalizations for public intervention in the occupations of the citizenry. Centuries of legal precedent and British and colonial practice had established
the right and duty of government to supervise, restrain, and promote in
order to protect the community's welfare and further the common good.
Yet while the right stood unquestioned, the nature of the intervention, by
the time of the Jubilee, was rapidly changing.

A central principle of English and American law was protection of the
rights of property. In the colonial economy, land was the usual form of
property, and agriculture its customary use. Early American law accordingly approached property as essentially static, something to be guarded
and preserved rather than developed. When conflicts arose—for instance,

when a new mill dam on a stream flooded neighboring fields, damaged the fishing, or impaired the operation of other mills—courts intervened to protect the injured parties. Such rulings deterred innovation by sheltering prior claims on property against new, competing uses.

The colonial courts' treatment of contracts and business agreements likewise served to preserve an existing order instead of promoting change. In contract disputes judges and juries looked not only to the stated intentions of the agreeing parties, but to their own sense of what was customary and reasonable. Courts sometimes voided or adjusted agreements, not because they were improperly drawn or illegal, but because they departed from what seemed a fair exchange. These decisions guarded community welfare by protecting unwary citizens from sharp bargainers. But they also discouraged complex business transactions involving chance or contingency. The legal system valued security and predictability.

The law of indebtedness also deterred risky business ventures. People who borrowed money bore full responsibility to repay. There was no éscape through bankruptcy, and delinquent debtors risked imprisonment.

In the half-century after independence, new laws and rulings traced a gradual shift from a static to a dynamic conception of the economy. Courts came to view property as active, not inert, and their emphasis shifted from protecting its old uses to promoting new ones. They adopted a flexible approach, which allowed scope to determine which of several conflicting claims on property was most conducive to community interest without deferring automatically to the one that came first. And more and more they assessed community interest—what Supreme Court Justice Joseph Story in 1827 called the "public convenience and general good"—in terms not of preservation but of development, reasoning frankly that the law should encourage new ventures in trade, manufacturing, and transportation. Courts came to see competition not as a danger to be suppressed or curtailed, but as a social boon, an arm of the improving spirit of the age; and they showed a willingness to bend old legal rules to foster it.

Lawmakers and jurists began to regard losers in competition, even injured bystanders, less as wronged victims deserving legal succor than as unavoidable casualties in the march of progress. As the New York Supreme Court put it in 1828, "every great public improvement must, almost of necessity, more or less affect individual convenience and property," and some private injuries must be "borne as part of the price to be paid for the advantages of the social condition." Placing the community's stake in economic development ahead of its interest in securing citizens from loss, Massachu-

setts passed legislation virtually inviting mill owners to flood their neighbors' fields. Courts rejected suits brought by farmers who suffered damage
from the operations of nearby factories.

In New York in 1805, when a mill owner brought suit because a new
dam impeded his stream flow, the court acknowledged the justice of his
complaint under traditional common-law rules, then rejected it anyway
because "the public, whose advantage is always to be regarded, would
be deprived of the benefit which always attends competition and rivalry."
When new businesses supplanted old ones—for instance, when canals and
bridges appeared alongside toll roads and ferries, stealing their custom
and destroying their value—courts denied recompense to the aggrieved
proprietors.

Courts withdrew from mediating the fairness of business agreements,
leaving the parties to negotiate for themselves and stepping in only to enforce the results. Justice Story pronounced in 1836 that the law should "act
upon the ground, that every person . . . is entitled to dispose of his property in such manner and upon such terms, as he chooses; and whether
his bargains are wise and discrete, or otherwise, profitable or unprofitable,
are considerations, not for Courts of Justice, but for the party himself to
deliberate upon." Or as New York legalist Gulian Verplanck put it in 1825,
"justice permits" a contracting party to exploit his "peculiar advantages
of skill, shrewdness, and experience." Implicitly jettisoning the notion that
goods or services bore an intrinsic value, courts left the market itself to
determine their worth. With the law no longer intruding to say what terms
and prices were customary and fair, parties were free to contract as they
wished.

The new legal approach encouraged enterprise by offering more freedom and less security. It freed entrepreneurs to strike their own bargains
and left them to take the consequences. At the same time though, as an
encouragement to business, lawmakers softened those consequences by re-
ducing penalties for delinquent debtors and offering ways to resolve debt
short of full repayment or jail. Once perceived as a moral failing, insolvency
now appeared more as an impersonal misfortune, a chance one took when
pursuing activities recognized as socially desirable yet freighted with risk.

Much of this evolution in the law, some of it highly technical and accru-
ing slowly over many years, was invisible to citizens and even to judges and
legislators. Often they acted without knowing what peers elsewhere were
doing, since the systematic compiling of statutes and reporting of judicial
decisions had barely begun. Rather than setting out to overhaul legal rules,

authorities simply did what seemed just and reasonable as problems and cases arose. But whether purposely or reflexively, their notions of justice and reason subtly adapted toward those of a dynamic and commercial society rather than a static and agricultural one. In other words, changes in law both reflected and furthered Americans' emerging perception of competition and innovation as positive social values. As Justice Story explained in 1825, "the law must fashion itself to the wants, and in some sort to the spirit of the age. Its stubborn rules, if they are not broken down, must bend to the demands of society."

Emergence of the Corporation

One sign of legal adaptation was the emergence of the business corporation, a key organizational tool of the expanding American economy. Its predecessor, the chartered stock company, had existed for centuries. In England and colonial America, kings and proprietors used charters to grant special powers and privileges as inducement and reward for doing some useful service. Chartered stock companies planted colonies, opened trade routes, furnished transport, and provided credit. Company enterprise thus mingled private profit with public benefit, the two being often so intertwined as to be inseparable. Educational, eleemosynary, and religious institutions—colleges, charities, churches—operated under corporate charters, as did governments of cities and colonies. Charters were individualized instruments, drawn to serve particular ends, and the rights they conferred were often exclusive or monopolistic.

After the Revolution state legislatures assumed the granting of corporate charters. They continued to use them to foster enterprises that would yield service to the public as well as, in some cases, profit to the incorporators. Bridges, ferries, turnpikes, waterworks, banks, and insurance companies sought and received charter privileges.

By the 1820s ideas of public service and private gain were starting to diverge onto separate tracks. Governments now undertook some projects themselves instead of delegating power to companies. For years after the Revolution, scant resources and poor credit had ruled state enterprise out of the question. But growth in population and wealth now made it possible; indeed, for the largest works there seemed no choice. New York's success with the Erie Canal after the failure of a private company on the same route seemed to show that state action was not only feasible but necessary.

Still, no one thought that states or localities should assume all the obligations of education, charity, religion, and philanthropy, nor that government should supplant private initiative in fostering economic growth. For both purposes states continued to dispense charters. Between 1816 and 1826, the state of Ohio incorporated, by special acts of legislation, eighteen turnpikes, seven bridges, two harbors, a waterworks, seven banks, an insurance company, two manufactories (one iron, one wool), a mining company, four colleges and a medical college, a seminary, eleven academies, six school and literary societies, eight libraries, eight charitable, benevolent, and religious organizations, and a historical society. Reflecting the state's interest in development as well as its hope for revenue, some governments accompanied charters with purchase of company stock. By the mid-1820s the state of Pennsylvania owned more than $4 million of stock in fifty-six turnpikes, twenty-five bridges, three canals, and three banks. Virginia, North Carolina, South Carolina, and Georgia all coupled incorporation with state investment as a means of promoting internal improvement.

Incorporation in such cases still implied a public purpose and usually conferred some special benefit. Bank charters, for instance, included the right to print and issue notes. Ostensibly these were IOUs upon the bank, redeemable in coin from its capital reserves. In practice, once lent out into circulation, they functioned as a quasi-official paper currency. (The federal government did not then, as it does today, issue its own paper. Technically, the country's only real money was minted gold and silver.) Turnpike and canal charters gave companies the power of eminent domain to procure rights-of-way. Ferry operators got exclusive locations. A perceived advantage to the public underlay all these grants. Citizens rarely sought incorporation for strictly private business. Planters, farmers, and professionals did not need charter privileges. Merchants and mill owners preferred the simple, easily dissolved personal partnership.

The establishment of the Boston Manufacturing Company in 1813 can be taken to mark the advent of the true business corporation. A few manufacturers had been chartered previously, though no very successful ones. Massachusetts in 1809 and New York in 1811 had already established general rules for incorporation. Yet in requesting a charter, the Waltham entrepreneurs avowed familiar public-service motives. Factories, like colleges or charities or canals, fostered the general welfare. They furnished goods and employment and thus enhanced the wealth, convenience, and security of the commonwealth.

Still, under a traditional guise Francis Cabot Lowell and his coadjutors were really seeking something new. Their need for incorporation stemmed not from the purported public purpose of their enterprise but from its scale. Much larger than any existing manufactory and more durable than any trading venture, the Boston Company needed an organizational structure that could pool a dozen men's capital under unified control and ensure continuity of the business if investors were to die or sell out.

A chartered stock company secured these features while lending the state's imprimatur to what was, at first, an uncertain venture. Significantly, the Boston group did not request, and the state did not bestow, any exclusive privilege. Unlike turnpikes or banks, manufacturers did not require monopoly rights or delegations of public power to operate profitably. All they needed was the legal and organizational security that a state charter provided.

Once manufacturing companies proved successful, there was thus no reason not to multiply their numbers indefinitely and let competition decide which would survive. Lawmakers could not grant corporate status to some and deny it to others without inviting accusations of favoritism. So with the Boston Company inciting imitators, legislatures moved toward granting charters to all comers. Massachusetts incorporated 18 manufacturers before 1810, 133 in the next decade, and 146 in the 1820s. By 1830 the New England states alone had chartered nearly 600 manufacturing and mining concerns, along with twice that number of companies providing public service—transportation, finance, utilities—for private gain.

Shorn of its quasi-governmental character, the corporation now stood forth as merely a convenient form of business organization, a pure tool of investment and profit. As charters became routine, their provisions became more standard, and special rights and privileges disappeared. This trend spread to older types of enterprise along with manufactories. The first bank incorporated in Massachusetts, significantly named the Massachusetts Bank, enjoyed a monopoly when it was chartered in 1784. But by 1829 sixty-six banks operated in the state, and in that year the legislature imposed a uniform organization on all banks for the future. Massachusetts had already standardized insurance company charters in 1818, turnpikes in 1805.

The redefinition of finance and transportation companies, along with manufacturers, from instruments of state policy to profit-seeking ventures led lawmakers and jurists to develop rules distinguishing the new "private" business corporation from traditional "public" corporations such as municipalities and charities. In the course of defining the new entity, they also endowed it with a prized and controversial attribute—the limitation of stockholders' personal liability for the corporation's debts. First established through the courts, the principle of limited liability was clarified and cemented by statute in New York in 1813, Connecticut in 1817, Massachusetts in 1830.

The Growth of Banking

The adaptation of rules and policies to fit the needs of enterprise spurred expansion in commerce and manufacturing. But it also raised questions about how to reconcile the promotional role of government with the republican ideal of fair and equal treatment for all. Without doubt, laws designed to foster development would, even if only incidentally, advance some interests at the expense of others. Measures sponsored under the rubric of the public good also bestowed private benefit, often most unevenly. The cost of canals and other tax-supported public works was borne by all, yet not all gained by their operation. And the privilege of incorporation, traditionally conferred in the service of the common weal, could appear illegitimate once it began to serve mainly private ends. Why should some citizens, and not others, enjoy special protection from government?

Events following the War of 1812 brought the incipient changes in the American legal and economic environment into open view and exposed their implications to public scrutiny. Though it had threatened for a time to wreck the federal finances, the war also triggered a commercial and agricultural expansion that continued after the peace. White settlers poured onto rich western lands newly wrested from the Indians, bringing four new states—Indiana, Illinois, Alabama, and Mississippi—into the Union by 1819. Driven by foreign demand, cotton prices doubled in two years after 1814, luring southwestern fortune-seekers to make frenzied purchases of land and slaves. Seaport merchants, hit hard by the war, revived as exports rose and British goods, long blocked from entry, flooded back into the American market.

Headlong expansion created urgent demands for capital and credit. Before the war the United States had boasted few banks and only a handful of men who could be called professional bankers. Now state legislatures, eager to finance prosperity, rushed to charter new banks, raising the number in operation from 88 in 1811 to 208 in 1815 to 392 in 1818. This sudden growth reflected a shortage rather than a surfeit of sound credit. Americans' thirst for land, goods, and slaves outran their means. Well-connected men, more versed in politics than finance, procured bank charters for themselves and their friends, not because they wished to invest in banks but because they wished to borrow from them. New banks met the call by printing and lending notes backed by scant or even phantom reserves of gold and silver specie.

In 1816 Congress joined in by chartering the second Bank of the United States, with headquarters in Philadelphia and power to open branches throughout the states. Its predecessor, the first federal bank, created in 1791 at the urging of Alexander Hamilton, was widely unpopular and had been allowed to die at the expiration of its twenty-year charter. But financial near-disaster during the war and the disordered currency that followed convinced Congress and President James Madison to change their minds.

The new federal bank, like the old one and like many state banks, blended private and public objects. As the government's own banker, it would hold, transfer, and disburse its funds, manage the federal debt, and issue notes to circulate as the country's only national paper currency, good for all debts due the United States. These privileges were exclusive, Congress having promised to create no competitor in the twenty years of the new bank's charter. While vital to the government, the Bank's public functions were also profitable for the investors who owned four-fifths of its stock. The federal government itself owned the other fifth, and the President of the United States appointed five of the Bank's twenty-five directors.

Its official capacity, its huge $35 million capitalization, and its national reach gave the new Bank of the United States enormous leverage over the state-chartered banks. In the normal course of business many of their notes came into its hands. By presenting them for redemption in coin, it could force them to maintain adequate specie reserves, thus reining in their issue of notes and stabilizing the currency. This was Congress's intent. But at first the Bank made no effort at control. Like the state banks, it extended its lending to the limit of its resources. Instead of restraining credit, the Bank helped expand it. Easy money fueled speculation in western lands and sustained rising prices across the country.

The Panic of 1819

For almost four years after the war Americans enjoyed a heady prosperity. Though some manufacturers suffered from renewed British competition, merchants and farmers and planters thrived on strong exports and loose credit. Chasing apparently limitless demand, cotton production doubled by 1819. But the pace could not be sustained. A reviving European agriculture curbed the foreign market for American grain and meat. At the end of 1818 British prices for American cotton sagged abruptly. The effect reverberated through the vulnerable debt-laden economy, setting off a wave of business failures and contractions that became known as the Panic of 1819. Prices fell, land values plummeted, debtors defaulted, and bubbles burst. Shocked at the collapse, Americans took stock and assessed blame.

Controversy enveloped the banks as bankers turned upon one another to save themselves. Compelled to reverse its own easy policy, the Bank of the United States sought rescue by holding the state-chartered banks to account. They in turn relieved the pressure by calling in loans, forcing borrowers to liquidate assets at distress prices. Credit, once readily granted, was now as quickly refused. Unable to raise enough coin, some banks simply folded or refused to redeem their notes (an action known as suspending specie payment), leaving unlucky holders of their worthless or depreciated paper to fend for themselves.

The bewildering descent from prosperity to panic and the greed, incompetence, and downright dishonesty exposed in its wake inspired a revulsion against banks, bankers, and banknotes. Davy Crockett of Tennessee, like many others, concluded that "the whole Banking system" was nothing more than "a species of swindling on a large scale." Attacking the irresponsibility and impudence of chartered corporations, critics pointed to banks that, in plain defiance of legal requirements, continued to operate after suspending specie payment. (Unwilling to drive them out of business, state legislatures acquiesced.) Resentment flared against the corporate privilege that allowed bankers, unlike other people, to escape paying their debts. One editor half-jokingly suggested amending a bank charter so that the stockholders themselves, instead of a list of their names, should be "hung up" on display before the next election of directors.

State bankers denied guilt and blamed the Bank of the United States instead. Some politicians and voters agreed. They saw their local banks as victims, and the national bank as the villain. The fault lay not with state bankers who sustained the boom, but with the national bank for puncturing it. At any rate, they said, the cause of the crisis was now irrelevant. The immediate need after the panic was not to restrain credit but to restore it. So while some turned in disgust against all banks, others argued for new ones, and proposals to curtail banking competed with plans to expand it. In the West, where a chronic regional trade deficit and resulting specie scarcity made distress especially acute, some legislatures stepped in to create new banks or loan offices with paper backed only by the faith of the state.

The banking debate posed friends of an abundant (paper) currency against defenders of a sound (specie-based) one. Proponents of remedial action to expand the money supply vied with those who would let retrenchment run its course. Both inflationists and contractionists sought the same end of restoring prosperity. The question was how. To provide a useful medium of exchange, the currency had to be both ample in quantity and sure in value. Yet given the country's shortage of specie and the underdeveloped state of its wealth-producing resources, it could be only one or the other.

Interwoven with the banking controversy was a parallel argument over relief for debtors caught in the general distress. Borrowers who could not repay clamored for "stay laws" forestalling legal process against them, or minimum valuation laws to prevent seizure and sale of their property at collapsed prices. Though strongest in the cash-poor West, the agitation was national. Ten states adopted stay laws, including Maryland, Vermont, and Pennsylvania.

The relief question, like the banking one, was framed within the assumptions of a commercial economy. Arguments on both sides assumed the need to rebuild business confidence but differed over means. Stay laws bought borrowers time to restore their solvency but abrogated lenders' right of recovery, thus shaking their trust in the security of debts and perhaps deterring them from lending again. On the other hand, failure to provide relief would protect creditors only by ruining debtors.

These were hard choices. Farmers and tradesmen and rough-hewn politicians now grappled, many for the first time, with abstruse questions about the nature of money and the function of credit. Was debt good or evil, a tool of industry or a mark of improvidence? Was the entrepreneur with few means and expansive dreams a benefactor or a plague? Were banks and banknotes agents of progress, as they had so recently seemed, or engines of privilege and persecution? In posing these questions Americans sought the right road back to a substantial, enduring prosperity.

The vocabulary of discussion was as much moral as financial, as people applied familiar ethical maxims to a novel commercial crisis. Some traced the panic to failings in human character. Foes of currency expansion and debtor relief blamed plungers for their own distress and linked paper money and indebtedness with recklessness and dishonesty. A Cincinnati critic castigated "the theatre and the circus, brokers and shavers, speculation, luxury, extravagance, effeminacy in dress and manners, auctions and pawn brokers, lotteries and lottery offices, insurance, great and sudden changes in circumstance." All these iniquities were "productions of the paper system."

Hezekiah Niles attributed the panic to "unprincipled speculation and unblushing fraud." His cure was simple: forsake the "supremely-to-be-hated rag, or paper system," return to "profitable industry, and prudent economy," and make both men and banks "pay their debts, or shut up shop." Andrew Jackson of Tennessee agreed: "habits of extravagance, and of transacting business too much upon credit" had created crisis. A return "to our former habits of industry and simplicity" would end it. Kentucky newspaper editor Amos Kendall drew a lesson from the panic:

Things will take their course in the moral as well as in the natural world. . . . *The people must pay their own debts at last.* This truth should be impressed upon them, their eyes should be turned from banks and the legislature to themselves,— their own power and resources. Few need despair. Industry never died with hunger. Economy never went without its reward.

A different view of the business principles appropriate to an enterprising people appeared in appeals for congressional relief from two groups of beleaguered debtors, merchants operating out of the Atlantic port cities and buyers of western public land. Overextended traders wanted a national bankruptcy statute to replace the confusion of state insolvency laws and establish a fair, uniform method of liquidating debts and distributing assets. Pioneers and speculators had bought millions of acres of government land on credit before the panic, incurring debts that were now due and unpayable. In Alabama, vast sales of prime cotton acreage at inflated prices had created a condition of "universal mortgage." Federal law required forfeiture as penalty for default. But buyers begged for additional time and for leave to subdivide their purchases and transfer payments from one tract to another.

Congress debated who was more worthy of relief—the merchants whose initiative energized the whole society, or that "most useful and virtuous class of citizens, the honest, industrious farmers, by whose labors life and vigor are imparted to every other." But both supplicants agreed on one thing: theirs was not a moral failing of malfeasance and irresponsibility, but a guiltless hazard inevitable in a country that was "young, enterprising, and comparatively deficient in capital." As merchant spokesman Joseph Hopkinson of Philadelphia argued, the risk of failure arose from the

nature and extent of their business; the hazards to which they were exposed from the enormous credits they were obliged to give in the course of their business; from their distant connexions and agents, to whose fidelity and capacity they must trust so much; from the dangers of all the elements; from the political change in their own and foreign countries; and, in short, from every quarter and source from which danger and ruin can come.

Foreign trade was vital to the nation's welfare, yet its risks were such that without legal shelter, entrepreneurs would fear to conduct it at all.

Both sound policy and "the obligations of humanity and justice," said Hopkinson, demanded bankruptcy protection for merchants. Not only were they men "of good principles and capacities for usefulness, whose offences are frequently nothing but inevitable misfortunes," but assisting them to get a new start would set loose "a mass of talent and industry." "Of what value is a distressed and harassed insolvent debtor to his country?"

Spokesmen for landed debtors reasoned identically. Confessedly they had been carried away by optimism and bought too much on credit. But if they had been imprudent, it was an imprudence that society as a whole (and particularly the federal government, which set the purchase terms) had sanctioned and encouraged. Why punish them for a miscalculation which all had shared?

A bill to relieve land debtors passed Congress and became law in 1821, though the bankruptcy bill failed. The debate over them and over the relief question in all its forms, both in Congress and the states, revealed the complexity and ambivalence of Americans' response to the novel demands of a commercial society. With no political parties to shape the alternatives, discussion was both heated and confused. Mixing arguments of morality and expediency, speakers on all sides sought somehow to capture the benefits of enterprise while avoiding its excesses. They wanted growth without extravagance, energy without recklessness. Still, amid charges of culpability and expostulations of innocence, few called for forsaking the chase and retiring to more sedate pursuits. Men like Niles, Jackson, and Kendall, innovative and successful in their own affairs, touted industry and economy as the slow but sure route to advance, not an alternative to it. Even farmer advocates spoke the language of improvement. Championing relief for land purchasers, Senator Richard M. Johnson of Kentucky praised the nation's husbandmen not just for their hardy toil, but for the "persevering enterprise" that had led them unwarily into debt.

Debates over banking, credit, and relief did not, in most states, draw clear or enduring political lines. Their urgency faded as prosperity returned. Nor did the unstructured dialogue reflect a discernable clash of classes. Debtors and creditors were not so much distinct constituencies as interests diffused throughout the community. Acute distress in the West lent the crisis a regional coloring, but relief measures there reflected no rejection of commercial aspirations. Most westerners, like other Americans who worked the soil, sought profit as well as sustenance. It was not devotion to some pastoral ideal but pell-mell expansion, agricultural as well as commercial and industrial, that encouraged borrowing and thus exposed them to the panic's worst effects. Land dealers, merchants, and manufacturers in the new inland empire were trapped in the collapse along with farmers and planters and joined them in the clamor for relief.

Short-lived but severe, the depression furnished a jolting reminder of the perils of unchecked development. Americans hailed the spirit of improvement and enterprise, but recoiled when that spirit produced rampant speculation, excessive debt, and abuse of privilege. Never fully extinguished, popular distrust of the symbols of commercial excess—especially of banks—lingered as a potentially explosive sentiment.

Commerce and the Supreme Court

The Panic of 1819 raised the enduring political question of how enterprise could be simultaneously cherished and controlled, and how such indispensable instruments of commercial advance as banks and corporations could be made socially responsible. Debated in the states and in Congress, these issues also engaged the United States Supreme Court. In a trio of momentous decisions handed down in early 1819, the Court took its own stand on the means of nurturing the spirit of improvement.

Guided since 1801 by Chief Justice John Marshall of Virginia (appointed by President John Adams), the Supreme Court had wielded its judicial weight carefully but effectively to fortify two intertwined principles—the supremacy of the national government over the states, and the Court's own authority as final interpreter and arbiter of the United States Constitution. For Marshall and his most energetic associate, Joseph Story of Massachusetts (appointed to the Court, with fitting symmetry, by Virginian James Madison), the ascendancy of national over state power was good in itself, a fulfillment of Revolutionary promise. But it was also means to another great end—the opening of a broad forum for business enterprise. As Story explained in 1818, "the spirit of commerce, once excited, is not easily extinguished or controlled. It is a useful spirit, which imparts life and intelligence to the body politic, increases the comforts and enjoyments of every class of people, and gradually liberalizes and expands the mind, as well as fosters the best interests of humanity." As nationality encouraged commerce, so commerce would cement union. Seeing enterprise as the carrier of progress, the Marshall Court set out to clear a field for its exertions.

The obstructions they found in its path were state laws. State legislators presumed the power to govern in their community interest. But in the Marshall Court's eyes, the community of trade transcended the states. The true scope of commerce knew no limits. It needed an open arena to work its improving magic. It needed stable, uniform rules throughout the country, and these only national authority could supply. In the constitutional grant of power to Congress to regulate commerce "among the several States" and the ban on state laws "impairing the Obligation of Contracts," the Court found the germ of that authority.

In the 1819 case of *Sturges v. Crowinshield,* the Supreme Court struck down a New York law relieving insolvent debtors. Richard Crowinshield was a New York merchant from a prominent Massachusetts family. Engaged in overseas trade at a time of international upheaval, he fell prey to embargo and war, declared himself insolvent in 1811 under the New York law, and obtained release from his debts. With this new start he returned to Massachusetts and prospered; but a New York creditor, Josiah Sturgis, sued him to recover an old loan.

Substantively the case raised the same issue with which Congress and the states were grappling—whether the aims of protecting property and promoting enterprise were best served by relieving debtors or holding them to their obligations. Overlaying this question of commercial utility were political and constitutional complications. Congress, which had power to impose "uniform Laws on the subject of Bankruptcies throughout the United States," had not done so. In the absence of federal law, the Court conceded that states might adopt rules on insolvency or bankruptcy (despite fine distinctions, the two words were nearly interchangeable). But the justices all agreed that by freeing Crowinshield from a legal debt, the New York law violated the "Obligation of Contracts" and was therefore unconstitutional.

Exactly how far this ruling restrained state power over debtor and creditor remained unclear. The New York statute under which Crowinshield took shelter had operated retroactively; it was passed after he had contracted his debt. Also, Sturgis had not sued in a New York court, but in federal court in Massachusetts. The Supreme Court did not say whether states could pass prospective laws affecting future contracts and governing their own courts. Congress could clarify everything and preempt state action by adopting a national bankruptcy system. In anticipation, Justice

Story drafted a bill himself. But Congress did not act, and the Court finally refined its edict. In *Ogden v. Saunders* in 1827, it sanctioned prospective state bankruptcy laws—a decision from which three of the seven justices, including Marshall and Story, dissented.

This unusual division among the justices (Marshall's dissent was his first on a major constitutional question in twenty-six years on the Court) mirrored the general uncertainty over the rules best suited to a commercial economy. Within the Court there was no dispute over ends. All agreed on protecting what Justice Robert Trimble called "the right of acquiring and possessing property." For Marshall, allowing state legislatures "the power of changing the relative situation of debtor and creditor, of interfering with contracts" would be "to break in upon the ordinary intercourse of society, and destroy all confidence between man and man." But the opposing majority saw relief laws as "useful, if not absolutely necessary, in a commercial community" and "vitally important to a people overwhelmed in debt, and urged to enterprise by the activity of mind that is generated by revolutions and free governments." So the Court straddled: states could not undo existing contracts, but they could set rules for future ones, including procedures for expunging debts.

On the rights of corporations the Supreme Court spoke with a clearer voice. It had already held, beginning with the 1810 case of *Fletcher v. Peck,* that a state law conveying land or other property was a "contract" in the constitutional sense of the word, which the state could not retract or modify at will. In 1819 the justices expanded that doctrine to cover corporate charters in the celebrated case of *Dartmouth College v. Woodward.*

Dartmouth, located in Hanover, New Hampshire, was incorporated by the colony's royal governor in 1769 and governed under its charter by a self-perpetuating board of trustees. Responding to a dispute between the trustees and the college president, the New Hampshire legislature in 1816 placed the school under state-appointed overseers, changed its name to Dartmouth University, and in effect converted it to a state institution. The trustees sued to get their college back.

The Supreme Court's ruling for the trustees fortified the rights of corporations against the governments that created them. Although Dartmouth served the community by educating young men, Marshall held that in the eyes of the law it was not, like a chartered city government, a public instrument, a mere arm of the state. Rather, it was a private entity, and as such it enjoyed the same property rights as an individual. Having vested these rights in the college administration, the state could not rescind them at will. Once called into existence by a charter that constituted a "contract," corporate privileges were untouchable, even by the governments that granted them.

The case concerned, as Daniel Webster said in arguing it for the trustees, only a small college; and its impact was limited by Justice Story's suggestion, in a concurring opinion, that legislatures could reserve the right to alter a corporate charter simply by saying so in the charter itself. Still the implications of *Dartmouth College* were broad and, at least on the part of Story (who behind the scenes had helped to orchestrate the case), wholly intentional. In 1819 corporations were new and untried entities, still evolving from their origins as delegations of governmental authority for public purposes. Their legal status and rights were yet poorly defined. In sheltering them from legislative interference by circumscribing their public character and clothing them with the sanctity of private property, the Supreme Court gave a powerful push toward incorporation as the preferred form of business organization.

If states could not cancel their own corporate creations, still less could they tamper with those of the federal government. That was the import of the Court's third great case in 1819, concerning the Bank of the United States.

The Bank's performance following its creation in 1816 had brought it into quick disrepute. Instead of resisting the state banks' expansion, the Bank had joined it; and when it did change course, the reversal angered debtors and state banks. The post-panic reaction against banking thus fell doubly on the Bank of the United States. Those who resented its power over state banks and those who hated all banks united to attack it. It was damned for failing to restrain state banks and damned again for trying to restrain them. The Bank's reputation fell further with the exposure early in 1819 of incompetence and malfeasance at its Philadelphia headquarters and outright fraud at some of the eighteen branch offices.

Even before the panic, several state legislatures tried to block the Bank of the United States from interfering or competing with state-chartered institutions. Six states, including Maryland, laid prohibitive taxes on its in-state branches while two others banned them altogether. This action raised the dual question of Congress's right to create the Bank and the states' right to regulate it. In March 1819, as popular outcry mounted against the Bank, the Supreme Court took on these issues in *McCulloch v. Maryland*.

Addressing the first question, one that had repeatedly dogged both the first and second federal banks, Chief Justice Marshall affirmed the constitutionality of the Bank of the United States. Though the Constitution did not in words authorize Congress to charter a corporation, it did empower it to collect taxes, borrow money, regulate commerce, and to "make all Laws which shall be necessary and proper" to effect these or other specific powers. According to Marshall and a unanimous Court, it was the right of Congress itself, not the courts, to decide what means were necessary and proper.

The Bank, therefore, though a privately owned and managed concern, was also in effect an arm of the federal government, and states could not touch it. If they could tax its branches into closure ("the power to tax involves the power to destroy"), they could frustrate Congress's aim in creating the Bank in the first place. "The states have no power, by taxation or otherwise, to retard, impede, burden, or in any manner control, the operations of the constitutional laws enacted by Congress to carry into execution the powers vested in the general government," Marshall intoned. Maryland's tax was unconstitutional.

To stunned critics the decision appeared to mean that the country must submit to "be prostrated at the feet of an overbearing stock-jobbing aristocracy." Pronounced in the midst of the panic, *McCulloch v. Maryland* evoked outraged opposition. The Court had cloaked a profit-seeking business corporation with the authority and immunity of the federal government itself. Timing and circumstance could hardly have been worse. James W. McCulloch was the cashier of the Baltimore branch of the Bank of the United States, whose refusal to pay Maryland's tax had triggered the case. But, as came to light just days after the decision, he was also an embezzler who used his position at the Bank to funnel huge sums to his business partners (including the president of the Baltimore branch) and to lend half a million dollars to himself. The Court in *McCulloch* thus threw its protection around a despised institution, embodied by a man who at that moment stood before the public as a symbol of flagrant corruption and corporate abuse.

In Ohio discontent spilled over into outright defiance. Just a month earlier, in February 1819, the legislature had levied a $50,000 tax on each of the state's two branches of the Bank of the United States. Undeterred by *McCulloch*, the state in September demanded payment. The Bank refused, state authorities seized the money by force, and federal authorities seized it back and jailed the state treasurer. The upshot of this comedy was another lawsuit, *Osborn v. Bank of the United States,* which reached the Supreme Court in 1824. Again the Court affirmed the Bank's immunity from state control.

By this time returning prosperity had cooled tempers; and the Bank, under prudent management, was proving an asset rather than a threat to the commercial community. Ohio dropped the confrontation. Another landmark case of the same term allowed the Court to strike a further blow for federal supremacy in commercial regulation. Sixteen years earlier, in 1808, New York had granted a state monopoly on steam navigation to Robert Fulton and his partner Robert Livingston. Both were now dead, but their heirs still controlled all steamboat traffic into and out of New York. In *Gibbons v. Ogden,* the Court voided the grant as an infringement on Congress's authority to regulate commerce between the states. Again the Court struck down a state law, but circumstances made this decision as welcome as *McCulloch* was hated. In 1808, when steamboats were new and unproven, government favors were necessary to lure inventors and investors. The New York law had done just that. But by 1824, with hundreds of boats in operation, the grant had lost its purpose; its only effect was to maintain a franchise resented by competitors and customers alike. *Gibbons* broke the monopoly and invited steamboat operators to run where they would, free from the paralysis of conflicting state privileges and restraints.

Taken as a whole, the Marshall Court's jurisprudence laid a firm constitutional foundation for the "spirit of commerce." The Court did not stand simply for protecting property and encouraging enterprise. No simple stand was possible. Different kinds of property rights and productive strategies inevitably clashed. When the Supreme Court curtailed the powers of state governments, it narrowed their ability to protect property as well as destroy it, to foster improvement as well as inhibit it. What bound the Court's rulings was not their promotional outlook, which state authorities generally shared, but their national scope, their determination to secure a wider arena for commerce by clearing away local fluctuations and impediments. "In all commercial regulations," Marshall pronounced in an 1821 case, "we are one and the same people."

The spirit of improvement working everywhere after the War of 1812 had raised perplexing questions about relations of debtor and creditor, the rights of corporations, and the extent of regulatory power. From a nationalist viewpoint, exactly how these questions were answered was less important than that they be answered. As Daniel Webster put it to Joseph Story in 1824 concerning a pending revision of the tariff on imports (on which he was feeling his own uncertainty), "it is a great object to settle the concerns of the community; so that one may know what to depend on." The "community" Webster meant was defined by livelihood, not residence—a brethren of traders, not a town or neighborhood. Businessmen wanted firm, clear rules that could be counted on and that were uniform throughout the country. These the Supreme Court endeavored to supply.

In doing so it placed its own authority at risk. The Supreme Court's claim to pronounce definitively on the meaning of the Constitution had never passed unchallenged. By 1825 the Court had struck down laws of nine states. Ominously, Congress in 1822 debated proposals to reconstitute the Court or narrow its jurisdiction. Perennially suspect as an undemocratic institution removed from popular control, and lacking direct means of enforcing its will, the Supreme Court's power rested ultimately on public acceptance. Rulings like *McCulloch* tested its limits.

Knowing this, the Marshall Court moved carefully. It overruled state authorities with a great show of reluctance. Carefully Marshall clothed his boldest pronouncements in the garb of judicial reticence. "Courts are the mere instruments of the law," he explained in the *Osborn* case in 1824, "and can will nothing." Justices tried to foster an image of the Court as an impartial oracle of constitutional truth. Usually they spoke as one, with no concurring opinions or dissents. Marshall and his fellows masked their differences by compromise or by simply putting off decision until consensus could be reached.

Behind the scenes, justices were anything but passive. Working with a coterie of attorneys (notably Daniel Webster) who specialized in Supreme Court litigation, they helped set up crucial test cases and contrived to get them quickly before the Court. Off the bench they acknowledged and welcomed the practical consequences of their decisions. "Let us extend the national authority over the whole extent of power given by the Constitution," exclaimed Joseph Story in 1815.

Let us have . . . a national bank; a national system of bankruptcy; a great navigation act; a general survey of our ports, and appointments of port-wardens and pilots; Judicial Courts which shall embrace the whole constitutional powers; national notaries; public and national justices of the peace, for the commercial and national concerns of the United States.

Marshall's strategy of sheltering policy-making behind a veil of judicial circumspection helped deflect censure, but it could not silence it entirely. Broadly speaking, the Supreme Court's promotion of commerce as the vehicle of American progress was at one with the spirit of the age. But in furthering national interests, the Court overrode local ones; in affirming federal authority, it challenged the traditional prerogative of state courts and legislatures to determine what rules best suited community interests. The question bruited by the Court's landmark rulings of 1819–1825 was not whether there should be banks and colleges and steamboats and corporations, but to whom they should be accountable—the federal government or the states, the people's own elected representatives or an unelected judiciary.

As it happened, this question of power, in part as old as the republic itself, was acquiring a new dimension at this moment. The Supreme Court's assertion of federal supremacy reawakened localist fears of central tyranny. It also aroused democratic hostility to a judicial "aristocracy." Around the country, a popular upheaval was brewing—one that would propound new definitions of progress and lay new claims to its control.

CHAPTER Four

The Statecraft of Progress

> The more enlarged the sphere of commercial circulation, the more extended that of social intercourse; the more strongly are we bound together; the more inseparable are our destinies. . . . Let us then bind the Republic together with a perfect system of roads and canals. Let us conquer space.
> —John C. Calhoun, 1817

> The great effort of my administration was to mature into a permanent and regular system the application of all the superfluous revenue of the Union to internal improvement. . . . With this system, in ten years from this day, the surface of the whole Union would have been checkered over with Rail roads and Canals. It may still be done, half a century later, and with the limping gait of State Legislation and private adventure . . . I fell, and with me fell, I fear never to rise again, certainly never to rise again in my day, the system of internal improvement by National means and National energies.
> —John Quincy Adams, 1837

After the War of 1812 a new generation of politicians gave voice to Americans' aspirations for greatness. Fired by patriotism and faith in the future, they planned a program of improvement under sponsorship of the federal government.

The leading spokesmen for the movement—John Caldwell Calhoun of South Carolina, John Quincy Adams of Massachusetts, Andrew Jackson of Tennessee, and Henry Clay of Kentucky—came from all parts of the country and articulated a vision of national progress that transcended local horizons. They saw limitless prospects, unbounded opportunities. But to seize them required direction and discipline—in a word, system. Clay dubbed his plan for coordinated economic growth the "American System." Adams, as secretary of state in 1821, proposed "a single and universal system" of weights and measures to further "that great result, the improvement of the physical, moral, and intellectual condition of man upon earth." Conceiving America's destiny in national terms, they exalted the supremacy of the federal government and favored an extensive use of its powers.

But the systemizers' plans for material and moral betterment faltered before resistance that drew on old ideas of localism and new ones of democracy. Ultimately the nationalists met defeat, not because they championed progress, but because their ideas of progress ran counter to Americans' desire to define and realize their future for themselves.

The Nationalist Program

President James Madison framed the nationalist agenda in his seventh annual message to Congress, in December 1815. For the first time he could afford to dwell on domestic concerns. After years of foreign crisis, the United States was at last "in the tranquil enjoyment of prosperous and honorable peace." Having gained respect abroad and confidence at home by waging the War of 1812 to a successful end, the government now needed to seek out ways of "patronizing in every authorized mode undertakings conducive to the aggregate wealth and individual comfort of our citizens." Madison proposed a national bank to stabilize the currency, a tariff on imports to protect home manufactures against renewed foreign competition, a road and canal program to bind the country together, and a national university in Washington to nurture knowledge and patriotism.

Madison's policy conjoined development, improvement, and enlightenment. In the House of Representatives young nationalists seized the initiative. John C. Calhoun and William Lowndes of South Carolina sponsored bank, tariff, and road bills, and Speaker Henry Clay pushed them through. Disparaging constitutional quibbles and calculations of local interest, Calhoun urged legislators to think nationally. No people on earth enjoyed a fairer prospect than Americans. Only disunion could threaten their future, and the surest guard against separatism was "mutual dependence and intercourse." Rightly regarded, the three great sources of wealth—agriculture, commerce, and manufacturing—were interdependent. Together, properly nourished by high-minded statesmen, they promised perpetual unity and "universal opulence."

The charter for the Bank of the United States and a new tariff passed Congress and became law in 1816. The next year Calhoun's bill to subsidize internal improvements also passed. But on his last day in office President Madison vetoed it. He now found no authority in the Constitution for federal roads, canals, or river improvements, though he had recommended them more than once. The new president, James Monroe, also praised improvements but announced his "settled conviction" against Congress's right to build them.

The Virginians' Dilemma

Madison's and Monroe's equivocation between progressive purpose and constitutional scruple reflected the uncertain outlook of their native state. Virginia had long been accustomed to lead, and others had looked to her for leadership. But now Virginians did not know where to go. While Virginia presidents hesitantly endorsed programs of commercial development, Virginia congressmen led the fight against them. At their moment of greatest triumph—their statecraft vindicated by foreign and domestic success, the British enemy repelled, the Federalist opposition in ruins—Virginians found themselves enmeshed in doubts about the future.

The last years of Thomas Jefferson, the sage of Virginia republicanism, exemplified his state's travail. More than any other man, Jefferson had given form to the aspirations that blossomed with the Revolution and flowered anew after the War of 1812. In old age he held to his optimistic faith in humanity's virtue and capacity for growth. The inexorable "progress of the human mind" ensured that each generation would surpass the last in knowledge, wisdom, and statecraft. As Jefferson told his old friend and rival John Adams in 1816, his was not one of those "hypocondriac minds, inhabitants of diseased bodies, disgusted with the present, and despairing of the future. . . . My temperament is sanguine. I steer my bark with Hope in the head, leaving Fear astern." "I shall not die," he repeated five years later, "without a hope that light and liberty are on steady advance."

Yet Jefferson looked on the enterprising nation that emerged from the War of 1812 with growing misgiving. In 1814 he celebrated Americans' healthy equality of condition, their freedom from twin evils of debasing poverty and decadent luxury. But soon he was decrying the mad rush for riches, the chasing after phantom fortunes. "We are now taught to believe that legerdemain tricks upon paper can produce as solid wealth as hard labor in the earth," he complained in 1816. "It is vain for common sense to urge that *nothing* can produce but *nothing*." Speculation and fraud usurped all measures of real value, leaving him to wonder what anything was worth. By 1819 Jefferson feared "a general demoralization of the nation, a filching from industry its honest earnings, wherewith to build up palaces, and raise gambling stock for swindlers and shavers, who are too close to their career of piracies with fraudulent bankruptcies."

Virginia's clouded prospects fed Jefferson's foreboding. He and his neighbors discerned no real gain in the price fluctuations of the postwar years. Plagued by stagnant markets and dwindling yields, Virginia agriculture continued its agonizing slide. Many planters, seeking new fortunes in cotton, decamped for the bonanza lands of the southwest. The exodus depressed land values (the essential measure of wealth in an agricultural society) and eroded Virginia's political weight. First in congressional representation in 1800, the state dropped to third behind New York and Pennsylvania by 1820. In 1815 a legislative committee observed that "while many other States have been advancing in wealth and numbers, with a rapidity which has astonished themselves, the ancient dominion and elder sister of the Union has remained stationary." Virginia's countryside offered "sad spectacles" of "wasted and deserted fields," abandoned homes and ruined churches.

In the next decade Virginia land values fell by half. When Jefferson, preparing for death in 1826, tried to clear off his debts by selling property, he could find no buyers. "The long succession of years of stunted crops," he wailed to James Madison, "of reduced prices, the general prostration of the farming business, under levies for the support of manufactures, &c., with the calamitous fluctuations of value in our paper medium" had produced an "abject depression" which "glutted the land market, while it drew off its bidders."

Inexorable economic decline belied glib confidence in a better tomorrow. Interpreting the present in light of the past, Jefferson came to see encroaching commercialism as simply resurgent Federalism, a new chapter in the old struggle of "Aristocrats and Democrats." Increasingly disillusioned, he warned in 1825 that a new generation,

having nothing in them of the feelings or principles of '76, now look to a single and splendid government of an aristocracy, founded on banking institutions, and money incorporations under the guise and cloak of their favored branches of manufactures, commerce and navigation, riding and ruling over the plundered ploughman and beggared yeomanry.

Where some saw progress, the apostle of progress now spied declension and approaching despotism.

While Jefferson battled private despair, other Virginia planter-politicians sounded public alarms. Like him, they traced their state's plight to political causes. Behind the patriotic platitudes that wrapped the nationalist program, they spied the old Federalist design of consolidation and oppression. John Taylor of Caroline, their most prolific and influential spokesman, damned bounties and subsidies, taxes and tariffs, charters and corporations. All were devices to transfer wealth from producers to parasitic "capitalists." In treatises like *Arator* (1818) and *Tyranny Unmasked* (1822), Taylor decried the rape and plunder of agriculture by paper profiteers and stockjobbers. Federal developmental policies, he charged, aimed to erect a commercial and manufacturing aristocracy, not on the honest profits of those endeavors, but on extortions from the farming majority. Taylor especially blasted the tariff, which struck farmers doubly by raising the cost of their purchases while dampening the foreign market for their surplus.

Though Taylor, like Jefferson, found American society increasingly alien after 1815, he was no reflexive traditionalist, expounding the virtues of torpid self-sufficiency. His thinking was both cosmopolitan and progressive. Taylor welcomed real improvement in all its forms, and devoted himself to resuscitating and reforming Virginia's ravished agriculture. He saw commerce, "the free animating principle of fair exchanges and unplundered industry," as the key to all progress. Trade in "necessaries, conveniences, and especially luxuries" was the "moral steam-engine" by which "civilization has been extended, knowledge produced, refinements discovered, wealth obtained, and a love of liberty inspired." Like the nationalists, Taylor saw "the finger of God" pointing Americans to a special destiny. Citing their birthright of civil and religious liberty and their continental expanse offering reward to industry and security from invasion, Taylor said, "I behold a miracle, worked for the salvation of liberty, and creating an awful responsibility on the people of the United States."

But Taylor accused the nationalists of squandering that opportunity instead of seizing it. A disciple of Adam Smith, Taylor believed that only individual energies, driven by self-interest and wholly unaided and unfettered by government, could yield the wealth and happiness Americans sought. Instead of presuming to guide and direct, government should follow the rule of "let us alone." Free trade, to Taylor, was the great "moral discovery" by which the United States could find its future. Every artificial interference with natural economic processes—every bounty, tax, tariff, privilege, subsidy, and charter—drove Americans further from "the great purpose to which they seem almost to have been destined" down the European road to despotism and destitution.

Jefferson and Taylor saw the nationalist program pointing directly the wrong way. When left alone, farming was Americans' natural pursuit. American farmers, like British manufacturers, were favored by circumstance to command the world market. Yet the government drained them of capital, siphoning the profits of agriculture to prop up artificial manufactures. In Taylor's eyes, as in Jefferson's, this "property-transferring policy" was not merely mistaken, but malevolent. Ambitious politicians leagued with avaricious capitalists to exploit the public for private gain.

Watching greed trample liberty in the name of progress and improvement, Virginians found their hopes for the future displaced by gloomy doubts. Out-argued and out-voted in Washington, they looked to the states to resist encroaching tyranny. To justify that resistance, they fell back on the old ramparts of state's rights and narrow construction of the Constitution. While Jefferson cheered them on, Taylor, Judge Spencer Roane, and Thomas Ritchie of the *Richmond Enquirer* attacked the Supreme Court's cloaked usurpations of power. In Congress, John Randolph and a small band of Virginians and North Carolinians assailed every nationalist measure as a transgression on the Constitution.

Outside of North Carolina, which shared Virginia's plight and followed her lead in politics, the state found its surest allies in New England. There too, the threat of being run over or plundered in the race for improvement prompted a querulous resistance to nationalist schemes. Fear of losing control of their fate united Virginia rejectionists like Randolph with the surviving New England Federalists, who had earlier sustained a similar loss at the hands of Virginia herself. Lacking a direct route to the West, New England, like Virginia, stood little to gain from an expensive national transportation program. Yankee import merchants, like Virginia planters, claimed injury from the protective tariff.

Nationalism vs. Sectionalism

In Washington from 1815 into the early 1820s, Virginians and New Englanders made common cause against federal internal improvements. Backed by presidents Madison and Monroe, they succeeded in stanching the clamor for congressional aid rising from the central Atlantic states and the whole western country from Louisiana to Illinois.

The tariff provoked a more complex range of responses. James Madison's 1815 message had endorsed protective duties as a great patriotic measure. Domestic manufactures were too vital for the country's defense and well-being to leave to unassisted private effort. Self-reliance, at least in essential items, was imperative for national security and prosperity.

The tariff of 1816 passed Congress by large majorities, with little objection raised in principle. But the duties it imposed failed to shield fledgling manufacturers from an onslaught of cheap British goods. Ironmasters and textile mill owners begged for higher rates. The Panic of 1819 forced congressmen from all over the country to consult the immediate needs of their constituents. Kentucky hemp growers, Pittsburgh glassmakers, and other inland producers blamed imports for their distress and joined in the call for protection. But planters laboring under collapsed staple prices and crushing land debts cried against adding new taxes to their burdens. When a higher tariff did finally pass Congress in 1824, the vote split starkly along regional lines. The mid-Atlantic, Ohio valley, and northwestern states voted overwhelmingly in favor, the plantation South just as strongly against. Only New England divided.

Though still buoyed by a rhetoric of transcendent patriotism, the program of tariff and internal improvement had in fact devolved in a few years from an almost consensual blueprint for national development to a bitterly contested sectional agenda. Its constituency centered in a band of states running westward from New York and Pennsylvania through Ohio and Kentucky to Illinois and Missouri. New England, now beginning to turn from foreign trade to manufacturing and from Federalist parochialism to a newfound cosmopolitanism, eyed the nationalist system with uncertainty. Planters, except in Kentucky and in Louisiana, where tariffs sustained the sugar industry, dug in their heels against it.

The crumbling of South Carolina's support for the program showed how local concerns constrained nationalist politicians. Spurning the narrow views of their Virginia and North Carolina neighbors, John C. Calhoun and his fellows had trumpeted the vision of a nation marching toward glory under the twin banners of internal improvement and domestic manufacturing. Observing Calhoun in Monroe's cabinet in 1821, John Quincy Adams thought him a man "of enlarged philosophical views, and of ardent patriotism . . . above all sectional and factious prejudices more than any other statesman of this Union with whom I have ever acted." But Calhoun's state soon turned against the nationalist system, and began to pull him and his friends with it. In 1820 and again in 1824 the lower house of the South Carolina legislature patriotically deprecated state opposition to federal economic policy. A year later it reversed itself and joined the upper house in denouncing both tariff and internal improvements as unconstitutional usurpations of power. In the United States Senate, Calhoun's colleague Robert Hayne railed against "this scheme of promoting certain employments at the expense of others as unequal, oppressive, and unjust."

Like Virginia's, South Carolina's emerging defensiveness was driven partly by economic stringency. With competition from new lands in Alabama and Mississippi, the state's cotton economy revived slowly after the Panic of 1819. Carolinians too now faced the prospect of waning population, land values, and political weight. To straitened planters a protective tariff no longer looked like a means toward general well-being and national self-reliance. Instead it seemed an unfair and onerous burden, a naked levy on one class of citizens for the benefit of another. Carolina planters began to view manufacturers not as partners in progress, but as oppressors and extortionists.

In short, South Carolinians, like Virginians, began to think after the Panic of 1819 that sacrifice for the national welfare was something they could no longer afford. But another, deeper worry underlay their turn against the tariff, causing some to articulate the issue (not quite accurately) in sectional terms of North and South. Allowing the federal government to steer the course of progress perhaps meant surrendering control of southern destinies to a northern majority. Carolinians, like Virginians, worried that northern designs for their future might include interfering with slavery. Here southern whites saw not just a challenge to their interests, but a threat to their lives.

Slavery and Colonization

Unease about slavery had long troubled Virginia planters' outlook on the future. The social and moral incubus of a growing, economically superfluous slave and free black population (the latter a legacy of Revolutionary-era manumissions) hung heavily on white minds and consciences. Some masters, like Thomas Jefferson, clung to antislavery ideals nurtured by the Revolution. To the end of his life Jefferson never relinquished, though he muted in public, his conviction that slavery was indefensible in principle and abominable in practice. Others, including John Taylor, defended the master-slave relationship as inherently benign and blamed predatory free blacks and misguided philanthropists like Jefferson for undermining it.

Taylor thought slavery a bane, not for its injustice to blacks, but for the threat of rebellion that mismanaged slaves posed to whites.

Torn by doubt and division even among themselves, restive planters felt they could trust no outsiders with slavery, even fellow Virginians. By 1820 a large, mainly nonslaveholding population had grown up in the western part of the state. Fearful of the burdens that backcountrymen might impose on slaveholding property, lowland planters clung to their predominance of power in state government. Repudiating Jefferson's ideas of egalitarian white democracy, they fought successfully for years against a more equal legislative apportionment and an expanded suffrage. Together, forebodings about slavery and economic decline warped some Virginia statesmen into unblushing reactionism. In Washington the misanthrope John Randolph, defiantly out of touch with the times, deprecated all forms of change and opposed even the admission of new states.

Among Virginia slaveholders neither critics nor apologists could regard their future with equanimity, and neither saw a way out. To do nothing meant sinking slowly in a sea of resentful black faces. Yet all assumed that emancipation would yield either racial amalgamation or race war. Both alternatives were unthinkable. Even Jefferson coupled his heartfelt indictments of slavery with revulsion at the thought of racial mixing. As early as 1785 he proposed to cut the knot by freeing Virginia's slaves and shipping them out of the country. Forty years later he still clung to the hope of "getting rid of them."

"Colonization," or assisted deportation, appealed to both northern and southern whites who were eager to expunge the reproach of slavery and yet avert a black citizenry. In December 1816 the American Colonization Society organized in Washington. It began with high optimism. Noting the "unexampled efforts" being made to advance knowledge, civilization, and Christianity, the society thought the time "peculiarly auspicious" for a "great national effort . . . in the great cause of philanthropy." The society's illustrious leadership augured success in its endeavors and stifled any doubt of its benevolent and patriotic purpose. Supreme Court Justice Bushrod Washington, George Washington's nephew, was its first president, and the officers, contributors, and well-wishers constituted a galaxy of statesmen, among them President Monroe, former presidents Jefferson and Madison, Chief Justice John Marshall, John Randolph, Henry Clay, Andrew Jackson, William Harris Crawford, Francis Scott Key, Richard Rush, and Daniel Webster.

Yet colonization found few friends in the planting states from South

Carolina west through Georgia, Alabama, Mississippi, and Louisiana. If slavery seemed a moribund institution in the older South—a besieged benevolence in the eyes of some, an encumbrance and a curse to others—in the new inland empire it was the foundation of wealth and progress. Untroubled by Virginians' forebodings, planters of the cotton domain were not about to surrender their means of advancement, even for a price.

Whatever their view of slavery's morality and prospects, on one thing all white southerners could agree: The choice of what to do about it was no one's but their own. Generations of bondage had carved deep social cleavages between black and white. For whites living in slave country—even, perhaps especially, for those who owned no slaves themselves—slavery was more than a regimen of labor. It was an essential tool of separation and control, the only barrier to unbridled racial mixture or racial violence. Right or wrong, it had become a fundamental fact, a way of life. Regardless of private convictions, no southerners could accept outside tampering with an institution that, in the words of the South Carolina House of Representatives, was "now inseparably connected with their social and political existence." Should Congress interfere with slavery, warned Jefferson, whites would have to abandon the South, and "most fortunate those who can do it first."

In 1819, just as the panic deepened and the Marshall Court issued its barrage of nationalizing edicts, the threat of federal interference with slavery suddenly arose. The slaveholding territory of Missouri had applied for statehood. Congressman James Tallmadge, Jr., of New York sought to impose gradual emancipation as a precondition of Missouri's admittance. A northern phalanx in the House of Representatives passed his amendment, but the southern-dominated Senate rejected it. With Congress deadlocked, the controversy spread from Washington to towns and villages across the country. Northern meetings and petitions demanded a halt to slavery's spread, while southerners warned of disunion if Congress dared intrude on Missourians' right to determine their own institutions.

After a year of escalating rhetoric, Congress reached a settlement in March 1820. A handful of northern congressmen joined the southerners in voting to admit Missouri to statehood without restriction (that is, with slavery), while a bisectional majority agreed to ban slavery forever in territories west and north of Missouri along the line of 36°30′ north latitude. This, coupled with the admission of the new free state of Maine, was the "Missouri Compromise."

The depth of conviction on both sides of the Missouri question unnerved nationalists throughout the country. John Quincy Adams, Henry Clay, and John C. Calhoun all feared it foretold eventual dissolution and civil war. Thomas Jefferson, "awakened and filled . . . with terror" by the debate, "considered it at once as the knell of the Union." The compromise was "a reprieve only, not a final sentence."

At the same time, skeptics who noted the pervasive discrimination against blacks in the free states questioned the sincerity of northern anti-slavery. Charging northerners with hypocrisy and fanaticism, Jefferson traced the agitation to a secret Federalist design to mount a political come-back on sectional confrontation. This was nonsense, but it was true that most northern whites did not look, any more than Jefferson himself, toward a racially egalitarian society. Having already rid themselves of slavery, few saw its existence elsewhere as a matter of pressing concern. As John Quincy Adams observed, "the question to the North and in the free states is merely speculative. The people do not feel it in their persons or their purses. On the slave side it comes home to the feelings and interests of every man in the community."

Still, despite their racial prejudice, most northern whites clung to a root antislavery conviction. They continued to believe what leading southern-ers had once freely admitted—that slavery was inherently unjust, that it contravened fundamental rights and principles on which the country was founded, and that the perpetuation and spread of what Jefferson himself had called a "foul stain upon our national character" were incompatible with America's mission of progress and enlightenment.

This sentiment was pervasive in the North, but usually inert. It was one thing to abhor slavery, another to meddle with standing property rights and social relations. The Tallmadge amendment thus perfectly suited the aims of people who in all things looked mainly to the future. With it they could shape the emerging West toward freedom without violating the self-determination of any existing state. Northern congressmen who opposed the westward spread of slavery were neither furthering a Federalist con-spiracy nor seeking sectional domination. They were speaking their con-stituents' views. As a New Hampshire Republican insisted, "for a member of either house, from a non slave-holding State to tolerate slavery beyond its present limits, is political suicide, & his constituents ought to limit his public services to his present term."

To some whites in both sections, the Missouri scare underscored the urgency of pushing ahead with colonization. In January 1824 the Ohio legislature offered a proposal "predicated upon the principle that the evil of slavery is a national one, and that the people and the states of this Union ought mutually to participate in the duties and burthens of removing it." The federal government, with consent of the slaveholding states, should gradually emancipate the slaves and settle them abroad, with the whole nation sharing the expense.

Seven free states and Delaware seconded this suggestion. Georgia, South Carolina, Missouri, Mississippi, Louisiana, and Alabama denounced it. The South Carolina Senate called Ohio's proposition "strange and ill-advised," and warned against outside tampering with slave property. A proposal by Senator Rufus King of New York in 1825 to dedicate revenues from western federal land sales to the purchase and removal of slaves brought more southern fulminations against "officious and impertinent intermeddlings with our domestic concerns."

Northern challenges spurred some southerners to try to reconcile principle with practice by working out moral and religious rationalizations for slavery. But most still defended the system less on grounds of abstract justice than of urgent necessity. South Carolinians felt the precariousness of their position most acutely. Only in South Carolina did slaves outnumber whites. In 1822 the uncovering of plans for a massive slave revolt in Charleston threw white Carolinians into a frenzy. The revelation that the plotters had drawn inspiration from the Missouri debate confirmed all their fears of outside interference.

A product of its peculiar political, economic, and social makeup, South Carolina's siege mentality was unique in its extremity. But even white southerners who welcomed a way out of slavery found themselves impaled on a dilemma. Wholesale colonization would be so massively expensive that only assistance of the kind suggested by Ohio could make it feasible. But accepting assistance meant inviting the very outside intervention that slaveholders most feared. It meant accepting a huge extension of federal power and entrusting the fate of slavery to strange and perhaps unfriendly hands. White southerners quailed at the prospect.

Stymied by southern hostility and the very size of the task, colonization went nowhere in Congress, but proceeded by private means. Within ten years of its founding, the American Colonization Society had secured endorsements from the legislatures of Virginia, Maryland, Kentucky, Tennessee, and six northern states, plus the governing bodies of the national Presbyterian, Methodist, Baptist, and Episcopal churches and innumerable religious and philanthropic groups in both North and South. Prominent politicians by the dozen endorsed its purpose. In 1821 the society purchased land on the West African coast for a colony named Liberia and began to recruit settlers.

Yet in a decade's work the society succeeded in sponsoring only a few hundred colonists. Ironically, the same ambiguity of purpose that won colonizationists such broad support fatally undercut their practical efforts. The uneasy mingling of proslavery, antislavery, and racist motives produced a stillborn program. By tying its plan to cleanse the country of slavery to the scheme of ridding it of blacks, the society avoided standing clearly for either slavery or freedom. It attracted friends, and soon enemies, from both sides.

The society lacked funds to purchase slaves for deportation and would not espouse emancipation without it. By default it turned to recruiting free blacks. Northern and southern whites of differing opinions on slavery but similar views on race could easily agree on expelling this degraded and undesirable population. But free blacks could not be sent off without their consent. Despite the daily indignities they suffered where they were, few were eager to exchange a new start in a struggling distant colony for the only home they had ever known. Predominantly native-born and generations removed from Africa, they saw themselves as Americans. What they wanted was recognition as citizens. Only a handful volunteered for expatriation to Liberia.

So despite high hopes and strong backing, the colonization movement produced negligible results. Meanwhile, in the years after Missouri, the fear of outside meddling with slavery infiltrated southern responses to every question of federal power, from congressional economic legislation to the expansive jurisdictional claims of the Supreme Court. Southerners did not all respond alike to these issues. Some wanted tariff protection for their products, and some sought federal aid for transportation. But for those, especially Virginians and now Carolinians, who saw themselves as victims of federal aggrandizement, the lurking slavery question infused their resistance with a deeper import. Faith in the efficacy of national action turned to fear, as exposed in John Randolph's warning on a landmark internal improvement measure in 1824: "If Congress possesses the power to do what is proposed by this bill, . . . they may emancipate every slave in the United States." Imbued with a growing sectional consciousness, southern foes of development measures began to see them not as instruments of uplift, nor even as isolated projects, but as joined components of a gigantic northern plot to suck dry the substance of the South.

The Election of 1824

Southerners were right to link the tariff and internal improvement policies, though wrong in their ascription of sectional purpose. Northern opinion, like southern, was far from monolithic. New England was only slowly shedding its own aversion to the nationalist agenda. In Congress the most stirring advocate of the development program, and the man who best articulated its rationale, was no Yankee but Kentucky slaveholder (and colonizationist) Henry Clay, Speaker of the House of Representatives.

In speeches on the tariff and internal improvement in 1824, Clay proclaimed his vision of progress. Americans were "essentially an agricultural people." Yet domestic manufactures would promote all interests, providing incentive to industry, freedom from foreign dependence, work for the idle, a home market for farmers and planters, and in the end greater wealth for all. Tariff protection, then, was the "genuine AMERICAN SYSTEM," the "path which leads to riches, to greatness, to glory." Internal improvement to foster domestic exchange was its complement. An implicit financial link also connected the two: excess federal tariff revenues could be used to build roads and canals. Clay appealed to doubters and foes, especially to "the South—to the high-minded, generous, and patriotic South"—to suppress local objections in the name of compromise, concession, and union.

Clay's program for American greatness was also his platform for the presidency. The 1824 election promised the first real campaign in twelve years. Federalists had put up only token opposition to Republican James Monroe in 1816 and none at all in 1820. Now Monroe's pending retirement and the close of the Virginia dynasty threw the race open to all comers. By spring of 1823 five contenders had entered the field. Two westerners, Clay and Andrew Jackson, hero of New Orleans and now a United States senator, faced three aspirants from Monroe's own cabinet, Secretary of War John Calhoun, Secretary of State John Quincy Adams, and Treasury secretary William Harris Crawford of Georgia. All five men claimed the mantle of Jeffersonian Republicanism.

Despite Clay's exertions and the growing polarization in Congress, his "American System" figured only indirectly in the contest. All the candidates, even the Virginia-born Crawford, had risen to fame as nationalists; all were now championed, at least where such views were popular, as friends of home manufacturing and internal improvement. The polite electioneering conventions of the day, which precluded a candidate's speaking too openly in his own behalf, allowed the three cabinet officers to avoid specifying the extent of their devotion to these policies. But in the Senate Andrew Jackson voted down the line for roads and canals and cast a crucial vote for the tariff of 1824. In a public letter Jackson acclaimed protection as a prescription for national independence and touted the power of the federal government to "give a proper distribution to our labor." He even said the country had too many farmers.

With a crowded field of contenders and no means to distinguish them, the mechanism for choosing became itself a point of contention. Since 1796 a caucus of Republican congressmen had named the party's presidential candidate. The caucus secured Republican unity and victory against Federalist opponents. But the demise of Federalism undermined its rationale. What was supposed to be a device to implement the people's will now seemed a way to avoid consulting it. In February 1824 the Crawford men, who controlled what was left of Republican organization in Virginia and New York, activated the caucus. Their self-interested motive escaped no one, and the result did more to discredit Crawford's candidacy than to promote it. Only sixty-six members of Congress, about one-fourth the total, attended the rump caucus that nominated him, while denunciations rained down from all sides against this usurpation of the people's right to choose. The caucus sank into disrepute, and Crawford's chances sank with it.

The reaction to the caucus served notice that old means of doing business would no longer serve in national politics. In the states democratic winds had been blowing with growing strength for a decade. The presidential election of 1824 was the first to feel their force.

Many Americans in the years after 1815 shared promoters' enthusiasm for national achievement. But they also grasped for another promise that came with independence: that of democracy, of genuine popular control of government. Doctrines of popular sovereignty and equal rights, propounded in the struggle against British rule, had destroyed the logic behind restricting the vote to men of means. The Revolution began a broadening toward universal white male suffrage. After 1815 it gathered speed. Men like James Kent in New York and John Randolph in Virginia fought the rule of "King Numbers," but the movement was unstoppable. A flurry of states—Connecticut in 1817, Massachusetts in 1821, New York in 1822— dropped all property requirements for voting or retreated to a nominal tax-paying standard. Indiana, Illinois, Alabama, Missouri, and Maine, entering the Union between 1816 and 1821, threw the franchise open from the start. By 1824 only a handful of states materially limited white men's access to the polls.

While more men gained the vote, the vote itself gained power. New state constitutions made more public officers elective, including governors and judges. One by one, state legislatures also relinquished the choice of presidential electors to the people. In 1816 ten of nineteen states held a popular vote for president. By 1824 only six of twenty-four states did not; by 1828 only two; by 1832, only one, South Carolina.

In 1824 the decline of the caucus and the spread of white male democracy produced a presidential campaign of singular chaos. Friends of the candidates scrambled to assemble "people's tickets" of electors. In the absence of national organization, regional loyalties stood first. New Englanders and what one editor called "the universal Yankee nation" of New England emigrants stretching westward across New York and Ohio favored John Quincy Adams. Virginia went for Crawford, Virginia-born and presumably most inclined toward principles of limited government. Jackson's stronghold was in the new southwest, Clay's in the Ohio valley. Calhoun, lacking a base outside South Carolina, posed as the only truly national choice; but after his effort in Pennsylvania fizzled, he withdrew and stood for vice president.

The real battle for votes was fought in the margins between the candidates' home territories. Organization was hasty and turnout variable, yet the returns yielded an unmistakable pattern. Outside the southwest Jackson led in New Jersey, North Carolina, Indiana, and Illinois. In Ohio he ran close to Clay and well ahead of Adams; in Pennsylvania his ticket rolled over the others by more than three to one. Overall he carried eleven of twenty-four states, with a plurality, though not a majority, of both the popular and electoral vote. Adams ran second, with seven states and eighty-four electoral votes to Jackson's ninety-nine.

Among the other candidates and their counselors Jackson's showing produced astonishment, then consternation. Despite a long public career he lacked the qualities or attainments expected in a statesman. He had never served abroad or in the cabinet; his congressional tenure was brief and undistinguished. Half-educated, strong-tempered, he had won fame only as a warrior. Mindful of his high-handed command style and wary of the fate of other republics ancient and modern, some saw in Jackson another Julius Caesar or Napoleon Bonaparte. At best he seemed patently unfit for the presidency, at worst an actual threat to the survival of republican government.

Accustomed to equating politics with statesmanship, Jackson's rivals (with the interesting exception of Adams, who tried to shunt him off to the vice presidency) had trouble taking him seriously. Yet Jackson enjoyed an enormous base of popular esteem. From one end of the country to another he was an icon, a patriotic symbol second only to George Washington. Since 1815 the Ohio state legislative journal had noted January 8 as the "Anniversary of Jackson's Victory" at New Orleans. No other event, not even Washington's birthday, was so honored. Though New York's legislature gave most of its electoral votes to Adams, he was told that in a popular contest there "no man could stand in competition with General Jackson," for "the 8th of January and the battle of New Orleans was a thing that every man would understand."

Jackson's managers had shrewdly yoked his totemic stature to the swelling demand for popular control of the electoral process. His campaign biography and his own public statements cast him not only as republican gladiator but as man of the people: agent of their will, servant of their wishes. Declaring their "imperative duty" and "sacred right" to "select our own candidate . . . independent of all interference, and aloof from all dictation," Jackson's converts proclaimed him "a uniform and consistent democrat" and "a friend to the *rights of man* and *universal suffrage*." In the eyes of both friend and foe, the frenzy for Jackson took on the look of a budding revolt against politicians' control of politics.

Still Jackson's electoral total fell more than thirty short of a majority. So according to the Constitution, the House of Representatives, voting by states, had to choose a president from among the three highest candidates: Jackson, Adams, and Crawford. Crawford, far behind the others and incapacitated by a stroke, was out of the running. Jackson was clearly the popular favorite, but fears of his incompetence and recklessness blocked his selection. Henry Clay, Speaker of the House, stepped in to play kingmaker. After procuring assurance of Adams's devotion to Clay's treasured American System, the Speaker helped sway enough state delegations, including his own, to give Adams thirteen states and election on the first ballot in the House. Adams then offered, and Clay accepted, the post of secretary of state.

An enraged Jackson accused Adams and Clay of stealing the presidency from him by "bare faced corruption." In fact the Adams-Clay "bargain" did not lack honesty (Clay's belief in Jackson's unfitness was sincere, and his own qualifications for the state department were unquestioned) but political sagacity. A campaign in which responding to popular sentiment had become the highest imperative ended with an arrangement that stank of collusion against the people's will. Charges of conspiracy and illegitimacy tainted the Adams presidency from its birth. Before his administration even began, his rivals hung on it the most damning epithet in the American lexicon: "aristocracy."

The Adams Presidency

John Quincy Adams commenced his presidential term with a chastening sense of weakness. To the committee bringing notice of his election he spoke candidly of his minority tenure; to himself he confessed that perhaps two-thirds of the voters disapproved. Adams's inaugural address coupled a celebration of American progress with a plea for reconciliation and forbearance. Yet already he knew that the disgruntled partisans of Crawford and Calhoun were coalescing under Jackson's banner, determined to make his administration "unpopular and odious, whatever its acts and measures may be," and to bring it down at the next election. Another man might have walked cautiously, trying to build support for a second term. But for Adams, the uncertainty of his mandate and forebodings of defeat merely added urgency to an overriding sense of mission.

Among the generation of visionary statesmen cast up by the War of 1812, Adams was perhaps the most farsighted of all. As James Monroe's secretary of state he had adroitly pursued territorial acquisitions in Florida and the West while pugnaciously asserting the country's independent and equal stature in the game of nations. Monroe's famous pronouncement in 1823 against further European colonization in the Americas was largely Adams's work. Characteristically he looked to the future, ignoring the nation's current weakness in the certitude of coming strength.

Adams believed that moral and physical power were ultimately one, and that in their combined force the United States was destined to lead the world. Faith in the progress of goodness and reason energized Adams's enormous intellectual talents and propelled him to embrace projects that others thought at best premature. His report on weights and measures in 1821 looked forward to the international adoption of the metric system as a "blessing of such transcendent magnitude" as to herald the arrival of world peace and the reign of Christ on earth.

Adams's vision of national development infused the universal talisman of "improvement" with overarching religious meaning. The Creator had blessed the United States with possibilities for "moral, political, intellectual improvement" beyond any in human history. The country's birthright of superabundant natural resources and republican political institutions offered full scope to initiative. To fail to seize these advantages, to let slip the unexampled opportunity to raise the condition of the American people and the human race, Adams thought, "would be treachery to the most sacred of trusts."

So in his first message to Congress, in December 1825, Adams threw down the challenge. "Liberty is power," he proclaimed, and power exists for the moral purpose of human betterment. While other nations, less free and therefore less powerful, were making "gigantic strides" in improvement, congressmen could plead no excuse for inaction, least of all that they were "palsied by the will of our constituents." Daring members to rise above penury and parochialism, Adams called for a national university and astronomical observatory, exploring expeditions, and laws for "the improvement of agriculture, commerce, and manufactures, the cultivation and encouragement of the mechanic and of the elegant arts, the advancement of literature, and the progress of the sciences, ornamental and profound."

Adams's call was as much a confession of faith as a summons to action. Expecting opposition, he looked to the long term for practical results. But dedicating his presidency to a transcendent purpose helped justify Adams's election to his own troubled conscience. He had launched the "perilous experiment" and, no matter the consequences for his political future, he could rest content that he had done his duty.

Much of the message, indeed, fell without effect. Adams's flights of rhetoric evoked only ridicule, and his recommendations for a national university and scientific establishment were soon buried. Stripped of these inessentials, however, the core of the president's program stood clear. It was Henry Clay's American System of protective tariffs and federal internal improvements. Upon the system's success in Congress and with the citizenry, the Adams administration would rise or fall.

The final months of Monroe's administration had broken the impasse between congressional majorities and Virginia presidents over internal improvement. Retreating from his "settled conviction," Monroe signed an appropriation for federal surveys of roads and canals "of national importance" in 1824. Later, after the election, he approved a bill subscribing stock in the Chesapeake and Delaware Canal. With these precedents in hand and with encouragement from Adams, improvement advocates moved boldly. In three years Congress approved a slew of transportation measures—more surveys, harbor and channel improvements, funds for the Cumberland, or National, Road across the Appalachians, stock subscriptions (including

$1 million for the Chesapeake and Ohio Canal), and land grants to help western states construct canals and river improvements.

Meanwhile manufacturers, finding the tariff of 1824 no more adequate to protection than that of 1816, pressed for still higher rates. New England textile interests now led the drive. A bill to raise duties on imported woolens passed the House of Representatives in 1827 but was derailed in the Senate by the deciding vote of Vice President Calhoun. Both sides organized to influence the next Congress. Delegates from thirteen states met in Harrisburg, Pennsylvania, to request higher taxes on foreign cotton and woolen goods, iron, raw wool, hemp, and flax. Speaking through Treasury secretary Richard Rush, the Adams administration lent its weight to the cause. On the other side, southern legislatures and public meetings bombarded Congress with strident and even threatening remonstrances. At a gathering in July 1827, President Thomas Cooper of South Carolina College decried further submission and warned that if northern oppression continued, "we shall 'ere long be compelled to calculate the value of our union."

Defying this challenge, Congress passed a new, highly protective tariff in May 1828. It came just in time to influence the upcoming presidential election; indeed, the bill was framed for that purpose by Jackson men in the House of Representatives looking to steal the issue from Adams. The rate schedules they devised were so brazenly calculated to reward Jackson-leaning states and to punish New England that manufacturers there nearly killed the bill themselves. In the end, after winning a crucial concession for the woolens industry, they acceded and the "tariff of abominations" became law.

Though fostering American industry was central to administration philosophy, the tariff of 1828 really announced the defeat, not the victory, of Adams and Clay's higher hopes for the American System. The new tariff was anything but systematic. Its provisions and the means of its passage bespoke political rather than patriotic motives. True, while John Quincy Adams tended to see the two as exclusive, Henry Clay did not. Above all men, Clay knew that bargain and tradeoff were essential tools of lawmaking. He never asked congressmen to sacrifice self-interest, only to take an enlightened view of it. But Clay, like Adams, also subscribed to an underlying belief in the federal government's duty to nurture the young nation toward maturity. To both men the American System at bottom was no arrangement of expediency; it was a venture in statecraft.

The "tariff of abominations" belied such pretensions. Even in triumph the American System had failed to rise above the pursuit of sectional, partisan, and personal gain. The array of local factions scuffling over tariff schedules made mockery of claims of higher national purpose. Boston textile magnate Abbott Lawrence told Senator Daniel Webster that the 1828 tariff would serve "the *true* interests of the country"—and, in the next sentence, that it would "keep the South and West in debt to New England the next hundred years." Seeing the same effect from different perspective, South Carolina denounced the tariff as "partial in its nature, unjust in its operation."

Road and canal legislation also showed little sign of plan or system. Congress distributed subsidies based as much on political grounds as on the projects' urgency or even feasibility. For internal improvement strategists, keeping their coalition together took first precedence; and in the haste to show results, policymaking devolved into horse-trading. Begging New England votes for roads and canals, Clay told Webster that "the West and Pennsa. should be made sensible of that support. . . . You have your equivalents in other forms. . . . We must keep the two interests of D[omestic] M[anufactures] & I[nternal] I[mprovements] allied." A Louisiana congressman warned Clay that "our Citizens are very impatient to *feel* in their State the beneficial effects of internal improvement. They are in favor of the system, but they want something here." Jacksonians too played the game of reward with improvement bills and tariff rates. In the last days of the 1828 session Adams and Jackson men bid frantically for Ohio votes with competing land grants for the state's canals.

No wonder, then, that southern critics railed against the American System as the "general bribery system" and Andrew Jackson privately complained of "flagicious *logg-rolling legislation.*" The fiscal link between tariff revenues and internal improvement expenditures, each supporting and justifying the other, turned the system in opponents' eyes from one of profligacy to one of plunder—"a system of fraud, robbery and usurpation," in the words of South Carolina's Thomas Cooper. Vice President Calhoun, turning from the American System and toward Jackson, worried that "the goverment [sic] is rapidly degenerating into a struggle among the parts to squeeze as much out of one another as they possibly can." South Carolina public meetings protested that "all that is taken from us is disposed of elsewhere. . . . The prosperity of the North is built upon the impoverishment of the South."

A vision of national cooperation for national progress, once shared by Calhoun and Jackson as well as Adams and Clay, had seemingly dissipated into a scramble for federal favors. Still, judging by congressional majorities, it was a scramble in which most Americans wanted to participate. Upon that premise, in effect, the Adams administration staked its hopes for re-election. An administration paper put the case squarely: "The real question, the only question of policy and principle, that is at issue between the supporters of Mr. Adams and those of Gen. Jackson, is this: 'Shall the American System be adopted as a great leading national measure or not?' "

Southern foes of the system accepted this issue, and they rallied around Jackson, a fellow planter and slaveholder, as the man to restore sectional fairness through economy and simplicity in government. Virginians and Carolinians, Crawfordites and Calhounites, buried old rivalries as they joined to overthrow Adams and with him the American System. But together they represented only one wing, and not a controlling one, of the diverse Jackson coalition; and Jackson himself, though he welcomed their support, did not endorse their cause. Elsewhere in the country Jackson's minions ran with the tide on economic questions, championing tariff protection and internal improvement in his name wherever it might win votes.

The broader, compelling appeal of the Jackson movement was not to any line of policy, but to the overriding principle of popular control of government itself. Politicians who had spurned Jackson's candidacy in 1824 now mounted his bandwagon and applied their talents to embellishing his theme of "the many against the few, of equal rights against privileged orders, of democracy against aristocracy." Jackson's press relentlessly pounded home the maxim: "Andrew Jackson is the *candidate of the people*." This message, rung over and over with every conceivable flourish and variation by Jackson's operatives, was highly congenial to the candidate himself. It fitted his persona of popular tribune and his very personal resentment of the insiders who had barred him from the White House in 1824 and who continued to ridicule his rough-hewn accomplishments, violent escapades, and homespun wife. Jackson's sense of exclusion resonated with voters who also felt slighted by the pretentious statecraft of the haughty Adams and conniving Clay.

In the campaign, Adams and his friends stood almost helpless before the Jacksonian combination of expert organization and outright demagoguery. "Public utility, faithful services, and acknowledged integrity" apparently counted for naught against the populist juggernaut. Profound systems of statecraft could not defeat newfound systems of electioneering. Vainly the administration's defenders tried to turn weakness into virtue by arguing that the victory of "an organized and disciplined party" would itself be a "usurpation of the rights of the People." Jackson's calculated evasion of policy discussion left the contest a personal one, and in such a match no man in the country could stand against the hero of New Orleans.

The popular vote for president in 1828 tripled that of 1824. Jackson carried every state south of the Potomac and west of the mountains, plus New York and Pennsylvania, for 178 electoral votes to Adams's 83.

Jacksonians whooped with glee. Adams accepted defeat with Christian resignation. Henry Clay found the result "mortifying, and sickening to the hearts of the real lovers of free Government." At the inauguration in March 1829 Daniel Webster saw "a monstrous crowd of people," some of whom had "come 500 miles to see Genl Jackson; & they really seem to think that the Country is rescued from some dreadful danger."

To both celebrants and mourners it was a portentous moment in the annals of the young republic. Jackson had won a great victory. What he would do with it, not even he knew.

The Realm of Reason

And here it is, in the heart of the United States, and almost the center of its unequalled internal navigation, that that power which directs and governs the universe and every action of man, has arranged circumstances which were far beyond my control, to permit me to commence a new empire of peace and good will to man, founded on other principles, and leading to other practices than those of the past or present, and which principles, in due season, and in the allotted time, will lead to that state of virtue, intelligence, enjoyment, and happiness, in practice, which has been foretold by the sages of past times.
—Robert Owen, 1825

Nature is the same. For her no new forces are generated; no new capacities are discovered. The earth turns on its axis, and perfects its revolutions, and renews its seasons, without increase or advancement. But a like passive destiny does not attach to the inhabitants of the earth. For them the expectations of social improvement are no delusion; the hopes of philanthropy are more than a dream.
—George Bancroft, 1835

Visions of a wonderful future led some individuals to fashion systems of polity and governance aimed at material and moral progress. They inspired others to conjure up projects of a perfected society, and seek to implant them on American soil. For a glimmering moment everything seemed possible. Reformers spoke of revolutionizing human character, eliminating exploitation and suffering, raising a generation of perfected youth—not as utopian dreams but as impending actualities, realizable here, tomorrow, today. Down every path of human endeavor improvement beckoned. The Jubilee decade set loose an explosion of organizing and experimenting.

Robert Owen and New Harmony

On December 8, 1825, just a month after the opening of the Erie Canal, the keelboat *Philanthropist* pushed off into the icy Ohio at Pittsburgh and pointed downriver for Indiana. This craft, soon dubbed the "boatload of knowledge," carried a cadre of intellects as distinguished in their fields as the statesmen and dignitaries with De Witt Clinton aboard the *Seneca Chief*. Heading the group was William Maclure, Scottish-born philanthropist, educational reformer, pioneer American geologist, and president of the Academy of Natural Sciences of Philadelphia. His recruits, drawn from the leading ranks of science and pedagogy, included naturalists Charles Alexandre Lesueur, Gerard Troost, and Thomas Say, and teachers Marie Fretageot, William S. Phiquepal, and Joseph Neef. All but Say, a native Philadelphian, were of European birth.

A quite extraordinary impulse drew this cosmopolitan band of talents from Philadelphia, American headquarters of science and learning, to the rude home that awaited on the Wabash. Maclure had recently returned from Europe to pursue his educational reforms in America, "considering the field of moral experiment in the United States to be the finest in the Globe." He and his companions were now bound for New Harmony, Indiana, to join the community proclaimed by industrialist and social theorist Robert Owen.

Born to a middle-class Welsh family in 1771, Robert Owen had risen quickly in the burgeoning British textile industry. At age twenty he ran a Manchester cotton manufactory employing five hundred hands. By 1800 he was manager and part-owner of the New Lanark spinning mills, largest in Britain. Disturbed by the long working hours, low wages, and miserable living conditions of factory workers, Owen structured his mill village on principles of benevolent paternalism. His improvements in housing, sanitation, and education, together with his agitation for parliamentary reform of child labor, brought international acclaim. New Lanark became a showcase, frequented by thousands of visitors seeking a solution to the suffering and degradation that came with pell-mell industrialization.

After 1812 Owen's horizons expanded. Targeting individualism, with its concomitants of competition and selfishness, as the source of social evil, he proposed "Villages of Unity and Mutual Co-operation," where shared work would banish unemployment and exploitation. He expounded what became his great central idea, that character was wholly a product of its environment. Circumstance, not innate deficiency, created human failings. By shaping social surroundings on correct principles, one could propel humanity forward to a realm of abundance, happiness, and "universal charity, benevolence, and kindness." Owen's notions of perfectibility and moral innocence ran counter to orthodox Christian doctrine. So he repudiated it, and denounced the Church for standing in his way. Given a free field to work in, Owen came to believe he could regenerate society in remarkably short order. But where could a free field be found? Like other visionaries before and since, he turned to America.

In 1824 Owen found a chance to try his ideas on American soil. He was invited to purchase the entire village of Harmonie, or New Harmony, in southern Indiana on the Wabash, together with all its buildings and equipment and twenty thousand acres of land. Harmonie was the home of the Harmony Society, disciples of the charismatic Christian George Rapp. One of several German pietist sects that came to America, the Harmonists, or Rappites, emigrated in 1804 from Wurttemberg to west Pennsylvania. Though they prospered there, after ten years Rapp ordained a move to Indiana, where they built another thriving town. Owen had already noted the Rappites' success, along with that of some home-grown American religious communitarians, the Shakers, as proof of what cooperative labor could do. When Rapp decided to return his flock to Pennsylvania, Owen jumped at the chance to step into his place.

Abandoning New Lanark, Owen sailed for the United States in October 1824. He received a celebrity's welcome in New York, Philadelphia, and Washington. In January 1825, on the Wabash, Owen clinched the deal: New Harmony and all it contained for $125,000. He next embarked on a triumphant publicity tour. In the United States Capitol Owen delivered his two lectures on "A New System of Society" before a galaxy of statesmen. In Philadelphia he recruited the men and women who would fill the "boatload of knowledge." Thomas Jefferson at Monticello and James Madison at Montpelier welcomed him. Newspapers and pamphlets published his theories and spread his somewhat reckless invitation to "the industrious and well-disposed of all nations" to join him in Indiana. By the time Owen returned to New Harmony in April 1825, nearly a thousand converts had crowded into the town. Enthusiasm ran so high that Owen thought his "new empire" of cooperation would replace the "individual selfish system" throughout the free states in two years.

The excitement that swirled around Robert Owen reveals much about the American mood in 1825. His plans for instant utopia were undeveloped and, as soon became apparent, transparently naive. Yet until it was tried, Owen's vision did not appear unreasonable. New inventions and forms of organization were appearing everywhere. Society was visibly turning, and no one could say what direction it would take. Owen's idea of grouping people into self-sustaining villages pursuing a mix of agricultural and industrial occupations drew support both from his experience at New Lanark and from the proven success of religious communitarians. In their modest size (up to twenty-five hundred people), their rural setting, and the efficiencies they were expected to achieve through mechanization and careful allocation of work, Owen's cooperative communities superficially resembled the dozens of factory villages already sprouting along waterpower sites from the Merrimack to the Delaware.

If Owen's ideas gathered plausibility from American experience, they also synchronized with American expectations of progress. Unlike the religious sects, Owen sought a model for the larger society, not a withdrawal from it. He conceived New Harmony as a leap into the future, not a retreat from the present. He was, as everyone knew, a very successful man of the world. And he shaped his thinking in direct response to one of the most striking and troubling new developments of the age, the factory system.

In Britain factory labor was creating a profusion of cheap machine-made goods and a population of visibly impoverished workers. This paradox of rampant misery amidst splendid wealth, though hardly evident yet in the United States, deeply troubled American observers. Proponents of mechanical innovation found their enthusiasm crossed by doubts about its consequences. Were dependence and degradation inevitable accompaniments of industrial advance? Critics like Thomas Jefferson and John Taylor feared they were. Owen held out hope that they were not. He promised a way to reap the material fruits of progress while avoiding its dread social by-products.

Owen premised his confidence upon the unity of truth and the transformative power of the intellect. His assumptions stemmed from a cast of thought rooted in the European Enlightenment of the eighteenth century, which had found earlier American exemplars in Jefferson and Benjamin Franklin. The hallmark of this stance was the creed of "reason," the conviction that the world moved in logical, knowable ways. By uncovering and applying the rules that governed its workings—social and moral as well as physical—people could discover the keys to almost illimitable improvement. As the Philadelphia chemist John Speakman, William Maclure's colleague in the Academy of Natural Sciences, put it, "lack of knowledge of the laws of nature is the source of all social evils." Above all Owen stressed the rationality of his system. He and Maclure approached social reconstruction, educational reform, and scientific inquiry as mutually reinforcing means to an indivisible end.

New Harmony began with transcendent expectations. But Owen, busy publicizing and recruiting in Britain and America, spent little time at the site. Without his buoying presence holes soon appeared in his theories. Filled with the beauty of his principle, Owen had never troubled himself about how to implement it. Faith in the imminence of his New Moral World overrode the need for mundane planning. Basic questions remained unsettled: how members would be screened and selected, how work would be organized and discipline enforced, how resources would be pooled and allocated, whether and in what form private property would exist, and whether Owen himself would be lord and lawgiver (as at New Lanark) or just another participant. Once hundreds of recruits gathered at New Harmony, answers to these queries could no longer be postponed. As soon as they came forth, the community began to divide.

On May 1, 1825, at New Harmony, Owen promulgated the constitution of a Preliminary Society to serve as a "half-way house between the old and the new." This soon gave way to a Community of Equality. But disputes over religion, governance, and economy compelled further change. Over the next year New Harmony went through a bewildering series of reorganizations, schisms, and secessions. Factions formed, and Owen's relations with William Maclure dissolved in bitterness. Hampered by demoralization and a lack of workers with requisite skills, production languished. In the spring of 1827 the experiment of formal community at New Harmony collapsed. It had never paid its way, and its losses absorbed much of Owen's fortune.

The Communitarian Collapse

The quick fate of New Harmony also befell several other communities inspired by Owen's principles. The most important was Frances Wright's Nashoba in west Tennessee. In 1824 Wright arrived on her second visit to America in the train of Lafayette. During the next year, partly spent at New

Harmony, she concocted the idea of combining communitarianism with antislavery. Blacks could work out the cost of their emancipation and colonization abroad while they received training and education for freedom. Gathering advice and guarded encouragement from the likes of Lafayette, Henry Clay, Andrew Jackson, and ex-presidents Jefferson, Madison, and Monroe, Wright began her experiment in the spring of 1826 with fifteen purchased slaves near the frontier town of Memphis.

Nashoba, like New Harmony, was nearly stillborn. Grand dreams of supplanting slavery with cooperative labor throughout the South were quickly laid aside as the pilot farm failed to meet its own expenses, to say nothing of generating a surplus for emancipation and colonization. In less than two years the community folded. "Cooperation," Wright conceded, "has well nigh killed us all." In 1830 she freed the slaves and took them to Haiti.

Communitarianism foundered on the quandary of incentive and coercion. Though benevolent, the schemes of Owen and Wright were also authoritarian. Owen proclaimed his good feeling toward every human being: "my intention is to do them good—to relieve them from the error and evil by which they are now on all sides beset." But he did not propose to consult them about the means of their uplift. Owen's theory of personality said that people whose characters were formed by the vicious society around them were not yet fit to govern themselves. At Washington he told his audience of congressmen and cabinet officers that they were all "in a state of mental bondage" from which he had come to rescue them. Owen spoke of the "liberty, affluence, and happiness" his system would bring. There was no mention of democracy or self-determination.

At New Harmony and Nashoba Owen and Wright decreed holistic regimes based on a priori principles. But the very openness and fluidity of American society that nurtured their dreams also doomed them to failure. The conditions that gave Owen and Wright leeway to experiment gave others freedom to dissent, reject, and destroy. At New Harmony Owen's human materials were not pliant wage hands but independent-minded volunteers, there by their own choice. Unlike religious disciples, they were held by no shared spiritual impulse or need for refuge from persecution. James Madison's judgment at the time, seconded by the religious communitarian John Humphrey Noyes a half-century later, was that a voluntary community could not cohere without such ties. At Wright's Nashoba most of the workers did have no choice. They were slaves. But to treat them as slaves would mock the whole point of the enterprise.

Renouncing religious mummery and physical force, Owen and Wright tried to hold their followers by an appeal to reason. In practice this translated into a promise of benefit, personal and communal, tangible and prompt. This promise in turn, however, rested on the untested ability of new social arrangements to work a regeneration of human character. When Owen's "immediate, and almost instantaneous, revolution in the minds and manners of the society" failed to occur, when instead of "unnumbered and unlimited blessings to every one" there appeared only contention and privation, confidence in the founder's transformative vision precipitously collapsed. Nothing else was there to hold the community together. The result was crippling disharmony at New Harmony and a sad resort to compulsion, even whipping, at Nashoba.

Failure in Indiana and Tennessee spelled a setback, but not an end, for American communitarianism. Religious ferment continued to throw off new adventures in cooperative living and to draw recruits to older sects like the Shakers. And after memories of New Harmony subsided, dissatisfaction with the anxieties and injustices of a competitive, selfish society again suggested a communitarian antidote. In the 1840s the same lure that had enticed Owen and Wright—the perception of American society as an embryonic organism capable of being molded in any direction—prompted another round of community experiments. Most soon foundered on the same contradictions that had wrecked New Harmony.

By this time, also, the spread of social choices was closing. Political parties pre-empted much of public discourse and the attention of leading men. The range of permissible behavior had narrowed. Frances Wright's Tennessee neighbors disapproved of her Nashoba experiment, especially when it extended to open interracial and extramarital sex. But no one tried to stop her. Twenty years later southerners would not encourage, or even tolerate, communities in their midst that aimed at overturning slave society. Americans did not relinquish their penchant for new experiments and expedients, nor their hopes for a better tomorrow. But never again would the promise of reborn humanity seem so tantalizingly close, and receive so respectful a hearing in such high places, as when Robert Owen stood in the Capitol in 1825 with all official Washington in attendance and proclaimed his "New System of Society."

In the height of Owen's ambition and the depth of his fall, the New Harmony venture paralleled John Quincy Adams's attempt to install the American System; and the chronological conjuncture of these two epic failures was more than coincidence. The apparent illimitability of American prospects at the Jubilee inspired grand efforts at social engineering. The same illimitability foredoomed their defeat. A plan of any kind required direction and discipline. It demanded a concentration of resources, a forswearing of alternatives, and thus a renunciation of the very plethora of possibilities that inspired it in the first place. Visionaries like Adams and Owen sought to impose exclusive, overarching systems, yet they lacked the means or desire to compel adherence to their schemes. All they could do was cast them into the market, put them up for vote.

The result in both cases signified that the tendency of American conditions, as well as the inclination of its people, was for diffusion rather than discipline, toward self-determination and away from supervision, however benign. The failure of system in social relations and political economy meant that the nation would approach its still-unsettled destiny not with concentrated force along a straight line, but erratically, unpredictably, even contradictorily, upon a dozen fronts at once. The society's own deep-rooted dispositions and the thousand choices of its citizens, rather than articulated design, would determine Americans' future.

Natural and Experimental Science

Americans welcomed Robert Owen, but would not follow him. They declined to surrender self-determination as the price of self-improvement because they thought they could have both. But if they spurned his autocratic means, many shared his hope of an American New Moral World. Owen's faith in progress through education and science especially resonated with American aspirations. Citizens agreed with William Maclure that theirs was "the finest and most rational Society on the Globe," and they saw their free institutions and vast resources opening an unexampled field for mental as well as material development. Scientific discovery would both help realize the country's productive potential and prove the superiority of its political and social forms.

Together, belief in patriotism and progress enlivened intellectual energies. In 1823 naturalist Thomas Say pledged his efforts "to the honour & support of *American* science." Zoologist James De Kay, speaking before the New York Lyceum of Natural History in 1826, noted an awakening "spirit of inquiry" borne by "the active, enterprising spirit of our citizens, happily co-operating with the genius of our free political institutions." In achievements of the mind, as in all else, Americans expected soon to lead the world.

The Revolutionary generation had marked out two fields as especially suited for native scientific endeavor. The first, championed by Thomas Jefferson and exemplified in his *Notes on the State of Virginia*, was natural history. European science in the eighteenth century had placed special emphasis on accumulating information about the natural world. In America a whole continent of geologic and biologic wonders awaited discovery and description. Jefferson's instructions for the Lewis and Clark expedition in 1803 charged it with gathering data on every aspect of the interior—its climate, topography, soils, minerals, fossils, plant and animal life, and native peoples. The inexhaustible novelty of American flora and fauna excited homegrown naturalists like Jefferson and lured such Europeans as John James Audubon, Thomas Nuttall, Constantine Rafinesque, Alexander Wilson, and the Philadelphia academicians who later accompanied William Maclure to New Harmony.

The second prominent branch of American science, mapped out by Benjamin Franklin, focused on observation and practical experiment in physics, chemistry, and applied mechanics. In the early nineteenth century versatile intellects like the astronomer/mathematician Nathaniel Bowditch, author of the *New American Practical Navigator,* and chemist/geologist Benjamin Silliman carried on in the Franklin vein. But where American conditions boosted the naturalists' inquiries, they handicapped the experimentalists. No city in the United States, not even Philadelphia, could match the centers of Europe in furnishing mechanical apparatus, reference works, publication venues, financial support, and intellectual fellowship.

The interest that political leaders took in their work gave scientists some recompense for crude facilities and professional isolation. Fulfilling the Enlightenment ideal of a broad-ranging pursuit of knowledge, Revolutionary patriots Franklin, Jefferson, John Adams, and Philadelphia physician Benjamin Rush were all scientific devotees and practitioners. In the next generation John Quincy Adams, authority on weights and measures, De Witt Clinton, founding president of the Literary and Philosophical Society of New York, and Nicholas Biddle, a Philadelphia littérateur who edited the journals of Lewis and Clark before turning to politics and finance, carried on the tradition of the scholar-statesman.

In his inaugural address to the New York society in 1814, Clinton lamented that Americans' "enterprising spirit" had thus far "exhibited itself in every shape except that of a marked devotion to the interests of science." But succeeding years brought a profusion of new societies and publications. The Philadelphia Academy of Natural Sciences began a journal in 1817. A year later the older American Philosophical Society resumed its *Transactions*. At Yale College Benjamin Silliman began the *American Journal of Science and Arts* in 1818 and founded the American Geological Society in 1819. New York state incorporated five natural history societies in as many years. In 1816 the New York Institution for the Promotion of the Arts and Sciences gathered the Literary and Philosophical Society, the Academy of Fine Arts, the Lyceum of Natural History, the Historical Society, a chemical laboratory, and a museum under one roof. The number of American scientific journals doubled from 1815 to 1825. In 1821 Silliman proclaimed "the *intellectual age of the world*": never before were so many men engaged in "so many and so useful researches."

Politicians, merchants, and urban professionals helped sustain the work of the country's embryonic corps of full-time scientists. Especially in the West, where fewer colleges, medical schools, and learned societies offered platforms for dedicated study, scientific and historical research still commingled with business. Caleb Atwater, Henry Rowe Schoolcraft, and Lewis Cass, students of history, geology, and Indian ethnology, were all Jacksonian politicians. In Cincinnati Daniel Drake, the "Franklin of the West," combined the roles of doctor, druggist, medical researcher and educator, bank director, author, and editor.

Patriotic ardor bolstered scientific endeavor. In *Notes on Virginia* Thomas Jefferson had repelled European aspersions on the size of America's animals and the vigor and intelligence of its native peoples. His successors fused nationalism with local boosterism. Civic leaders sponsored academies, colleges, and learned societies as a way of trumpeting their progress in sophistication and besting rival towns and states. Philadelphia, though losing its lead in population and trade, was still the Athens of America. New York scrambled to catch up, while Bostonians schemed to make Massachusetts "the 'headquarters of science' in the U.S." In the West, William Maclure's hope of making New Harmony "an Emporium of Arts and Sciences that will attract the attention" of the whole hemisphere mirrored the pretensions of Lexington, Louisville, Cincinnati, and a dozen others.

Politicians, editors, lawyers, and doctors incorporated the Historical & Philosophical Society of Ohio in 1831. Its first president was Benjamin Tappan, lawyer, judge, canal commissioner, and amateur mineralogist and conchologist. Tappan laid out an ambitious program of research on Ohio's natural and human history—its Indian culture, pioneer settlement, geology, botany, zoology, and mineralogy. The society needed a headquarters, a journal, and a botanic garden; it should dedicate itself to advancing science by "collecting all the facts which may be known upon every branch of human knowledge, and by publishing such collections."

Bolstering this plan of universal study was an exhilarating feeling of power, a sense that knowledge was suddenly breaking old restraints and leaping forward on all fronts. "This is emphatically a matter of fact age," remarked Tappan:

Men delight not now as formerly in abstract theories, and wayward imaginings; the subtleties of dialectics are giving way to the truths of science; and education, is ceasing to content itself, with learning the languages, or storing up the opinions of past ages; and is endeavoring to reach the unknown truths it seeks to find, through those which are known and acknowledged.

The Pursuit of Useful Knowledge

Faith in the wonder-working powers of information suffused the American scientific enterprise. Steered by patriotism and a thirst for improvement, it produced science of a distinctly utilitarian cast. Benjamin Silliman devoted his *American Journal of Science and Arts* to the "PHYSICAL SCIENCES, with their application to THE ARTS, and to every useful purpose," including agriculture, manufactures, and domestic economy. The *Journal of the Academy of Natural Sciences of Philadelphia* intended "to exclude entirely all papers of mere theory,—to confine their communications as much as possible to facts." American scientists and the public men who surrounded them demanded facts, and useful ones at that.

To be sure, the definition of usefulness was supple and expansive. To a lover of learning like John Quincy Adams, investigation and inquiry were worthy in themselves. Attainments in knowledge and wisdom were marks of character. Disciplined mental exertion elevated intelligence and morals. Study yielded benefits independent of the subject studied. Adams studied everything, from classical languages to weights and measures.

Most American research still centered on natural history and mechanics. Botanists and zoologists fanned out to collect and catalogue the endless abundance of plant and animal species. The village of New Harmony found new life after 1827 as an outpost of science. When Robert Owen and his followers departed, the core of specialists from the "boatload of knowledge" remained, along with Owen's four science-minded sons and the library and collections of William Maclure. Together they made the town a base for wide-ranging fieldwork through the Ohio and Mississippi valleys. The *Disseminator of Useful Knowledge,* produced by Maclure's School of Industry, published the scientists' findings on ichthyology (fish), entomology (bugs), and conchology (shells).

A voracious curiosity underlay the naturalists' extensive, often grueling fieldwork. Still, they were always alert to practical applications. Plants and insects yielded information useful in agriculture and medicine. Knowledge of flora and fauna presumably would assist the country's development. In return, development aided science. Improved transport promoted intellectual exchange and opened new regions for study. Major Stephen H. Long's army expedition to the Rocky Mountains in 1819–1820, which included naturalists and ethnographers, went up the Missouri by steamboat as far as the Council Bluffs. In the Jubilee summer of 1826 Amos Eaton, who had earlier conducted a geologic survey of the Erie Canal route, organized a floating school of science. Twenty students, including a son of Governor Clinton, traveled back and forth on the canal boat *Lafayette* giving lectures on botany and chemistry, collecting geologic samples, and studying the countryside.

Geology promised a more direct return than botany or zoology. The legislatures of New York and North and South Carolina subsidized geologic investigations in the 1820s. In 1830 Massachusetts sponsored the first comprehensive state survey. Tennessee followed in 1831, Maryland in 1833, New Jersey, Connecticut, and Virginia in 1835, and nine more states before 1840. While surveys added to understanding of geologic processes, their immediate aim was to locate soil types, mineral deposits, building materials, and transportation routes. The Massachusetts report was subtitled "The Economic Geology of the State." The Maine legislature declared its survey to be "intimately connected with the advancement of the arts and sciences, of agriculture, manufactures, and commerce."

Developing and dispensing useful information was also the goal of technical institutes and agricultural societies. The Franklin Institute of Philadelphia, organized in 1824 and dedicated to "the promotion and encouragement of manufactures and the mechanic and useful arts," stood for that union of scientific and mechanical pursuits that had distinguished the work of its namesake. Through its experiments and its journal the institute amassed and disseminated technical data of direct economic value. One of its committees studied the causes of steamboat accidents, prompting federal safety legislation in 1838. Another ran hundreds of tests to measure and improve the efficiency of water wheels.

While it aimed at practical knowledge, the Franklin Institute did not take a narrow technician's outlook. Along with men of the Baldwin, Du Pont, Evans, Gilpin, and Sellers manufacturing families, institute members included the scientist Alexander Dallas Bache (great-grandson of Franklin), Nicholas Biddle, now president of the Bank of the United States, publisher Mathew Carey, architect William Strickland, and engineer-inventor Franklin Peale. At the dedication of its new building in 1825, lawyer and institute official Peter A. Browne linked science, education, and republican liberty in the march of humanity:

Knowledge ceases to be monopolized by few and is becoming the property of the many; theory and practice formerly disunited and unsocial, now walk hand in hand enlightening and correcting each other; the workman and the philosopher are united in the same person. . . . *Americans*, let us all unite in this determination, to encourage institutions *calculated to diffuse knowledge among* the people. . . . It will insure to us *religious, political and personal freedom;* and will, sooner or later, by our example lead to the emancipation of the world.

Like their companions at New Harmony and elsewhere, the Philadelphia philosophes saw improvement as indivisible. Truth was one, and all progress was of a piece. The pursuit of knowledge, wisdom, and beauty carried them effortlessly across the disciplinary boundaries of physical and natural science, mechanics and engineering, art, education, and even politics. In nature's wonders they found an object of scientific curiosity, esthetic appreciation, and artistic inspiration. In coupling the search for new knowledge with its dissemination among the people, they defined a mission of social uplift.

Even family relations embodied the harmony of interests. The Baches, descendants of Benjamin Franklin, and their Duane and Dallas in-laws were astronomers, financiers, journalists, and politicians. The man who did most to shape Philadelphia culture, aside from the late Franklin, was Charles Willson Peale. Sire of a brood of artists, naturalists, and mechanicians, Peale was himself painter, inventor, paleontologist, entomologist, and ornithologist. His celebrated Philadelphia Museum, housed from 1802 to 1827 in historic Independence Hall, was a copious "school of wisdom," a "world in miniature." It held collections from the Lewis and Clark and Long expeditions, plus birds and animals (alive and stuffed), fish and marine creatures, insects, minerals, shells, fossils, Indian artifacts, relics, curiosities, inventions, machines, apparatus, and portrait, landscape, and historical paintings—perhaps one hundred thousand items in all.

Across the country societies and institutes disseminated useful knowledge along with the cosmopolitan rational faith. At the United States Military Academy at West Point, New York, the revamped curriculum after 1817 stressed science, mathematics, astronomy, and engineering, preparing officers to lead explorations as well as campaigns, and construct canals and railroads along with fortifications. Expansion of the Harvard Medical School, inauguration of the *New England Journal of Medicine* in 1812, and the opening of Massachusetts General Hospital in 1821 made Boston Philadelphia's rival as a center of medical research.

The merchants and manufacturers who subsidized Boston's medical complex also led in applying science to farming. Their Massachusetts Society for Promoting Agriculture, incorporated by the state legislature in 1792, doubled in membership and broadened its activities between 1817 and 1822. The society published a journal, supported a botanical garden at Harvard, collected and distributed seeds and cuttings, promoted new farm implements, sponsored the importation and breeding of superior livestock, and put on fairs with cash prizes to foster a "spirit of emulation." Aided by state bounties after 1817, Massachusetts county societies mimicked these activities. Fifty New York counties organized agricultural societies after the state offered a subsidy in 1819. North Carolina chartered twelve agricultural societies from 1818 to 1822 and in the latter year created the State Board of Agriculture to support them.

In Baltimore in 1819 John S. Skinner began the *American Farmer,* the country's first regular agricultural journal. In 1821 it offered a paper, "On the Composition of Soils, and Their Improvement by Calcareous Manures," by the young Virginia planter Edmund Ruffin. Inspired by John Taylor's writings on agricultural reform, Ruffin launched a one-man crusade to rescue Virginia's exhausted land. Ruffin's work exemplified the methods and purposes of American practical science. He tested soils for chemical composition, applied marl (shell lime) in careful doses, kept precise records of the results, and tirelessly publicized his findings. His discovery of acidity as the source of infertility and of liming as its cure brought dead, discarded farms back to life.

Science and the Challenge to Authority

Gaps between expectation and performance marked much of American science. Many agricultural societies soon folded, while farmers clung to old ways. Even Edmund Ruffin's best friend resisted his reforms. Benjamin Silliman coupled celebrations of American achievement with complaints about poor support for his journal. But if Americans' attainments were yet limited, their aspirations were profound. The proliferation of societies, institutes, and journals bespoke a boundless faith in scientific advance. The Enlightenment creed of progress through knowledge still flourished in America after the War of 1812. Native conditions sustained an optimism that catastrophic war had undermined in Europe. "The present is, pre-eminently, an age of inquiry, and of enterprize, of discovery, of invention, and of universal improvement," intoned a Connecticut Phi Beta Kappa orator in 1825. "It is an age, full of destiny; and, if we are just to ourselves, of most auspicious augury to our country."

In conception the spirit of inquiry was both unifying and democratizing, for its promise was universal. All touted progress; all yearned for its re-wards. Yet here, as elsewhere, broad hopes of betterment masked budding disagreement over specific ends and means. In agriculture, improvement was everyone's watchword. But the societies' methods met resistance from self-described "practical farmers" who spurned supercilious instruction from gentleman dilettantes. Heralds of agricultural reform learned, as had Robert Owen and John Quincy Adams, that leadership even in the name of progress was unwelcome when tainted by imputations of authority.

The very definitions of science and reason became contested when efforts were made to apply them to human institutions. In the 1820s law, medicine, and even language became battlegrounds for public disputation between the claims of learned expertise and those of popular wisdom. Legal scholars like Joseph Story, Nathan Dane, and James Kent strove to rationalize the tradition-based English common law for American usage. Consonant with an age whose "most striking characteristic," according to Story, was its "superior attachment to practical science," the law they envisioned would be systematic, sensible, and useful. It would, as Story proclaimed in his inaugural lecture as Dane Professor at Harvard in 1829, be like "the natu-ral sciences, where new discoveries continually lead the way to new, and sometimes astonishing results."

But this conception of scientific law was implicitly elitist. Trained judges and lawyers would play the scientists in uncovering new legal principles and applications. Story's program ran up against another idea of the type of law best fitted for Americans, one equally scientific and progressive and avowedly democratic. Critics condemned the whole common law, with its arcane terminology and complex rules of procedure, as a relic of medieval barbarism, unsuited to the needs of a free people and the temper of modern times. Americans wanted no "aristocracy" of judges and lawyers to tell them what law was, nor to make new law for them under guise of explicating the old. Away with tradition and precedent! A self-governing people demanded an explicit code of laws, enacted by their own representatives and written in plain language for any citizen to understand. "Simplification, order, arrangement, labor saving contrivances, and increased efficiency of exertion" were transforming "every other branch of human knowledge and effort," argued one codifier. Why not apply the "universally prevalent" "benevolent principle" of improvement to the law as well? A fresh code of laws "would be almost as real and as great an improvement in jurisprudence, as the introduction of steamboats in water transportation." In this debate both sides recruited under the banners of reason, science, and progress.

So also in medicine, where botanic practitioners challenged the authority of trained physicians. Samuel Thomson and other crusaders purveyed simple natural remedies and invited ordinary Americans to doctor themselves. Thomson's *An Earnest Appeal to the Public Showing the Misery Caused by the Fashionable Mode of Practice of the Doctors at the Present Day* (1824) and *New Guide to Health; or Botanic Family Physician* (1825), spurned the medical profession's claim to a monopoly of knowledge and wisdom. The people, said Thomson, "should in medicine, as in religion and politics, act for themselves." Daniel Drake, medical educator and western exemplar of the Philadelphia style of scientific medicine made famous by Benjamin Rush, answered in 1830 with savage sarcasm:

Down with the profession, *vive la Charlatanerie.* The world has been long enough duped by lawyers, and priests, and doctors. Let us rid ourselves of the last of them. . . . Push aside the "riglar" Doctors!—Conceal all their cures, and publish all their failures! . . . Break down the *aristocracy* of learning and science: give the people their rights. . . . Every quack is, indeed, a *demagogue;* and relies, for his success, on nearly the same arts, with his political and religious, or rather *irreligious,* brethren. He is one of the *people,* and pre-eminently the guardian of the *people;* while those who spend their lives, in acquiring the knowledge which has been handed down by the great physicians and benefactors of the world, are not *of* the *people,* but arrayed against the *people,* and bent on killing them off.

In the same vein Drake ridiculed the new president Andrew Jackson, "the people's friend," who "fought a great *battle,* and is therefore a great *doctor!*"

Thomson and Drake both spied an underlying unity in the democratic revolt sweeping across the boundaries of law, politics, religion, and medicine. Defense of his learning placed an ironic burden on doctor Drake, as it did on statesman John Quincy Adams or reformer Robert Owen. These men saw themselves as tribunes of progress through knowledge, not upholders of hierarchy. They sought to elevate Americans, not repress them. Far from defending tradition, they wanted nothing more than to lead people to a better world. But the people, it seemed, did not want to be led.

The assault on authority extended even into language. In the 1820s a spate of native writers challenged the ongoing effort by grammarians to improve Americans' English. Avowedly populist and rational, they derided the idiosyncratic formal rules imposed on the language by English fops and aristocrats. Americans were a new people, demanding a style of their own.

Popular attack on the claims of the learned, inverting their expertise from an entitlement for leadership into a disbarment, put scientists in a peculiar position. Their own enterprise had once rested, in large part, on a similar rebellion against the authority of the Church. Many Revolutionary apostles of progress drew an affinity between reason and religious skepticism. Jefferson, Franklin, and Paine scorned unthinking acceptance of received dogma in any aspect of human affairs. While they embraced Christian moral teaching, they challenged the Bible as revealed truth, and they decried the superstition, ignorance, and persecution that Christian establishments had thrown in the way of advancing enlightenment.

The assumption that ancient faith and modern reason were essentially at odds lingered long after the Revolution, especially in certain scientific circles. Free thought and skepticism flourished among some naturalists and geologists, whose discoveries suggested a world much older and more complex than that of the Biblical creation story. William Maclure railed at the "prejudice, superstition & bigotry" of clerics, while his friend Benjamin Tappan wrote off the Scriptures as "all damned nonsense." Robert Owen's "Declaration of Mental Independence" on the Fourth of July in 1826 condemned "ABSURD AND IRRATIONAL SYSTEMS OF RELIGION" as one of the three *"monstrous evils"* that inflicted misery on the whole human race. Owen's rejection of Christianity extended even to its calendar. From the Jubilee day forward the *New Harmony Gazette* dated its issues in years of "mental independence."

The New Harmony set proposed to liberate humanity from the shackles of the past by joining scientific inquiry and social experiment with religious skepticism and democratic politics. Maclure, Tappan, Frances Wright, Thomas Say, and Owens's sons all spurned conventional Christianity. They also supported Andrew Jackson. They saw the overthrow of "aristocracy" in religion as inseparable from its downfall in government. Both were essential to progress.

But others, equally improvement-minded, disagreed. John P. Crozer, manufacturer and enthusiast of science and education, called the failure of New Harmony "another instance of the folly of men in their efforts to establish communities repudiating or failing to recognize the Christian religion as the basis of society and good government." In his view, shared by many others, the absence of religion at New Harmony was not the hallmark of its promise, but the seal of its doom.

In 1814 President Timothy Dwight of Yale College, the "pope of Connecticut," leader of the state-supported Congregational establishment known as the "standing order" and a champion of science, hailed the new age of invention:

Improvements are making on so large a scale, as to outrun every thing which had been known before. . . . Knowledge will increase, and great improvements will still be made. I believe it will not be more than one or two centuries before there will be such a restraint on human passions . . . that it will make the world appear as if all the good men in it were brought together.

Like Owen and his associates, Dwight identified scientific with social and moral advance. He too saw the progress of knowledge as a signpost to the millennium—not, however, by way of overthrowing Christian influence on society, but of spreading it.

Scientists who were also Christians saw their work furthering the fulfillment of their religious aims. At Yale Dwight's protégé Benjamin Silliman devoted his life to science, confident that in reaching to master the physical world he was enriching Christian reverence, not undermining it. Silliman found no contradiction between a rational, improvable universe and a Christian God. "The whole circle of physical science is directly applicable to human wants, and constantly holds out a light to the practical arts; it thus polishes and benefits society, and every where demonstrates both supreme intelligence, and harmony and benificence [sic] of design in THE CREATOR."

Religious controversy did not disrupt scientific enterprise. Believers and skeptics labored in consort. All could see that their work served the end of improvement. Whether improvement brought them closer to or further from a Christian God, they did not yet need to decide.

But for Americans at large that question was already urgent. While they might celebrate the country's achievement in science and welcome its fruits in new and useful knowledge, they could not help asking: progress toward what? To what goal did they aspire? The fulfillment of destiny, the pursuit of happiness, perhaps the salvation of the soul, all hung on the answer. Even as the spirit of inquiry rose, it became entangled in a struggle to define Americans' moral mission in the world.

The Kingdom of Christ

There is no country in the world where the Christian religion retains a greater influence over the souls of men than
in America; and there can be no greater proof of its utility
and of its conformity to human nature than that its influence is powerfully felt over the most enlightened and free
nation of the earth.   —Alexis de Tocqueville, 1835

For Protestant Christians the United States at the Jubilee was a place of
unique promise. Ever since the days of the Pilgrims, believers had looked
to the new world as a site for godly communities. For two centuries, inter-
vals of revival and awakening had helped sustain hope of America's special
Christian destiny. Now that destiny appeared near, as the rapid spread of
improvement across the land foretold an imminent apotheosis, a permanent
and universal triumph of the faith.

The ubiquitous sense of possibility and urgency goaded divines and laypeople into a frenzy of organizing and evangelizing. The compulsion to
spread the gospel and gather in the fold gave rise to new developments
in Christian theology and polity and to a host of efforts to purge society
of sin. Ultimately, in religion as in politics, competing systems of uplift
clashed not only with one another, but with Americans' wish to choose for
themselves their own path to redemption.

The Challenge to Calvinism

On the day of Jubilee in 1826, while Robert Owen declared mental independence at New Harmony, Lyman Beecher was preaching a revival at

his new church in Boston. During nearly thirty years of ministering to village congregations in Long Island and Connecticut, Beecher had mastered the technique of bringing recalcitrant souls to Christ. Now he was testing his skill in the big city. The stakes were high—in Beecher's eye, nothing less than "the resurrection of New England to an undivided and renovated effort for the extension of religious and moral influence throughout the land and through the world."

Beecher entered Boston as the champion of Calvinism, the faith of the Puritans and, in its Congregational and Presbyterian forms, the dominant religious tradition in America. Beecher was a graduate of Yale and a protégé of Yale's president Timothy Dwight. Dwight represented New England tradition in person as well as in station. He was the direct descendant of theologians Solomon Stoddard and Jonathan Edwards, who had kept the old creed vital in the eighteenth century.

But by the time Lyman Beecher mounted his first pulpit in 1799, religious establishments were retreating on every front. For half a century previous, European immigration and native awakening had multiplied the number of Christian sects in America. Even as Beecher began his work, fast-moving Methodist circuit-riders and Baptist missionaries raced out to recruit new followers. Expansive, mobile organization and low educational standards for the ministry enabled these and other new groups to train and deploy preachers more quickly than the stolid Congregationalists and Presbyterians. Relying largely on emotional suasion, Baptists and Methodists pressed for quick conversions. They reached downward and outward to those beyond the grasp or interest of the older churches—backcountry farmers, the urban poor, slaves. They reaped spectacular success. Within three decades after 1790, Baptist and Methodist membership ballooned from a few thousand communicants to more than half a million, leapfrogging denominations two hundred years older in a single generation.

Congregational, Presbyterian, and Episcopal churches were hard pressed to hold their home ground, to say nothing of competing in the growing inland regions. Baptists came to outnumber Congregationalists even in parts of Massachusetts. In 1801 New England Congregationalists and Philadelphia-based Presbyterians pooled their resources for westward expansion in a "Plan of Union." But their efforts brought mixed results. In the southern backcountry, Scotch-Irish immigration and the Revolutionary disestablishment of a weak Church of England opened a rich field for Presbyterians. Mass exercises like the famous communion at Cane Ridge, Kentucky, in 1801 recruited thousands of new Christians. But most of these landed finally with the more nimble Methodists and Baptists or even with separatists like the Shakers. Methodists, not Presbyterians, made the camp meeting a favorite conversion tool.

Inside the old churches, aggressive evangelizing incited controversy on central points of style and doctrine. Presbyterian leaders reproved the emotional excesses that accompanied revival preaching—the moaning, screaming, jerking, and swooning—and doubted the worth of conversions procured by such means. They also condemned revivalists' inclination, in their eager search for souls, to throw off essential Calvinist dogmas of divine omnipotence and man's powerlessness to work his own salvation. Traditionalist efforts to uphold church decorum and discipline provoked schism and revolt. Presbyterian divisions spawned new independent sects—Cumberland Presbyterians, Christians, Disciples of Christ—adding to creedal confusion and competition.

While staid old Calvinism lost country followers to the fervid preaching of camp-meeting exhorters and circuit-riders, its cosmopolitan constituents drifted away in the other direction, toward rationalism. In the Revolutionary generation, deism and other polite forms of crypto-religiosity flourished among urban sophisticates and gentleman planters. The Enlightenment set that surrounded Franklin and Paine was notoriously skeptical in religion. Not one of the four Virginia presidents from Washington to Monroe was a regular churchgoer.

In Boston, once the proud capital of Puritanism, deists and outright unbelievers were rare. Instead, Harvard College, the leading churches, and many of the leading citizens succumbed to Unitarianism. Without going as far as deists, the Enlightenment-influenced Unitarians spurned the forbidding Calvinist deity for a God who was rational, humane, and knowable. Unitarianism and its country cousin Universalism were so benign, emotionally distant, and undemanding upon their adherents that to an ardent believer like Lyman Beecher they appeared to be no Christianity at all.

Beecher, Finney, and the New Preaching

Losing souls in every direction, heirs of the Puritans softened their stiff ancestral ways. As Lyman Beecher often complained, Calvinism's creed of inscrutable divine sovereignty and human depravity inspired a fatalistic lethargy in parishioners—they were damned or not, and that was that—and left energetic pastors like himself with nothing to do. Beecher and other reformers within the Congregational/Presbyterian tradition sought to breathe life back into old forms. They shaped a new divinity along a middle path between overintellectualized Unitarianism and the hyper-emotionalism of the evangelistic sects. They embraced the technique of revival, but tempered it from a quick catharsis to a slow, careful unfolding, in which the attending minister monitored and shepherded the convert's progress toward understanding and faith.

Charles Grandison Finney, a Presbyterian itinerant who began preaching in upstate New York in 1824, took Beecher's methods farther toward emotionalism with his direct, riveting pulpit style and loose theology. A revival, said Finney, was "not a miracle, or dependent on a miracle, in any sense. It is a purely philosophical result of the right use of the constituted means." Together Beecher and Finney domesticated the revival from an unpredictable, mysterious working of divine providence to a calculated, refined instrument for making new Christians.

Bending to the times and their own craving for souls, practitioners of Finney's "new measures" quietly backpedaled from the old Calvinist creed toward notions of human free agency and plenitude of divine grace. They discovered they could not win converts to a predestinarian God whose doings seemed both unfathomable and cruel. To cover their retreat the reformers downplayed the importance of doctrine. Beecher always denied deviating from true Calvinism, but he preferred simply not to discuss the question. In practice he adapted his teaching to the needs at hand.

Politically too, the new Calvinists accommodated to a democratizing society. In the face of collapsing hierarchies and orthodoxies, clinging to old authority structures could be as fatal in religion as in politics. Baptist and Methodist insurgents flung charges of "aristocracy" at clerical establishments just as Jeffersonians had thrown them at Federalists. Beecher bitterly resisted the dismantling of Connecticut's Congregational "standing order" after the War of 1812. But he came round to viewing it as *the best thing that ever happened to the State of Connecticut.*" Shorn of taxes and public officials for its support, the old church had to roll up its sleeves and get out and fight for converts. Activity gave life to faith. In an open marketplace of souls, evangelists bid for true conviction, not hollow obedience. Beecher himself sounded the theme for the age in an 1817 sermon on "The Bible a Code of Laws," whose refrain was a challenge to "dare to think for yourself." It was but one step further—a step he did not quite take—to say, "save yourself."

Indeed, the practical import of the new teaching, doctrinal technicalities aside, was to thrust upon every hearer direct responsibility for securing his or her own salvation. Like their evangelical competitors, Beecher and Finney preached initiative, not resignation; hope, not despair. Suppressing the fatalism and mystery of old Calvinism, their message of individual empowerment laid enormous expectations on clergy and laypeople alike. "Sinners ought to be made to feel that they have something to do, and that is to repent," declared Finney. "That is something which no other being can do for them, neither God nor man, and something which they can do and do now. Religion is something to do, not something to wait for." The unrepentant could blame none but themselves for their fate.

Likewise, ministers could gauge their effectiveness by counting converts. In effect, numbers became the standard for judging pastoral competence and even doctrinal purity. As Beecher argued to his traditionalist critics, a creed that could not win souls was worthless, and a worthless creed could not be true. Finney defended his new measures—what one old-school critic called "his shocking blasphemies, his novel and repulsive sentiments, and his theatrical and frantic gesticulations"—on the simple ground that they worked: people heeded his message. By making converts the measure of correctness, preachers nearly offered up the tenets of Christianity for popular referendum. Finney explicitly likened his techniques to those of a politician seeking votes.

Thus far, though Beecher was loath to admit it, he and Finney mainly copied the innovations of Baptist and Methodist insurgents. Calvinist revivalists defended the old faith only by surrendering much of the contested ground, both stylistic and theological. Doctrines of divine omnipotence and original sin sank from view as confidence in human efficacy grew. These concessions bore a price. Creedal retreat set traditionalists and innovators within the church against each other. Beecher and Finney were themselves sometimes allies, sometimes foes. Clerical resistance to their departures from orthodoxy culminated in Beecher's ecclesiastical trial for heresy in 1835, Finney's abandonment of Presbyterianism in 1836, and a formal division of the national church into "New School" and "Old School" factions in 1837.

But though it finally rent Presbyterianism in two, the new preaching also exerted an influence stretching far beyond church ranks. By adapting old faiths to suit new times, Beecher and his fellows succeeded in keeping the country's deepest religious tradition vibrant in an optimistic and democratic age. But they did more than that. By linking the evangelical impulse, essentially borrowed from Methodists and Baptists, to a program of holistic moral improvement, and firing both with millennial energy, they retooled American Protestantism from an instrument of individual salvation to a scheme of national regeneration.

Toward a Christian Nation

Like John Quincy Adams or Robert Owen, Lyman Beecher felt the imminence of destiny hanging over him. He approached the struggle for souls with (as his son described it) a "singularly progressive and buoyant enthusiasm," in "full belief that the millennium was coming, that it was at hand, that the Church was just about to march with waving banners to final and universal dominion." Beecher saw "civilization, science, and religion" advancing together. Even theology should reflect progress in knowledge and reason. In his contest with Boston Unitarianism Beecher applauded the awakening "noble spirit" of investigation and inquiry—"a spirit that determines to examine for itself, to hear for itself, to think for itself." He never doubted victory, for the faith he offered was not only scriptural but "reasonable" and in full accord with *"common sense"* and *"the experience of mankind."*

Beecher aimed to convert a nation. From Boston he went to Cincinnati in 1832 as president of the new Lane Seminary to battle infidels and Catholics for the soul of the West. The region's great capacity and unformed character inspired in him, as in others, a sense of boundless possibility and dire urgency. Here the future of the world was to be decided, and soon. "The moral destiny of our nation, and all our institutions and hopes, and the world's hopes, turns on the character of the West," he told his daughter Catharine. "If we gain the West, all is safe; if we lose it, all is lost." The West was "the Valley of Decision in respect to this, and probably all other nations," urged Beecher's colleague Thomas Skinner. Success there would "bring the Millennium to the very doors."

Christian philanthropists backed Beecher and his fellows in their quest to evangelize the West and the nation and thus secure a blessed future for all humanity. Headquartered in eastern cities with affiliates across the country, Protestant societies pursued interlocking strategies to "enlarge the kingdom of our Lord and Savior Jesus Christ." The Boston-based American Board of Commissioners for Foreign Missions, founded by Beecher and others, despatched ministers to the heathens abroad and Indians at home. The American Education Society financed their training. From New York City the American Home Missionary Society answered the western need for preaching. The American Sunday School Union in Philadelphia supplied teachers, books, and curricular materials for Christian instruction. The American Tract Society and American Bible Society, both founded with Beecher's aid and operating from New York, sought to place their publications in the home of every family in America.

All these agencies, save the foreign mission board, were organized after the War of 1812, some by federating older state and local groups. With the founding of the last two, the tract and home missionary societies in 1825 and 1826, philanthropists were poised to flood the country with Christian propaganda. The Home Missionary Society soon supported seven hundred preachers in the field. Exploiting the latest technology in printing and paper-making, Christians let loose a deluge of publications. The tract society printed forty-four million pages in its first two years. By 1830 the agencies were distributing a million Bibles and six million tracts a year, and the country had more than six hundred religious newspapers.

Ostensibly ecumenical, the benevolent agencies were dominated by Presbyterians and Congregationalists. Rival denominations maintained their own, less expansive operations. The national societies drew contributions from auxiliaries across the country, but the essential seed money, as well as the executive talent to direct the enterprise, came from a circle of prosperous merchants centered around the brothers Arthur and Lewis Tappan in New York City. Raised in Massachusetts of Puritan descent, the Tappans failed to imbibe their parents' emotional piety but substituted in its place a compulsive craving to do good. Arthur Tappan, one of New York's richest men, ran a wholesale drygoods business netting tens of thousands of dollars a year. He devoted nearly all of it, along with his time away from business, to the campaign to Christianize America. In 1828 brother Lewis joined him, moving down from Boston where Lyman Beecher had rescued him from Unitarianism.

Amplified by the relentless evangelizing of a half-dozen sects and bolstered by the sense of expectation accompanying the Jubilee, missionary benevolence helped ignite a religious fire in the late 1820s. Excitement peaked in upstate New York. Newly accessible via the Erie Canal, the region was settled largely by Yankee emigrants and saturated by agency propaganda. In 1826 Charles Finney's preaching gathered waves of new converts in Rome, Utica, Auburn, and Troy. After stints in Philadelphia and New York (at the behest of the Tappan group, who later built him a church there), Finney returned to Rochester in 1830 for a six-month crusade that drew in all the Protestant denominations and doubled the town's church membership. This triumph drew national notice and capped a year of awakening that Lyman Beecher hailed as "the greatest work of God, and the greatest revival of religion, that the world has ever seen, in so short a time."

New Faiths and Creeds

The Christian ferment of the 1820s produced new principles, new sects, and briefly a new political party. Even the insular Society of Friends, or Quakers, felt the impact. Evangelistic urgency split the society into hostile factions over long-controverted issues of doctrine and authority. In 1827 and 1828, following a series of showdowns that approached physical violence, Elias Hicks and his followers separated from orthodox Quakerism, creating a cleavage never fully healed.

In 1830 Alexander Campbell of western Virginia, who had been a Presbyterian, then a Baptist, broke off again to found the Disciples of Christ, or Campbellites, devoted to the restoration of primitive Christianity. The same year, in Palmyra in upstate New York, young Joseph Smith, Jr., climaxed a series of visions and revelations by publishing the *Book of Mormon* and establishing the Church of Jesus Christ. He and his disciples soon departed for Ohio "to begin the gathering of Israel." By this time millennial visions were sprouting on every side. Along the Vermont–New York border a Baptist named William Miller, who had been working on biblical calculations since 1816, announced in 1831 that Christ would come again and the world would end around 1843.

From modest beginnings, Mormonism and Millerite Adventism grew to formidable dimensions in the 1840s. Antimasonry, which sprang from the same ground at nearly the same time, followed a swifter trajectory. The Order of Freemasons had spread across America after the Revolution. Its aura of urbanity and fellowship attracted professionals, public officials, and military men, including George Washington and later Andrew Jackson. Carefully guarded secret rites fostered comradeship among members, but invited outsiders' resentment and suspicion. In 1824 Masonic lodges joined in welcoming Lafayette, a fellow Mason, to American shores. Then in September 1826, a man named William Morgan, who was about to publish the order's mysteries, was kidnapped at Canandaigua, New York, and never seen again. His disappearance and probable murder, followed by signs of connivance and cover-up by state authorities and prominent Masons, touched off a furor.

Spreading quickly across the North, the "blessed spirit" of Antimasonry burned hottest in heavily evangelized regions. Beginning as a religiously powered outburst against Masonry's supposed immorality, sacrilege, and diabolism, Antimasonry quickly burgeoned into an all-purpose crusade against secret societies in general, against political establishments (which in New York meant Martin Van Buren's Jacksonian regime), against landlords and bankers and other symbols of oppression—in short, against every form of "aristocracy" and exclusiveness.

Antimasons soon branched into party politics, winning statewide elections in Vermont and posting strong showings in New York, Massachusetts, and Pennsylvania between 1828 and 1834. Thriving on the new democratic ethos, the Antimasonic party pioneered techniques of mass organization and participation, including the first presidential nominating convention in 1831. (Their candidate, William Wirt of Maryland, carried Vermont in 1832.) Antimasonry's impressive but brief showing in politics actually understated its achievement. Under its onslaught American Freemasonry nearly disintegrated. Lodges folded as men resigned by hundreds. With their aim secured and their constituency fragmenting over other matters, political Antimasons in the mid-1830s disbanded or fused with one of the emerging national parties.

Seekers and Questioners

Sprouting from seeds sown by regular Christian evangelists, Adventism, Mormonism, and Antimasonry showed what unpredictable and rebellious fruits religious fervor might yield. Relentless proselytizing created a spiritual milieu that was exhilirating and highly fluid. Most Americans encountered revivalism not as a methodical competition of creeds and systems, but as a kaleidoscope of new ideas and experiments, each one promising the fulfillment of prophecy, the purification of earthly existence, the end of the world. Driven by novelty and excitement, and without much regard to consistency, converts leaped readily from one enthusiasm to the next.

Young William Cooper Howells grew up in Ohio among Quakers and Methodists. In 1821 he converted at a camp meeting, but he backslid and was expelled from the church. Moving to a new county, Howells found his neighbors immersed in theological disputation. "Religious feeling pervaded the whole community intellectually" and dominated public discourse, even crowding out politics. Around 1829, in Wheeling, it suddenly struck Howells "that the world was on the eve of some great social, political and civil revolution, in which the 'ills that flesh is heir to' were to be all cured." Egged on "by a few who were making war upon certain forms of sectarianism in the church, and by all who were dissatisfied with politics and the world in general," he began a newspaper, the *Eclectic Observer*. It soon folded. Next he published "a queer compound of politics and theology" called *The Rise, Progress and Downfall of Aristocracy*, written by a local eccentric. After further political and religious wanderings, Howells settled down as an anti-Jackson man and a believer in spiritualism.

Howells's odyssey shows just how easily Americans slipped from one creed to another, and even between religion and irreligion, in their search for a true faith and a perfected community. Joseph Smith's first revelation grew from his consternation and bewilderment at the divisive claims of Palmyra's noisy sectarians. The cacophony of creeds found voice in his parents' restless sampling of Universalism, Methodism, Presbyterianism, and skepticism. Promising release from argument and uncertainty, Mormonism itself drew converts from a half-dozen denominations. Creedal cross-fertilization readily passed the boundary between sectarianism and secularism. Owenites recruited from Shakers, and vice versa. Many seekers, like Howells, passed several stations on route to their final home. Sidney Rigdon, an important Mormon convert, had been by turns a regular Baptist, Campbellite, and communitarian.

In April 1829 Robert Owen himself arrived in Cincinnati to debate the evidences of Christianity with Alexander Campbell. Campbell took up a challenge Owen had thrown down in New Orleans a year earlier, offering to prove that all the world's religions "have been founded on the ignorance of mankind; that they are directly opposed to the never-changing laws of our nature; that they have been, and are, the real source of vice, disunion, and misery of every description; that they are now the only real bar to the formation of a society of virtue, of intelligence, of charity in its most extended sense, and of sincerity and kindness among the whole human family." The dare was irresistible to Campbell, who thrived on disputation. Later he would pen an attack on Mormonism and debate a bishop on Catholicism.

For eight days, morning and afternoon, Owen and Campbell addressed an audience of twelve hundred. Seven leading citizens moderated the proceedings while a stenographer took them all down. The debate created a sensation. Owen hailed it as the first open discussion of its kind in history, proof itself that knowledge and reason were advancing toward "a greatly improved period of human existence, call it, if you please the Millennium." The Englishwoman Frances Trollope, who was in the audience, agreed it was a "spectacle unprecedented, I believe, in any age or country." She was less sure of what it augured. "This I think could only have happened in America. I am not quite sure that it was very desirable it should have happened any where."

Mostly the two men talked past each other. Owen propounded twelve laws of human nature that showed man to be a creature of circumstance. Undaunted by the New Harmony debacle, he paraded his new social system as the cure for all evil. Campbell tried to prove the Bible's accuracy as history. Only near the end did they cross swords directly. Christianity was either "the greatest curse with which our race is at this time afflicted" or a universal blessing of "peace on earth and good will among men." Owen charged religion with inspiring "ignorance, weakness, insincerity," while Campbell attacked Owen's benevolence as a "plagiarism" of Christianity and dismissed his new system as a "whimsical arrangement of circumstances" calculated, at best, to deny man's higher impulses and leave him "a happy animal . . . a stall fed ox."

The audience went with Campbell. At the close he asked *all the persons in this assembly who believe in the christian religion or who feel so much interest in it, as to wish to see it pervade the world,* to stand up. All but three rose. From this verdict Owen politely demurred. Truth, he cautioned, is not determined by majority vote. But in America it was. Campbell's rout of Owen in the public eye reflected the trend of sentiment across the country. Though they sought it in a hundred different places, most citizens looked to religion as a means of progress, not an impediment. Owen and his freethinkers were left aside, prophets of a discarded future, as Americans by the thousands decided for a Christian destiny.

Choosing faith meant forswearing neither reason nor the hope of improvement. Behind their opposite conclusions, Campbell and Owen argued from remarkably similar premises. Each took human happiness as the highest goal of existence, and graded social and religious systems according to their likelihood of producing it. Campbell's ultimate brief for Christianity was simply that without its promise of eternity, life would be miserable. Both men assumed a millennium in the offing, a "state of society far superior to any thing yet exhibited on earth." Owen expected it daily, Campbell "some time soon." Each argued that only resistance to his own reformation blocked the way to perfect social bliss. And both disdained any argument that was not self-consciously, even ostentatiously rational. In fact it was Campbell, defender of the faith, who seized the high ground of reason, presenting the Christian religion as "an institution built upon facts" and attacking Owen for offering "assertions without proof, and declamation without argument." Campbell prefaced the published debate by urging the reader to "reason, examine and judge, like a rational being, for himself."

The congruities between Owen and Campbell, the doctrinal straddles of Lyman Beecher and Charles Finney, and the passage of seekers back and forth all showed one thing: The common base of assumptions and expectations was so broad that only the width of a hair separated one creed from another. Slight, even imperceptible, turns could send like-minded men and women, even members of the same family, journeying in different directions. Around Philadelphia the coterie of textile manufacturers, though knit by common interests and pursuits, was splintered among freethinkers, Episcopalians, Presbyterians, Methodists, Baptists, and Quakers. Lewis and Arthur Tappan of New York, patrons of Christian benevolence, were brothers of that Benjamin Tappan of Ohio who thought the Scriptures "all damned nonsense." All the Tappans embraced improvement and uplift. Yet, as Lewis observed, they differed over whether to seek them through "the Creator of all things" or through "law, deism, politics, mineralogy, & conchology."

Fruits of Commitment

The decision for the Christian path burrowed deep into believers' lives, reshaping behavior, convictions, and affiliations. Converts had found the key to happiness, the way to redeem themselves and transform America's glorious prospects into millennial reality. The discovery sent some, like Joseph Smith, Jr., out in search of a new Zion. But it set others to the task of creating Zion where they were out of materials at hand. Most directly, it pointed them to prepare the way for God's kingdom by purifying themselves and the nation of sin.

The idea that righteous conduct should accompany faith was not new. All Christians presumed a code of morals to which believers should adhere, even if adhering was no substitute for, or proof of, an inward state of grace. Congregations had long acted as moral police, overseeing their members' behavior not only within church doors but in business, recreation, public deportment, and family relations. Enrollment in the community of the faithful meant submitting to church discipline. To control those unchurched and unreached by weak civil authority, clergy led in establishing what Cotton Mather in 1710 called "Societies for the Reformation of Manners and for the Suppression of Vice."

Revival preaching prompted a tightening of congregational discipline that had gone slack over the years. But Lyman Beecher and his fellows envisioned a broader role for Christian governance. Even while battling for converts one by one, they set their sights on a reformation that would embrace the United States and all its inhabitants. To prepare the way for the millennium at hand they needed to reach everyone, not just church members. Looking beyond godliness in the congregation and good order in the community, they aimed at nothing less than the moral regeneration of the country as a whole.

The broadening horizon of evangelical reform emerged from changes both within and without the church. Together, the material improvements visible at every hand and the expansive notions of human moral capacity introduced by revivalists swept away old limits on what people dared to envision in the way of betterment. Steamboats, canals, paper mills, and printing presses not only promised a better future but enabled clergy for the first time to project their message to a national audience.

The excitement of conversion itself inspired activity. Lyman Beecher and Charles Finney preached a faith that would be useful as well as sincere— indeed, whose sincerity could be judged by its usefulness. "If filled with the Spirit, you will be useful. You cannot help being useful," said Finney. He promised that "if the church will do all her duty, the millennium may come in this country in three years." Beecher enjoined his converts to set about "VIGOROUS ACTION FOR GOD." In Beecher's view, a "sermon that did not induce any body to *do any thing*" was a sermon "thrown away."

The creed of usefulness made concern for others a crucial test of faith. "The sole object of the government of God, from beginning to end, is to express His benevolence," said Beecher. If benevolence was godliness, then obsession with self was sin. "All sin," said Finney, "consists in selfishness; and all holiness of virtue in disinterested benevolence." True Christianity moved one "from selfishness to benevolence, from having a supreme regard to one's own interest to an absorbing and controlling choice of the happiness and glory of God's Kingdom." In other words, the convert who did not sway others to Christianity was no good Christian himself. Contentment with one's own state of grace was proof of its imperfection.

To be a Christian, then, was to commit unreservedly and wholeheartedly to the reform of everyone. As Finney put it, the Christians' "spirit is necessarily that of the reformer. To the universal reformation of the world they stand committed." The social mission of the believer knew no bounds. "A man is responsible for all the good he can do." It began in one's own family. Beecher labored mightily for the souls of his children. To extend the reach of his benevolence he demanded not only that his sons convert, but that they follow in his footsteps as ministers. Lewis Tappan hectored his faithless brother Benjamin without letup, because "if *I think* you are losing your soul it is my duty to attempt to save you." Lewis feared that his brother's blood "would be found on my skirts at the Judgment Day."

After rescuing family and friends, the credo of benevolence required Christians to seek out and war against sin and social abuse. The first evil they faced was drunkenness. Reformers saw the pernicious influence of alcohol everywhere. Corn whiskey was cheap and plentiful, and Americans drank habitually and heavily. Even clergy engaged in convivial tippling. Drunkenness bred suffering, waste, poverty, and violence too glaring to overlook. Benjamin Franklin and his physician friend Benjamin Rush had years before spoken out against drink. Rationalists charged that alcohol excited the emotions and befuddled the brain; evangelists warned that it deafened the ear to Christ's appeal. As one preacher complained, intemperance "stands in the way of revivals. . . . Every drunkard opposes the millennium; every dram-drinker stands in the way of it, every dram-seller stands in the way of it. . . . There is no hope of the conversion of a man who habitually uses ardent spirits."

As a young man Lyman Beecher helped turn the moralist's disapproval of drink toward a national religious crusade. Beecher had early imbibed the New England ministerial tradition of doing good. In 1806, at age thirty, he preached a sensational sermon against dueling, then helped form a society to have this "great national sin" outlawed. At clerical gatherings he felt "alarm, and shame, and indignation" at his fellow pastors' free use of tobacco and alcohol. Appointed to a church committee on the subject in 1812, he produced a stirring manifesto against liquor, "the most important paper that ever I wrote." That year Congregationalists and Presbyterians pronounced against drunkenness. Another rousing Beecher sermon on "A Reformation of Morals Practicable and Indispensable" prompted the founding of state moral reform societies in Massachusetts and Connecticut.

The crusade thus set "marching through New England, and marching through the world" was at first not wholly clear of ulterior motives. The new societies were top-heavy with Congregational clergy and Federalist politicians, both fearful for the fate of the old order at the hands of democrats and dissenters. Temperance and moral reform began their organized careers in New England as buttresses of the ruling establishment's faltering authority. On the other hand Beecher himself, though then fully engaged in the fight to save Connecticut from "innovation and democracy," also saw moral reform from the beginning in a more forward light, as "part of that great and new system of things by which God is preparing to bless the world and fill it with his glory."

The New England "standing order" fell apart after the War of 1812. But temperance trundled on, a broadly based movement peopled by clergy of all stripes and by a growing number of local societies. The Methodists, never connected with any official establishment, tightened their standards against alcohol and in 1832 called for total abstinence. In 1825 Beecher preached a new attack on drunkenness, "the sin of our land," whose unchecked career threatened to "defeat the hopes of the world, which hang upon our experiment of civil liberty." A year later the campaign assumed national scope with the founding of the American Society for the Promotion of Temperance. By 1831 the society had 2,200 local branches with 170,000 members; its New York state affiliate alone pumped out four and a half million publications in five years. American alcohol intake began to fall off rapidly.

Beginning in Virginia in 1826, temperance agencies multiplied across the slaveholding states. In the South high illiteracy rates (both white and black), inferior communications, and a dispersed rural population hampered the spread of reform enterprises that recruited mainly through printed publicity and neighborly contact. Still, southern evangelicals joined in the crusade to banish drunkenness and immorality. Cosmopolitan outposts such as Tuscaloosa, Alabama, boasted temperance, tract, Bible, and Sunday school groups by 1830. Clergy helped form antidueling societies in Charleston, Savannah, Natchez, and New Orleans between 1826 and 1834.

Besides dueling and alcohol, Christians campaigned against tobacco, licentiousness, and frivolous amusements. In New York City the Tappan brothers scored a coup by converting a theater into a church for Charles Finney. Arthur Tappan founded the Magdalen Society to fight prostitution in 1831; its graphic report on the city's flourishing vice trade caused an uproar. The same year in Philadelphia, temperance lecturer and former Presbyterian minister Sylvester Graham began propagating his system for mental and physical self-control through dietary strictures, vegetarianism, exercise, and sexual abstinence.

Abolitionism

The last and greatest of the evangelical crusades was the one against slavery. In Boston on New Year's Day, 1831, William Lloyd Garrison began publishing *The Liberator,* dedicated to ending American bondage. Though Garrison's zealotry soon set him apart even among reformers, his early spiritual quest much resembled that of others inspired by Christian awakening to dream of a purified world. Raised by a devout Baptist mother, Garrison came under Lyman Beecher's influence while attending his church in Boston. As editor of the *National Philanthropist,* a Boston temperance journal, Garrison espoused Beecher's whole spectrum of moral reform. He also embraced the Christian pacifism of William Ladd, who founded the American Peace Society in 1828—yet another offshoot of the evangelical impulse. In 1829 Garrison began editing *The Genius of Universal Emancipation* in Baltimore for Quaker Benjamin Lundy.

Like most white antislavery activists, Lundy favored colonization. Emancipating and expatriating all the blacks seemed the best solution to the tangled dilemma of race and slavery—even though most free blacks, the first candidates for colonization and those best qualified by circumstance to speak for their enslaved and silenced fellows, wanted no part of it. To northern whites the pantheon of illustrious southerners in the American Colonization Society offered hope that, in time, people of good will of both sections could unite to end slavery.

Garrison began as a colonizationist, but the ultraist thrust of reform thinking quickly pushed him further. If slavery was sin, then slaveholders were sinners, and those who tolerated and condoned their sin shared in its guilt. Halfway measures and expedient compromises—anything short of wholesale renunciation of evil—could never bring redemption, either national or individual. The mission of the emancipationist, like that of the revivalist, was to demand complete, wholehearted, and immediate separation from sin. In the temperance movement this remorseless logic was driving Beecher and other reformers from their initial effort to moderate Americans' drinking toward a call for total abstinence. It led Garrison, in an address to the Colonization Society on July 4, 1829, to excoriate slavery as a fraud upon American principles, a wrong to the slave, and an outrage against God. It was, said Garrison, "our duty, as Christians and Philanthropists, . . . to assist in its overthrow."

In Baltimore editing for Lundy, Garrison demanded "immediate and complete emancipation," with no compensation to slaveowners and no colonization. His quite specific denunciations of slave traders soon landed him in jail, whence he was rescued by Arthur Tappan, another ex-colonizationist whom Garrison's editorials had converted to abolition. Tappan paid Garrison's fine and, after an interview in New York, offered a donation for his work. Six months later the first issue of *The Liberator* appeared in Boston.

Now unfettered, Garrison launched an all-out assault on the Colonization Society. In *The Liberator* and an 1832 pamphlet called *Thoughts on African Colonization* he mercilessly dissected the society's contradictory goals, ineffectual measures, and racist premises. Garrison painted colonization as a proslavery program with an antislavery mask. Behind a facade of false philanthropy its real consequence, and implicit purpose, was to fortify slavery by lulling honest friends of freedom into complacency. Toward actual emancipation, the colonization scheme accomplished nothing and was meant to accomplish nothing. To Garrison the society's slaveholding constituency and leadership were proof not of its earnestness, but of its essential hypocrisy.

Garrison gave the new abolition crusade an editorial voice of ringing clarity. Others soon followed. The Tappans and their friends supplied organization and money. In December 1833 sixty-two abolitionists, including Garrison and Lewis Tappan, met in Philadelphia to form the American Anti-Slavery Society. Their "Declaration of Sentiments" announced a cause—"the abolition of slavery by the spirit of repentance"—which in "magnitude, solemnity, and probable results upon the destiny of the world" would surpass even the American Revolution, "as moral truth does physical force." Branding slaveholding a crime, the society demanded "immediate and total abolition," without recompense for owners, and the prompt admission of blacks to "all the rights and privileges which belong to them as men, and as Americans."

The society's first president was Arthur Tappan. Under his direction abolition soon acquired all the institutional trappings of evangelical reform—hundreds of state and local affiliates, an ocean of tracts and periodicals, and a traveling cadre of lecturers and organizers under command to drive home "the SIN OF SLAVERY." By 1837 the American Anti-Slavery Society claimed a thousand auxiliaries, all in the North, with a membership of more than one hundred thousand.

Despite this feat of recruitment abolition had made but a beginning in luring converts, and in practical progress toward emancipation, even less than that. Public reaction showed what formidable obstacles lay athwart the young crusade. A few southern mavericks, notably James G. Birney of Alabama and the South Carolina sisters Angelina and Sarah Grimké, heard the call and swore themselves to antislavery. But slaveholding society as a whole answered abolitionism's first appeal with ferocious outrage. Legislatures from Virginia to Louisiana barred abolitionist literature and lecturers and demanded federal and free-state cooperation in suppressing this invasion of their domestic peace. Georgia offered a reward for Garrison's capture. Southern evangelicals—Presbyterians, Methodists, Baptists —rushed to denounce abolitionism and disavow its claims upon Christians.

One cause of southern reaction was a gripping fear of insurrection. In keeping with their religious precepts, abolitionists preached only nonviolence and moral suasion as means of liberation. Yet by way of exposing slavery's hypocrisy, they did not hesitate to measure the master's tyranny against that which prompted Americans to revolt against Britain in 1776. In 1829 David Walker, a free black Methodist of Boston, made the Revolutionary parallel explicit. His *Appeal to the Coloured Citizens of the World* argued straight from the Christian Bible and the Declaration of Independence to the righteousness of slave rebellion. Two years later, and just eight months after Garrison launched his *Liberator,* Nat Turner unleashed the bloodiest of American slave revolts, killing fifty-five whites in a single day's rampage through the Virginia countryside. Turner was a slave preacher who identified with Christ and, by his own account, was inspired to violence by divine revelation. Whether he was actually moved by knowledge of Walker and Garrison, as some surmised, was unprovable and really immaterial. Revolt was certainly a plausible response to their teachings. White southerners drew the moral: Tolerating abolitionism meant toying with their lives.

Abolitionism did not frighten free states with nightmares of blood-drenched rebellion. Still its initial northern welcome was hardly less hostile than in the South. Abolitionists' inflamed rhetoric and their apparent willingness to disrupt sectional harmony in pursuit of their cause affronted businessmen, politicians, patriots, and lovers of order throughout the Union. "If the South is not left to the exercise of its own discretion in regard to its domestic institution," warned a Virginia Methodist journal, "then farewell to the brilliant hope of an enduring confederated republic; farewell to the prosperity of our favored country; farewell to all the glory of the American name."

Calls for black equality aroused deep-seated northern white hatred. An angry mob broke up the Tappans' first attempt to organize an antislavery society in New York in October 1833. Neighbors' hostility, backed by state law, blocked their efforts to found a school and college for blacks in Connecticut. Abolitionist lecturers braved heckling, rotten eggs, rocks, and worse. In 1834 rioters swept through New York City, wrecking black neighborhoods and sacking Lewis Tappan's house. In 1835, as the American Anti-Slavery Society launched a gigantic postal campaign to bombard the slaveholding South with abolitionist literature, mob reaction across the land mounted to a crescendo of violence.

Like no other cause or crusade, abolitionism threatened white Americans' peace of mind. Abolitionists began with typical exuberance and hopes of early success. "We shall spare no exertions nor means to bring the whole nation to speedy repentance," vowed the American Anti-Slavery Society in 1833. "Truth, Justice, Reason, Humanity, must and will gloriously triumph. Already a host is coming up to the help of the Lord against the mighty, and the prospect before us is full of encouragement." Yet while abolitionists looked forward with confidence, their view of existing conditions was anything but complacent. They saw all American society, North and South, steeped in complicity with slavery. Its tyranny and viciousness, they charged, were not peripheral or exceptional to the American experience, but central to it. If this was really true, then the United States was not, as so many liked to think, an advanced nation on a smooth road to perfection. It was, in the words of Angelina Grimké, *"rotten at the heart,"* sunk so deep in sin that only a revolution in morals could root it out.

Abolitionism thus confronted white Americans' deepest presumptions, their optimism, and their patriotic pride. It showed them as frauds and hypocrites, not lovers of liberty. It was hardly surprising, then, that citizens of both sections, including some who deplored slavery, looked on abolitionists as little short of traitors, or that civic leaders sometimes led anti-abolition mobs.

To Christian evangelicals abolitionism presented an especially troubling challenge. It was hard for them to deny the injustice of slavery. In their early days, before too many slaveholders joined their ranks, southern Methodists and Baptists had denounced it themselves. But by the 1830s those voices had been stilled. Southern clerics joined their neighbors and constituents in repelling abolitionist interference.

Slavery's presence at the heart of southern life, buttressed by northern whites' loathing for blacks, made plain the futility of easy change. Americans were not going to slough off slavery as casually as they could swear off drinking. Abolitionism called its recruits to acknowledge a moral canker at the core of American existence and dedicate their lives to excising it, no matter the risk or cost. Abolitionists must, said convert Angelina Grimké, be "ourselves willing to suffer the loss of character, property—yea, and life itself, in what we believe to be the cause of bleeding humanity." Abolition asked Christians to sacrifice all their comforts and aspirations for the chance at cleansing the country of this one great sin. It demanded perfect devotion and utter commitment. *"This,"* said Grimké, *"is a cause worth dying for."*

Even real sympathizers paled at the price. Northern free blacks, seeing the slaves' liberation as inseparable from their own, were first to enlist for abolition. Some thousands of northern whites—especially white women—joined them. Driven by millennial urgency, they cheerfully undertook a reformation of racial attitudes and practices that earlier and later generations of Americans would have deemed impossible.

Many more refused. Southern evangelicals opposed to slavery had already bowed to necessity and made their peace with the institution. In the North, the high demands of antislavery commitment cleaved even the most dedicated Christian ranks. As the Tappans immersed themselves in abolition, some of their Bible, tract, and missionary associates turned on them as pariahs.

Slavery fractured Lyman Beecher's campaign to evangelize the West before it fairly began. In 1832 Beecher arrived in Cincinnati to head the new Tappan-financed Lane Seminary. He soon confronted a student abolition movement organized by Theodore Dwight Weld, a convert of Charles Finney. Beecher's attempt to temporize between militant students and hostile townspeople failed. When Lane's trustees moved to silence the students, nearly the whole first class arose and decamped for a new seminary at Oberlin, again endowed by Arthur Tappan with Finney himself as professor of theology. Oberlin became an abolitionist haven. But Finney, like Beecher, refused to subordinate his revival enterprise to the antislavery cause or even to seat blacks with whites in his own church. Though both men thought slavery an "unblushing wrong," neither would trade his mission of saving souls for that of freeing slaves.

The Reform Ethos

Much like other Americans of their day, Christian crusaders beheld a vision of a better society, and tried to turn the country along a path to reach it. Prosperity and material advance aided their efforts and helped fire their faith in the future. Lay sponsors of evangelical reform like the Tappans were successful men of affairs. Confident, forward-looking, commanding the means, will, and time for social uplift, they were as willing to innovate in techniques and strategies of reform as in their own business. As Lewis Tappan chided his brother Benjamin, "you infidels should keep up with the age. This is a century of inventions."

Reformers saw themselves as altruists. They wished to help others find the same conviction and discipline that had brought them success, happiness, and peace of mind. They preached liberation, not repression. They yearned to help everyone escape the bondage of sin. As they had learned, only those who mastered base impulses and achieved genuine self-control could count themselves truly free.

In short they wanted, quite innocently and honestly, to shape America in their own image. Their motives, if not disinterested, were far from selfish. Finney gave up a promising career at the bar to preach the gospel. Garrison and other abolitionists courted injury and even martyrdom. The Grimkés accepted exile from their Carolina home. Theodore Weld, an orator and writer of immense promise, knowingly destroyed his health in service to antislavery. Illinois abolitionist editor Elijah Lovejoy lost three printing presses to mobs. Defending a fourth, he lost his life. The Tappans spent a literal fortune on reform, and got paid in resentment, ridicule, riot, and ruin. They never regretted the bargain.

Still, many Americans rejected the reformers' self-image of selfless benevolence. If they saw themselves as humble advocates for Christ, others saw them as prudes and busybodies, meddling in other people's lives and telling them what to do. Baptists and Methodists, recalling their long struggle against state clerical establishments, hesitated to join reform ventures led by their old oppressors. Catholics, still few in number in 1830 (Irish immigration, which at mid-century would exceed one hundred thousand a year, totaled only fifty thousand during the 1820s), shunned crusaders who condemned their ways as sinful and refused even to recognize them as Christians.

To the unconverted, the unconvinced, and the uninterested, the moral certitude of Christian zealots could be truly insufferable. Lewis Tappan foisted tracts on everyone he met, at his boardinghouse and even on vacation. Lyman Beecher invited hearers to choose for themselves—but he threatened damnation on those who chose wrongly. Slaveholders and non-slaveholders who thought themselves good citizens and good Christians reddened with rage at William Lloyd Garrison's presuming to pass divine judgment on them.

Reformers for the most part favored tools of persuasion; they sought to convince, not coerce. Still, behind the helping hand of voluntarism lurked the fist of compulsion. Some temperance-minded businessmen organized boycotts against the liquor trade and demanded that their employees quit drinking. The Tappans required church attendance of their clerks and wielded their financial muscle to punish the ungodly, a tactic that slaveholders later turned upon them.

One branch of evangelical reform, the Sabbatarian crusade, was plainly coercive. Since the War of 1812, Congregational and Presbyterian clergy had tried to enlist the federal government in their campaign to stop business on the Lord's Day. On July 4, 1827, Reverend Ezra Stiles Ely preached in Philadelphia on "the duty of Christian freemen to elect Christian rulers" and build *a Christian party in politics.* In New York, after failing to get Erie Canal locks closed on Sundays, Sabbatarian businessmen organized six-day stage and boat lines and threatened to boycott Sunday traffickers. In 1828 the General Union for the Promotion of the Christian Sabbath circulated petitions to ban federal Sunday mail service. Opponents charged them with trying to abrogate the separation of church and state.

Plans to evangelize the West hinted of both sectional and cultural imperialism. Eastern sophisticates found the explosion of raw western growth both exhilarating and disturbing. A young Ralph Waldo Emerson noted that "the vast rapidity with which the deserts & forests of the interior of this country are peopled have led patriots to fear lest the nation grow *too fast* for its virtue & peace." Proper Bostonians, New Yorkers, and Philadelphians worried that without proper instruction, these "raw multitudes"— the "offscouring of civilized society," "an ignorant & licentious people"— would "pour out upon the world an accursed tribe of barbarous robbers." But if they could be schooled "to speak a voice of wisdom & virtue, the reformation of the world would be to be expected from America." It was to instruct the West in Christian civilization that Lyman Beecher went to Cincinnati, and that eastern societies showered westerners with Bibles, tracts, Sunday schools, and missionaries.

Recipients of such largesse were often strangely ungrateful. They resented reformers' condescension and their sometime willingness to wield wealth and even state power along with moral suasion to achieve their ends. Behind the front of benevolence, unwilling objects of evangelical attention saw only arrogance. Employees, clients, and customers chafed at submitting to someone else's code of discipline. Insurgent denominations, content with minding their own business and tending their own flocks, rebelled at the imperial aspirations of Presbyterians and Congregationalists. Westerners, some of whom had fled to new country precisely to escape overbearing religion, cherished their independence and balked at eastern dictation. Everywhere those who spurned the reformers' summons asked defiantly: in a free country, who dared tell them what to believe and how to behave?

So while evangelical reform grew from impulses that most Americans shared, its thrust was to split them into two camps—those who embraced and those who rejected its holistic prescription for progress. The cleavage was not simply between believers and scoffers, or even evangelicals and nonevangelicals. Many active Christians still conceived their mission in personal, not national terms; they sought to save souls, not purify society. It was the homogenizing urge of the reform movement, aimed at gathering a whole country within its fold, that set it off from traditional Christian moralism and from the individualist focus of Baptists, Methodists, Disciples, and American Catholics. These dissenters, despite their growing numbers, had no history of power and no inclination to exercise authority beyond their own ranks.

For some the evangelical crusade offered a path to millennial purity. To others it seemed a threat to moral autonomy and democratic self-determination. In a crowded, raucous marketplace of ideas and creeds, men and women searched their minds and souls, and pledged their faith accordingly.

The Republic of Labor

Let the young man, who is to gain his living by his labor and skill, remember that he is a citizen of a free state; that on him and his contemporaries it depends, whether he will be happy and prosperous himself in his social condition, and whether a precious inheritance of social blessings shall descend, unimpaired, to those who come after him; that there is no important difference in the situation of individuals, but that which they themselves cause, or permit to exist; that if something of the inequality in the goods of fortune, which is inseparable from human things, exist in this country, it ought to be viewed only as another excitement to that industry, by which, nine times out of ten, wealth is acquired; and still more to the cultivation of the mind, which, next to the moral character, makes the great difference between man and man.
—Edward Everett, 1830

Look abroad on the misery which is gaining on the land! Mark the strife, and the discord, and the jealousies, the shock of interests and opinions, the hatreds of sect, the estrangements of class, the pride of wealth, the debasement of poverty, the helplessness of youth unprotected, of age uncomforted, of industry unrewarded, of ignorance unenlightened, of vice unreclaimed, of misery unpitied, of sickness, hunger, and nakedness unsatisfied, unalleviated, and unheeded. Go! mark all the wrongs and the wretchedness with which the eye and the ear and the heart are familiar, and then echo in triumph and celebrate in jubilee the insulting declaration—*all men are free and equal!*
—Frances Wright, 1829

Innovations in transportation, manufacturing, and commerce brought new chances for wealth. They also raised questions about what constituted wealth and how it should be allocated. In the 1820s Americans began to work out their conceptions of economic justice. Thinkers produced analyses and critiques. Citizens confronting change in their lives sought to make sense of the emerging society and to find their place within it. Together their efforts produced new forms of organization and ideas of political economy. What began as a formless and inchoate questioning assumed shape and structure, as constituencies gathered behind newly articulated programs of social advance. Theories, systems, and interests coalesced, then clashed.

The Lowell Experiment

In 1858 some prominent Bostonians asked the industrialist Nathan Appleton to reminisce on the founding of Lowell. They wanted to hear "not merely of the setting up there of factories and spindles," but of "the wise and prudent foresight . . . which in the beginning made provision for religious worship, schools, a hospital for the sick, and established a system of management, well calculated to preserve the morals of the people there to be gathered." Accepting their invitation, Appleton also seconded their idea of Lowell's importance. It lay not just in the making of cloth or profit, but "establishing the cotton manufacture, on the principle of making every possible provision for the moral character and respectability of the operatives." To hear these men tell it, a path-breaking venture—one that concentrated a huge capital under corporate control, deployed new inventions and machines, integrated the processes of textile manufacture, harnessed waterpower on a grand scale, challenged the industrial supremacy of Great Britain, and did all this so well that it paid rich dividends for decades—was most memorable not for any of these reasons, but as an experiment in employee welfare.

According to Appleton, social motives had prevailed from the start. America's first factory owners faced the challenge of replicating Britain's industrial achievement while avoiding its social consequences. European factory towns festered with poverty and misery. Laboring long hours under wretched conditions, mill workers "were notoriously of the lowest character, for intelligence and morals." Francis Cabot Lowell, founder of the Boston Manufacturing Company, saw their degradation on his British tour of 1810–1812. The task he and his fellows set themselves, first at Waltham and then on a grander scale at Lowell, was to create an American textile industry without creating an American working class.

They shunned the models available to them, both abroad and at home. Small spinning mills from Massachusetts to Maryland employed whole households at one time, including very young children for the simplest tasks. Most workers came from the lowest ranks of society. Early factory publicists in both America and Britain touted mill work as a form of charity, an alternative to the poorhouse for indigents, widows, and orphans.

To the Boston Associates a pauperized, captive labor force was neither available nor desirable. They discovered another source of hands on New England's crowded farms. High birthrates and westward migration by enterprising men left a supply of young females who, like country women everywhere, were well habituated to work. Here among "the daughters of respectable farmers," remarked Appleton, was "a fund of labor, well educated and virtuous," that could be "readily induced to come into these mills for a temporary period."

To lure them in the associates fashioned a workplace that extrapolated rather than broke from the patterns of New England village life. Company boardinghouses functioned as surrogate families. Matrons watched young women's welfare, guarded their morals, and escorted them to church. Tending textile machinery in the mill replaced home labor at the wheel and the loom. The Lowell firms offered good wages and, unlike many underfinanced early manufacturers, paid them punctually and in cash. The work was not too grueling, and far more sociable than farm drudgery. Town life offered diversion and amusement, while Lowell's pastoral setting cushioned the transition from farm to factory. Built in the country and running on water power instead of smoky steam engines, the mills preserved a rural flavor. In Lowell's early years fields were visible from a window, accessible in a stroll.

Many young women found mill labor in these conditions attractive. It offered a blend of independence, conviviality, respectability, and reward available nowhere else. At any rate it was only temporary. Most hands saved their earnings and quit after a year or two to get married, just as their employers planned.

The Lowell experiment's social influence blanketed its investors as well as its workers. At a time when foreign trade had lost its lure and most new business ventures carried high risk, the mills paid steady, reliable dividends. Corporation stock provided a safe refuge for Boston merchant fortunes. In turn, profits from textiles and connected operations in transportation and finance flowed out to local philanthropies and charities: the Boston Athenaeum, Massachusetts General Hospital and McLean Asylum for the Insane, Harvard College with its law and medical schools. Through this complex of businesses and benevolences the Boston Associates built a uniquely insular and sheltered world, not only for their employees and beneficiaries, but for themselves.

In this security lay the genius of Lowell. It promised to guide New Englanders from an idealized agricultural past to an unfolding industrial future—from hand work to machine work, farm to factory, village to town—without any disruption of relations or sacrifice of values; without hardship, conflict, or risk.

In time the shine of novelty wore off at Lowell. Rising competition in the textile industry prompted directors to conserve their profit margin by adding work, extending hours, cutting wages, and recruiting a less mobile force of Irish immigrants. As early as the 1830s strikes and ethnic turbulence marred the new industrial utopia. By mid-century Lowell had become to some appearances a depressingly familiar factory city, crowded, dirty, ridden with poverty and disease—an American Manchester, after all.

Even from the first, Lowell drew critics. Behind the facade of a harmonious village, they charged, lay a reality of savage exploitation, of lordly proprietors and brutally overworked and underpaid employees. Some of the sharpest accusers were southerners, who took this chance to throw back Yankee aspersions on their treatment of slaves. Still, most early visitors, including foreigners, accepted Lowell's claims at face value.

The Changing Face of Work

Whatever its success, Lowell held little value as a blueprint for general use. Only a well-capitalized and consistently profitable venture could afford experiments in paternalism. Only a highly mechanized operation could sustain efficiency with a rotating labor force. Most of all, the surfeit of mobile, single young women in New England opened a convenient detour around the central social problem of the American workplace. It let Lowell's managers escape deciding how to structure long-term relations between employer and employee by avoiding the relation itself.

Outside the uniquely favored New England textile industry, few had that luxury. For most overseers and operatives, masters and apprentices, proprietors and hands, the workplace was not a setting for experiment, nor an investment haven, nor a youthful interlude. It was where one made a living, and relations there shaped a way of life. Most Americans had no choice but to face unsettling changes in the way they earned their money and ordered their time.

These changes, suddenly becoming visible in the 1820s, grew out of the new advances in transportation and, to a lesser extent, in manufacturing. Coupled with rapid population growth, canals and steamboats and machines raised material standards of living and opened new ways of garnering wealth. But in rushing to exploit these, Americans imperiled their treasured birthright of independence and equality.

Revolutionary patriots and publicists had celebrated the productive household as the foundation of all that was best in American life. Working his own land and coordinating the supplemental labor of wife and children (and sometimes slaves, though this was rarely mentioned), the American farmer, unlike downtrodden European peasants, was prosperous and free. Abundant land meant easy access to ownership. Property guaranteed a man's livelihood and thus his autonomy, fitting him for the rights and responsibilities of republican citizenship. Economic independence secured political independence. No landlord or grandee supervised the American farmer's management, lived off his labor, or controlled his vote.

This image of the United States as a nation of small farmers, articulated most eloquently by Thomas Jefferson, was easily transportable to urban life, where, as in the countryside, it portrayed a substantial reality. The town counterpart to Jefferson's hardy and self-reliant agriculturist was the craftsman who also owned his home and shop and produced and vended his own products. He too presided over a working household that might include journeymen and apprentices in the trade along with the master's wife and family. Journeymen, though laboring for wages (paid for piecework rather than by the hour), preserved their sense of independence by owning their own tools, changing employers and locales whenever they chose, and aspiring to master status. In an artisan tradition epitomized by the printer Ben Franklin, journeymen and masters together guarded their pride of craft ("the mystery of the trade") and toasted themselves as bulwarks of republicanism, the bone and sinew of the nation.

The small farm and shop economy of the early United States, while never as idyllic as patriots pictured it, did secure for common people rewards unparalleled in Americans' ken. Compared with the mass of Europeans or their own colonial forebears, most citizens lived free from basic want. If luxury was rare, so was indigence. The essentials—land, food, fuel, housing materials—were plentiful and cheap. Family heads enjoyed an autonomy (not to be confused with subsistence, or self-sufficiency) that came from controlling their household labor and the sale of its fruits, and that provided a base for relative social and political equality.

But this leveled society, more horizontal than hierarchical, was as much the product of circumstance as of design. Distance and terrain isolated communities from one another and confined most exchange to face-to-face transactions. Country folk swapped goods and services with their neighbors. In the absence of currency, much trade took the form of barter. Scattered settlement and poor transport encouraged occupational versatility rather than specialization. Besides growing or making much of what they consumed, farm families fabricated simple goods for local sale. The wives of town artisans gardened or kept livestock.

Since demand for money always outran supply, Americans dealt largely on credit, which they got in small amounts and mainly from each other. Few banks existed before 1815, and those that did handled a narrow range of mercantile transactions. Within this radically decentralized system of exchange, opportunities for innovative entrepreneurship and for amassing great wealth were few. Apart from foreign trade and land speculation, both requiring a large capital and involving much risk, there were not many ways to make a fortune in the early United States, nor to spend one.

In short, Americans' general affluence (by the standards of that day) whetted what Hezekiah Niles in 1815 called "the almost *universal ambition to get forward*" at the same time that existing means of production, transport, and finance restrained it. But by the 1820s these ancient limits were crumbling. Inventions, canals, corporations, and banks opened new avenues. As orator Edward Everett noted in 1830, the United States had become "in every thing,—a new country,—a country of urgent and expansive demand, where new branches of employment are constantly opening, new kinds of talent called for, new arts struck out, and more hands employed in all the old ones." Seizing new tools for creating wealth, Americans embarked in search of riches.

Innovators employed credit to organize production of consumer items for an expanded home market. In the shoe, clothing, and furniture trades, merchants and masters turned themselves into manufacturers by coordinating large-scale assembly of ready-made goods. They broke down the process of production into discrete stages, enforced a specialization of labor among their hands, and let the simplest tasks out as piecework at cheap rates to less skilled town and country women and off-season farmers and fishermen. By these means merchant-manufacturers multiplied output and cut costs without building factories or introducing machinery. They also, not incidentally, undermined the tradition of custom work and bypassed the old craft fellowship of master, journeyman, and apprentice.

These arrangements made expanded production possible. New modes of transport made it profitable. Canals and steamboats carried textiles, shoes, ironware, books, furniture, and imported merchandise in exchange for foodstuffs, farm products, lumber, coal, and raw materials. The challenge of vending across long distances spurred new facilities for finance and distribution. Banks furnished credit and insurers covered the risk, while middlemen—boatmen, warehousers, jobbers, brokers, agents, auctioneers, commission and wholesale and retail merchants—shipped, stored, and sold the goods.

Exchange, divorced from manufacture or shipping, emerged as a distinct and often lucrative calling. Specialized vendors displaced the old-fashioned general merchant and custom craftsman's shop. Entrepreneurs like Arthur and Lewis Tappan learned the fortunes to be made in domestic trade. Sons of a provincial goldsmith, they abandoned general merchandizing to specialize in the sale of imported silks. From their New York City storefront they supplied retail clients across the country.

Expanding trade networks penetrated the countryside. Proprietors rather than peasants, American farmers had always been alert to chances for gain. Even when they operated without cash, country Yankees thought in commercial ways. They kept scrupulous record of credit and debit, relentlessly noting in monetary terms even the smallest transactions—a load of wood, a morning's work. Farmers and planters with ocean access had tailored production to faraway markets since colonial days. Pioneer families braved hardship in hope of future reward. The flow of migrants to new soils and the brisk trade in land revealed a people more attuned to bettering their prospects than intent on preserving their past.

Now a quickening commerce opened new chances. Farmers and planters centered their energies where promise of success was greatest. Rich land and slave labor laid the basis for southern fortunes in cotton and sugar. Plantation cropping offered a return on capital second to none. Westerners sowed wheat and raised hogs for distant stomachs. Farmers on older, less fertile soils met western competition by intensifying land and labor use or developing new crops.

Country stores spread through the hinterland. The array of goods they carried offered a spur to farmers' labor. Rural wives and daughters, freed from semi-isolation, gave up inefficient home production of a range of household items and purchased store products with money earned through outwork or mill labor. The link of town and country created new ways for farmers to secure their savings and enhance their earnings. Prosperous husbandmen bought bank, mill, and insurance stock.

While burgeoning trade raised living standards and excited expectations, not all perceived its effects as gain. Even in the country, heightened competition dictated a quickened pace of work and forced wrenching changes in routine. Innovation made losers as well as winners. While some farmers hailed roads and canals as instruments of progress, others bemoaned the destruction of their property, increase of their taxes, and loss of their markets to distant competitors. Wider exchange networks took away local pricing and decision-making power even as they brought in new goods. The caprice of the market threatened farmers' sense of self-control. Along with new chances for success came a new dread of dependency.

In cities too, uncertainty and risk intruded into formerly sedate callings. Few innovators enjoyed the security that the Boston Associates derived from a large capital and proprietary control of an advanced technology. In most businesses development was rapid and unpredictable and competition fierce. Credit underwrote growth, and many men operated on the thin edge of solvency. Even for the prudent, failure loomed as the price of bad judgment or bad luck.

Racing to beat their rivals, entrepreneurs pressed for advantage wherever they could. Pioneers in business, like pioneer farmers, labored long hours and practiced ruthless self-deprivation. (European visitors, not realizing the pressures they faced, found their single-minded attention to work repulsive.) To bolster their fortitude for the struggle, men mustered behind behavioral bulwarks of religion, moral discipline, and mutual support. They joined churches and banded together in groups such as the Society for the Promotion of Industry, Frugality, and Temperance, founded by shoe-trade merchant-manufacturers of Lynn, Massachusetts, in 1826.

Pressure on businessmen translated into pressure on their employees. Workers were forced to accept the regimentation and work discipline necessary for their employers' success. Craft journeymen felt the squeeze directly. Streamlined production sped their pace of labor and threatened their skills with obsolescence. Subdivision of tasks enabled employers to shift some of their work to half-trained apprentices and outworkers, undercutting their versatility and independence. The environment also changed as merchants, armed with capital and managerial talent rather than arti-san expertise, invaded the ranks of craft employers and expanded the size of the workplace. Journeymen who had sometimes boarded with mas-ter craftsmen and joined them as partners in production now confronted wage-paying strangers in the relation of boss and hired hand.

Workers in this situation felt especially vulnerable to the caprice of progress. As far as they could see, new efficiencies were being achieved and fortunes amassed mainly at their expense. Their standard of living, even if not declining, was visibly diverging from that of their employers. Journey-men felt exploited; but they were also well positioned to resist. Clustered in towns, possessed of craft skills and traditions, with some education and re-sources and a sense of fellowship within the trade, they could act in concert for their own protection.

Trade Societies and Labor Parties

In June 1827 Philadelphia journeymen house carpenters called for a re-duction in their summer working hours to ten per day. The present "griev-ous and slave like system" of dawn-to-dusk labor (minus two hours for meals) left no time "for the cultivation of their mind and for self im-provement." Master carpenters took only a day to answer. They would not shorten hours. They could not afford it, and the existing system was not "oppressive." Further, they condemned the journeymen's action for its "tendency to subvert good order, and coerce or mislead those who have been industriously pursuing their avocation and honestly maintaining their families."

Appealing for public support, the journeymen voted to withhold their labor. The ensuing carpenters' "stand out" failed. But the ten-hour demand enlisted other building tradesmen, and the strike provided a springboard for further organization. In December 1827 representatives of Philadelphia crafts joined to form the Mechanics' Union of Trade Associations. De-crying the exploitation of labor by capital, organizers vowed to "raise the mechanical and productive classes to that condition of true independence and inequality [sic] which their practical skill and ingenuity, their immense utility to the nation and their growing intelligence are beginning imperi-ously to demand." They soon opened a library and began the *Mechanics' Free Press*, the country's first labor newspaper. But the Philadelphia Me-chanics' Union sponsored no more strikes, and in two years it disappeared.

From this uncertain start workers' organizations spread swiftly as far

as St. Louis in the early 1830s. Some groups grew out of older craft benefit societies. Others sprang up anew. In Lynn, Massachusetts, center of
the burgeoning shoe trade, male cordwainers and female binders created
mutually reinforcing societies in 1830. In 1833 New York City counted
twenty-nine craft associations, including printers, cabinetmakers, masons,
bookbinders, stonecutters, house painters, tailors, jewelers, hat makers,
blacksmiths, coopers, bakers, chair makers, and tin-plate workers. Soon
these were joined by carpet weavers, locksmiths, saddlers, piano makers,
umbrella makers, and paperhangers. By 1837 the Philadelphia area had
sixty organizations, Baltimore more than twenty. While most of these took
root in traditional crafts, some represented textile mill hands.

The growth of trade societies prompted efforts to unite workers across
craft and geographic boundaries. In New York City in 1833 a carpenters'
strike over wages led to the creation of a city General Trades' Union.
The same year a new Trades' Union appeared in Philadelphia. By 1836 it
had fifty constituent societies with ten thousand members. Citywide labor
councils followed in a dozen other towns. Amid a rising tide of strikes
over wages and hours—more than fifty in 1836 alone, many of them successful—the organizational drive reached its apex with the creation of a
loosely structured and short-lived National Trades' Union.

The trade societies mostly eschewed general social questions to concen-
trate on matters of immediate import to their members. They demanded
higher wages and shorter hours, defended their legal right to organize and
strike, and struggled to uphold the quality of work, the dignity of labor,
and the "rules of the Trade." Through such means they sought to prevent
a "system of ruinous competition" among employers from degrading and
impoverishing their employees.

Meanwhile, before its demise, the original Philadelphia Mechanics'
Union spawned another kind of activism. In 1828 the federation, still less
than a year old, undertook to name candidates for public office. The resulting Philadelphia Working Men's Party outlived the Mechanics' Union
itself, nominating and endorsing friends of "the Working Classes" for city
council and state legislature for three years before folding in 1831.

This venture into electoral politics caught on even faster than trade
organization. Workingmen's parties, often bolstered by new labor presses,
sprang up in dozens of towns. In New York and Boston they were especially
active. Like the Philadelphia prototype, most of the Workingmen's parties
flourished briefly around 1830 before withering just as the formation of
trade societies and labor federations gathered speed.

The Workingmen's parties and their adjunct presses urged an array of legislative measures to elevate the condition of laboring people. Demands included ending imprisonment for debt, abolishing the militia system (which required men to participate in what had become a charade of military training), and passing mechanics' lien laws to secure wage claims against employers. Workingmen wanted protection against unfair competition from convict labor, overworked children, and abused apprentices. Above all, they demanded free schools—"an equal and republican system of mental instruction." By this reform alone, according to Philadelphia's Workingmen, Americans could "rid ourselves of every existing evil." New Yorkers hailed "Equal Universal Education" as "the great lever by which the Working Men are to be raised to their proper elevation in this republic."

The Workingmen's program reflected tradesmen's determination to share in the material and moral promise of the republic. Their flaming denunciations of economic injustice and aristocratic oppression evoked an image of class war. Still, they were ambivalent and flexible in defining the membership of the "working classes." Their legislative agenda spoke to masters and journeymen without distinction, and their underlying message of education and uplift was calculated for the widest possible appeal.

Trade societies, by contrast, pitted masters and wage-earners against each other. Journeymen denounced "tyrannical employers and wealthy capitalists," while the latter complained of employee coercion as "oppression, tyranny, and misrule." Each side accused the other of forcing its hand and claimed to organize only in self-defense. But even the trade societies reflected their members' individualized aspirations and their reticence to accept a separation of classes. Workers demanded a fair share of the nation's multiplying wealth. They complained of long hours and child labor on the ground that overwork left no time for the schooling and self-improvement that wage-earners needed to advance themselves. Though tradesmen espoused novel means of cooperative action, they clung to old goals of independence and proprietorship. As Ely Moore, first president of both the New York and national general trades' unions, said, "The principle for which we contend holds out to individuals proper motives for exertion and enterprise."

Many wage-earners showed their individualism by shunning organization altogether. Given the fleeting tenure of the trade societies and labor parties and the sketchy record of their activities, exactly how many people joined them or subscribed to their beliefs must always remain in doubt. But available tallies of strike participants and society members do not bear out boasts of labor solidarity. Most working men did not vote the Workingmen's ticket. Organizers recognized, while they did not advertise, wage-earners' reticence to unite on their own behalf. These people saw their first task as educative. Aspiring to lead workers, they first had to convince them.

Emergence of a Labor Critique

A cadre of publicists and agitators led in organizing and framing the rhetoric of the Workingmen's parties. In Philadelphia there were Langdon Byllesby, Stephen Simpson, and William Heighton; in Boston, Theophilus Fisk and Seth Luther. In New York, editors Thomas Skidmore and George Henry Evans battled for ascendancy in the short-lived but influential Workingmen's Party of 1829–1830. (Evans's brother Frederick followed his own path to reform. After helping George, he became a communitarian, joined the Shakers, and rose to be an elder.) Also active in the New York party were Robert Dale Owen, eldest son of Robert Owen, and Frances Wright. Fresh from New Harmony and Nashoba, Owen and Wright arrived in New York in 1829 and established a Hall of Science where they gave lectures, sold books, and published the *Free Enquirer,* successor to the *New Harmony Gazette.*

These pioneer labor advocates were as much propagandists as organizers. Most were printer-journalists of modest means. Some had never earned a wage. Both their critique of American conditions and their hopes for deliverance reached far beyond mundane issues of working wages and hours. They embraced labor's cause, not from want or ambition, but out of a burning desire to comprehend, and perchance to control, the changes in the American social landscape. Current trends thoroughly alarmed them. Old formulas for achievement seemed no longer valid; America's unique promise was being betrayed. They saw the wage-earner's plight as symptom of a deeper malaise: the destruction of republican equality.

Independence and equality had always been linked, both in Jeffersonian theory and American practice. Wide opportunity to obtain property underwrote a rough parity of condition. But now opportunity and equality, instead of reinforcing each other, appeared to be pulling apart. The invitation to self-advancement that had once promoted social leveling now threatened to subvert it. A fast-growing economy opened the way to unprecedented riches, but only for a few. Increased overall wealth brought increasing disparities of wealth, widening the gap between rich and poor.

As some people gained great fortunes, they also gained power over others. Superabundance for a few meant subservience, personal and political, for the many.

Already the laborites saw telltale signs of "aristocracy." While a few wallowed in luxury, growing numbers dwelt in "wretchedness and starvation." To dramatize inequality, labor writers stressed what Seth Luther called the "injustice, cruelty, ignorance, vice, and misery" of working life. Factories and cities indeed made hard work and poverty more visible, if not more prevalent, than ever before. But the laborites' root concern was not over working conditions or standards of living. Even the lowest-paid mill hands suffered less from cold and hunger than frontier families. No one claimed the latter as victims, because they presumably chose privation as the cost of a propertied independence. What alarmed the laborites was not so much hardship as hopelessness: the subjection of citizens to the degradation and uncertainty of wage employment while "aristocracy, privileges, extortion, monopoly, and overgrown fortunes" flourished. At heart their critique was not economic but moral. They lamented the fall from proud independence to a dependence so abject it amounted nearly to slavery.

In short, they worried that America's treasured exemption from fixed social cleavages was fast disappearing. Why? What had gone wrong? Like the capitalists of Lowell, the journeymen of New York and Philadelphia, and indeed nearly everyone, labor activists refused to accept the inevitability of an American working class. Abundant land and equal political rights for white men should have guaranteed freedom from want and subjugation for many generations to come, perhaps forever. Here was no scarcity of resources nor legal impediments to equality—no European *"entails, nobility, hierarchy, monopolies."* The prerequisites for universal independence were seemingly in place.

And yet they saw a moneyed class multiplying its possessions, influence, and clout while a mass of common people stagnated or regressed in wealth, status, and power. What especially rankled the laborites was that the men accumulating riches were not, as they saw it, the real creators of wealth, the ones who actually made useful goods. The blossoming of regional and national markets, the expansion of workshops, and the elevation of trade and finance from adjuncts of production to independent enterprises had thrown up a new, highly visible group of managers and manipulators. According to the Workingmen's idea of productive labor, these people—bankers, brokers, financiers, insurers, investors, lawyers, speculators, "capitalists"—really did not work at all. They wielded no tools, produced no wealth. They were simply leeches. Their ascendancy shook the country's ethical foundations. The uniqueness of America, the core of its virtue, had always been the promise of a just reward for honest labor. Here were men who performed no labor, yet reaped all the reward.

In their gloomier moments the labor advocates warned of a stark class struggle looming over the American future. On one side were the workers, bone and sinew of the country, rightful guardians of its republican and egalitarian heritage; on the other the "aristocracy" who oppressed and exploited them. Given the newness of these classes, however, it was sometimes easier to posit their existence than to say precisely who was in them. The line between parasite and producer did not always run between employer and employee. Merchants and manufacturers still claimed the title of workers, and thinkers like New York's George Henry Evans were inclined to give it to them, as long as their labor was "useful." Boston trades' unionists welcomed "mechanics, farmers, artisans, and all who labor, whether as boss or journeyman." All had "a common interest in sustaining each other" against the idle rich.

Given the prevalence of family-owned farms in America, few writers fixed their fire on landlords, traditional targets of peasant protest. Here the main villains of the labor critique were monopolizers of money, not property, men who lived by manipulation rather than rent. Though their bustling activity gave off an illusion of industry, their real work was extortion. They siphoned off others' substance while creating none of their own.

How did they get away with it? Explanations abounded. Thomas Skidmore, most radical of the Workingmen, persisted in tracing all evil to a monopoly of land, the true birthright of everyone. To this Stephen Simpson added the funding of the Revolutionary debt, by which "patrician officers and greedy capitalists and hungry speculators" stole the pay of "the poor veteran, his helpless widow, his shivering orphans." Frances Wright and Robert Dale Owen blamed exclusive systems of education and the poisonings of sectarian religion. Prosecution of unions for criminal conspiracy prompted labor writers to tab the judiciary as "the headquarters of the aristocracy" and the common law as an engine of oppression. "The secret trades union of the bar" foiled open, equal access to justice. Workingmen in Boston and New York attacked "the multiplication of statutes, and the mysterious phraseology" that made the law intelligible only to experts charging "enormous fees."

Cures for inequality were as varied as the diagnoses. Some sought to replace the wage system with labor exchanges or manufacturing cooperatives to eliminate middlemen and "secure to the producer the full products and control of the fruits of his labor." Robert Dale Owen and Frances

Wright took the leveling implications of universal schooling to a logical extreme. They proposed a system of state guardianship: at age two, all children should be taken from their parents to be raised and instructed in public institutions under conditions of exact equality. Thomas Skidmore advocated redistributing all property each generation to ensure an equal start for everyone. Less drastically, George Henry Evans urged the federal government to stop selling western lands and distribute them free to actual cultivators. This would break the capitalists' land monopoly and elevate wages by luring surplus workers to the countryside.

Whatever the particulars, each proponent argued that one stroke of reform, correctly aimed, would right all wrongs and restore America's betrayed promise. Let workers but realize their strength and act, said Stephen Simpson, and "the present oppressive system will vanish like the mists of the morning before the rising sun." Wright saw her school system "as capable, and alone capable, of opening the door to universal reform" and creating "an enlightened, a virtuous, and a happy community." Beyond injustice and oppression, a new world beckoned, visible and within reach.

Though their tone was dogmatic, the laborites spoke from a vast uncertainty. Groping to make sense of changes that had no precedent, they offered analyses and remedies that were both original and tentative. Like the Workingmen they hoped to lead, they were not sure what to think. The system they challenged was so new it did not yet have a name: Critics who yearned for an alternative still had to invent it for themselves.

Thus the laborites confronted the American future with optimism and dread, elation and foreboding. They celebrated the country's progress toward perfection, yet warned of imminent disaster. They were at once entranced by new productive capacity and appalled by the specter of dependence and degradation that it raised. They decried the evils of unrestrained competition, yet called for it to be more open and free. With no sense of incongruity they offered drastic plans to redistribute wealth and modest ones for public schools, and claimed that each would cure all ills. They believed the United States stood at a historic threshold, with utopia or nightmare just ahead. But they were not sure which it was.

The Attack on Privilege

Though Skidmore, Owen, Wright, and Evans aspired to speak for all working people, they gathered few followers. Ideas of confiscating property and taking children from their parents held little popular appeal. But one part of the labor critique struck a chord that echoed far beyond the narrow and contentious constituency of craft journeymen and urban wage-earners. That was the attack on monopoly and inequality before the law.

According to this complaint, it was above all else the arrogation of legal privilege that allowed capitalists to siphon off wealth created by the producing classes. Every legislative grant, every corporate charter, every exclusive license opened a new avenue of exploitation and created a new monopoly. Such aristocratic devices, conferring a special power on the few while withholding it from the many, were "direct and palpable infringements on the true spirit and genius of our institutions." New York City's Workingmen lashed out at every species of advantage from railroad charters and ferry franchises to auctioneers' control of import sales and the licensing of food vendors.

The most vicious of all monopolies was banking. It was, as Stephen Simpson put it, "the *banking system,* that fruitful mother of unutterable affliction to the sons of industry, which brought us, at one fatal step, into the vortex of English aristocracy" and created extremes of "overgrown fortunes and hopeless poverty." As chartered corporations, banks were automatically objectionable. But they also held an insidious leverage over all other forms of business. Bankers' control of credit, their ability at whim to extend or deny the lifeblood of enterprise, gave them command over every endeavor and every breadwinner.

What was worse, bankers' power was not the fruit of industry. Any man had the right to lend what he had earned. But bank credit derived from legal privilege, not accumulated wealth. Charters authorized banks to print and circulate notes far beyond their real capital. Legislative favor protected them in creating these fictitious representations of value—in reality, mere pieces of paper—and passing them off as if they had worth. Outrageously, though banknotes were in the form of IOUs promising redemption in specie, they carried no interest and were often backed by no assets, and it was not the issuer but the receiver at second or third hand who, willing or not, assumed the risk of their circulation. When a note depreciated or lost value altogether, the banker was at fault. But the workingman who got the note in payment took the loss.

Seen from this vantage, bankers were licensed extortionists, corralling the fruits of laborers' "toil and sweat" with paper of no real cost or value. To the New York Workingmen, this something-for-nothing exchange explained how "knaves, imposters, and paupers" could command the earnings of the hard-working "American merchant, manufacturer, mechanic, and laboring man." Legal privilege sanctioned a "rapacious and cruel plunder of the people" and sustained a moneyed aristocracy of the most odious kind: artificial, predatory, corrupt.

The laborite attack on corporate privilege and banking drew directly on suspicions and resentments lingering from the Panic of 1819. It also fed a broader misgiving over the trend of American development. The warning against oppression from an aristocracy of "capitalists" resonated with planter disciples of Thomas Jefferson and John Taylor and with farmers and wage-earners facing the threat of dependency.

Even foreign observers felt uneasy. In 1831–1832 the Frenchman Alexis de Tocqueville visited the United States. The first sentence of his *Democracy in America* recorded that "nothing struck me more forcibly than the general equality of condition among the people." But Tocqueville also warned "the friends of democracy" to keep an anxious eye on the new workplace. American affluence sustained a high demand for goods. But, said Tocqueville, specialization to meet this demand narrowed the worker's skills. He became degraded and dependent, unfit for personal advancement or useful citizenship. "What can be expected of a man who has spent twenty years of his life in making heads for pins?" Meanwhile the profits of manufacturing would lure "men of great opulence and education," but without experience in the trade. Their approach would be mercenary and exploitative. Unconnected to their employees by habit, obligation, or interest, they would have "frequent relations, but no real association." Thus "out of the bosom of democracy" springs "a permanent inequality of conditions," a gulf between master and worker, one born to command and one to obey, one an emperor, the other a brute. "What is this," asked Tocqueville, "but aristocracy?"

The Celebration of Enterprise

Tocqueville's grim forecast belied Americans' most cherished hopes for their future. The question they faced was whether the conditions he described really existed in the United States. Was America a class society?

The essence of the labor critique was that it was, or soon would be. Equality was already threatened, perhaps destroyed. Much of the ambiguity in reformers' outlook and program turned on the uncertainty whether the aristocracy had already arrived or was merely imminent. Moderate correctives might ward off an impending collapse of independence. Once lost, only severe measures could restore it. But either way laborites saw current trends, left unarrested, leading to a bad end.

Others, however, including many who worked the soil or earned a wage, viewed the status quo less darkly. They saw a future of widening opportunity, not declining autonomy. The thrust of a dynamic, innovative economy was not to establish class distinctions but to erase them. In the United States Senate in 1832, Henry Clay laughed off the charge of a manufacturing "aristocracy." "Nothing can be more essentially democratic," said Clay, than corporations which enabled people of ordinary means to pool their capital and thus "counterpoise the influence of individual wealth." American manufacturers were not lordly aristocrats but "enterprising and self-made men, who have acquired whatever wealth they possess by patient and diligent labor."

Clay was answering an attack by cotton planters, not Workingmen. But his bouyant view of a rising general affluence countered the latter's charge of workplace oppression as well as the former's fear of sectional oppression. Writers and publicists elaborated. In an 1835 treatise, businessman-economist Henry Carey repelled the idea that the capitalist's gain was the worker's loss. In the United States wages and profits did not war for their share of a fixed national wealth. All grew together. The crucial link was improved productivity, which ensured rising returns all around. Capital provided the machinery and direction that multiplied labor's output and hence increased its value. Everyone gained. The proof, said Carey, lay in the fact that American workers' real wages were rising, not falling. Within a generation the fall in commodity prices from more efficient production had doubled journeymen's purchasing power.

In Carey's view the capitalist and the worker shared such an identity of interest that it was fruitless to distinguish the two. One could not flourish without the other; indeed, since capital was nothing more than accumulated labor, one *was* the other. Over time the growing wealth of a free economy would submerge even these nominal distinctions of function, producing a perfectly classless and unimaginably prosperous society. Carey's technical analysis simply reinforced what speakers like Henry Clay and Edward Everett considered so obvious it needed no formal demonstration: the United States was still, as it had always been and indeed more than it had ever been, the land of opportunity, the laborer's paradise.

This roseate view carried further implications. The first concerned banking. In the United States working capital usually took the form of credit. Celebrants hailed the spread of credit as an unalloyed good. It was credit, they said, that liberated people's energies, multiplied their resources, and extended their reach. Without credit the country's expansion would slow to a crawl, and only the few with accumulated savings could engage in business. Another visiting Frenchman, Michel Chevalier, found attacks on the banking "aristocracy" simply perverse. Credit was really a great leveler. It enabled Americans to speedily "cover their country with roads, canals, factories, schools, churches, and, in a word, with everything that goes to make up civilization." It offered a farm to the poor ploughman, goods to the merchant and consumer, a job to the mechanic. Credit was the "lifeblood of the prosperity of the United States," the very engine of growth. Bankers who created credit and legislatures who licensed them to do so were not the workers' slavemasters but their liberators. "In this country," said Chevalier, "every enterprising man of a respectable character is sure of obtaining credit and thenceforth his fortune depends upon his own exertions." Banks did not subvert independence, they sustained it.

If capitalists and bankers were truly labor's benefactors instead of its oppressors, then it was a libel to deny them the accolade of working men. Their labor too was "useful," indeed vital. In an 1830 address on the new Workingmen's parties, Edward Everett asked who could claim membership in such a group, and answered: everyone who works "in an honest way and for a lawful object." Like hand and brain, labor and capital were necessary to each other. Separately they were helpless; together they formed "one great party, one comprehensive society" within which, "as there is but one interest, so there should be but one feeling." At Lowell on the Fourth of July, Everett proclaimed that the union "between labor and capital (which is nothing but labor saved) may truly be called a *holy alliance*."

Everett's conception of work excluded no one by occupation, save idlers and thieves. But he did exclude the "dishonest and immoral," the intemperate and vicious. Everett defined workingmen not by calling but by character. In any line of endeavor, "industry, temperance, and perseverance" were the real keys to success and usefulness. Since these traits were available to everyone, those who lacked them had only themselves to blame. "Let no one think he wants opportunity, encouragement, or means," Everett admonished. Henry Carey agreed: the rise of some journeymen to master status should prove to the rest that "nothing is wanting to them but industry and economy." If Americans failed, the fault was not in their bankers but in themselves.

On its face, here was a precise inversion of the labor critique. The United States was not an aristocracy but a perfect meritocracy where, as

Everett said, "the place to which each individual shall rise in society is precisely graduated on the scale of capacity and exertion,—in a word, of merit." Since "talent of every kind is sure to be required, honored, and rewarded," disparities in wealth revealed differences only in ability and effort. In other countries inequality of condition might reflect social injustice, but in America it simply proved equality of opportunity. Here people reaped precisely what they sowed.

Taken to their logical ends, as orators and agitators often did take them, these views were irreconcilable. Edward Everett and Frances Wright could not both be right. The United States could not be egalitarian and aristocratic, classless and classbound, a place of widening and vanishing opportunity, all at the same time.

Behind the rhetoric, celebrants and critics were less far apart than they seemed. If their appraisals of current trends ran opposite each other, their prescriptions for the future could be remarkably alike. Both George Henry Evans and Henry Carey embraced a "field of fair competition" as the solvent of inequality and the guarantor of prosperity. They differed on the sole point of whether such a field already existed, whether present arrangements unleashed or stifled what Evans called "the energy and enterprize of humble industry." Apologists and detractors of the status quo also agreed on education as the key to progress, the essential instrument of uplift. Here there was debate over means and systems, but none over ends and principles.

In clasping the twin talismans of enterprise and education, commentators of all stripes revealed their commonality. All avowed a faith in the limitless capacity of the American economy for growth and of individual Americans for elevation. Critics like Evans and Wright censured evil institutions for blocking workers' aspirations. Celebrants like Carey and Everett defended the institutions and told the unsuccessful to heal themselves. But all agreed that a true system of political economy would banish social divisions by rewarding effort and giving every honest man the chance to rise. They equally agreed that to make the offer meaningful, the tools of mental and moral advance must be available to everyone. The fate of the American experiment rested on guaranteeing that opportunity lay open to all citizens, and that all citizens were equipped to seize it.

CHAPTER

The Elevation of Character

It is the duty of a government, to do all in its power to promote the present and future prosperity of the nation, over which it is placed. This prosperity will depend on the character of its citizens. The characters of these will be formed by their mothers. . . .

Anticipation . . . points to a nation, which, having thrown off the shackles of authority and precedent, shrinks not from schemes of improvement, because other nations have never attempted them; but which, in its pride of independence, would rather lead than follow, in the march of human improvement: a nation, wise and magnanimous to plan, enterprising to undertake, and rich in resources to execute. Does not every American exult that this country is his own? And who knows how great and good a race of men, may yet arise from the forming hand of mothers, enlightened by the bounty of that beloved country,—to defend her liberties,—to plan her future improvement,—and to raise her to unparalleled glory?

—Emma Hart Willard, 1819

The Correction of Criminals

In the summer of 1824 the scientist and philanthropist William Maclure visited Robert Owen's showcase factory village in Scotland. Maclure spent a few days, "the most pleasant of my life, . . . contemplating the vast improvement in society" there. What he found helped sway him to join Owen's American venture at New Harmony soon after. At New Lanark "I never saw so many Men, Women, and children with happy & contented countenances, nor so orderly, cheerfull, & sober a Society without any coertion or physical constraint. It is on a par with the moral experiment in the new Jail of Philadelphia."

Maclure was not trying to be funny. Nor in comparing a model community to a well-ordered prison did he intend irony. What captivated Maclure at New Lanark was Owen's effort to break through the historic limits on human possibility. Common folk, doomed since the dawn of time to a life of brutish toil, could be schooled to a new plane of usefulness and happiness. Like Owen, Maclure believed that people were the product of their environment. By molding circumstance, one could mold character. There was no better place to test this hopeful premise than a prison. If convicts, the most depraved and alienated members of society, could be made over into good and useful citizens, then anyone could.

In Philadelphia and elsewhere, Americans were testing that premise. Their efforts transfixed European observers. A prison visit was high on any tourist itinerary—for some, the very reason for coming. To Alexis de Tocqueville and his companion Gustave de Beaumont, Harriet Martineau, and later Charles Dickens, American prisons represented one of the most daring facets of the national experiment: the attempt to forge in this new country a new and improved human character. Americans were as proud to show their jails as Europeans were eager to see them. Translating Beaumont and Tocqueville's *On the Penitentiary System in the United States* for a domestic audience in 1833, Francis Lieber (himself a German émigré) proclaimed it "a matter of pride to every American, that the new penitentiary system has been first established and successfully practiced in this country." America's "novel experiment" in corrections established the country's "elevated place in the scale of political or social civilization." American prisons, said Lieber, represented "a new victory of mind over matter—the great and constant task of man." In the redemption of wrongdoers, as in all else, Americans marched ostentatiously in the van of progress.

Eighteenth-century Americans, like Europeans, had penalized crime with fines, public humiliation, whippings, execution, and even banishment rather than incarceration. Official strategies and public attitudes centered on deterring or punishing offenders, not reforming them. No government thought to eradicate or cure crime, only contain it. For this purpose extended confinement seemed as pointless as it was expensive. Jails were mere holding pens, where malefactors and detainees of all kinds and both sexes mingled indiscriminately under minimal restraint until their cases were resolved.

After independence American humanitarians, with Pennsylvania Quakers in the lead, began to explore using prisons as a way to mitigate the cruelty of punishment while combining it with rehabilitation. The experiment began with the conversion of Philadelphia's Walnut Street jail to a state prison in 1790. Convicts there served long sentences under rules of conduct intended to reform instead of just restrain them. The Walnut Street system was widely acclaimed and followed. But over the years the Philadelphia exemplar and its imitators failed to cure their inmates, many of whom relapsed into crime after release. Critics attributed the high recidivism to overcrowding, lax discipline, inadequate work regimes, mingling of hardened and novice offenders, and hasty pardons. Crowded, disordered prisons became themselves breeding grounds of vice.

Reformers sought a more thorough control of the inmates' environment. Between 1817 and 1821 Pennsylvania and New York authorized new prisons with separate cells for each convict. This revolutionary innovation substituted solitary habitats for the promiscuous housing of the old-fashioned prison. Pennsylvania spared no expense at its Eastern Penitentiary in Philadelphia in 1829. Containing eventually 586 cells, it was the largest, most imposing structure in the country.

The two states carried the principle of prisoner separation to different lengths. Both cut off contact with the outside world except through the mediation of prison authorities and chaplains. At New York's Auburn and Sing Sing, operative by 1826, inmates worked together but in strictest silence. Talking was forbidden at all times. Philadelphia imposed total solitude. Convicts were so isolated through their stay as to not know of one another's presence.

This was the regimen that William Maclure hailed as a breakthrough on a par with Robert Owen's model village. Other visitors concurred. Captain Basil Hall, generally critical of things American, pronounced the discipline at Sing Sing "one of the most efficacious combinations of moral machinery that has ever perhaps been seen in action." Harriet Martineau, humanitarian champion of oppressed slaves and women, declared the Philadelphia system "the best method of punishment which has yet been tried" and judged that "in the treatment of the guilty, America is beyond the rest of the world." Charles Dickens recoiled from the horror of total solitude. But overall he thought "that in her sweeping reform and bright example to other countries," the United States had "shown great wisdom, great benevolence, and exalted policy."

A debate grew up around the New York and Pennsylvania systems, both of which were widely copied at home and abroad. The Prison Discipline Society of Boston, founded in 1825, touted New York's Auburn as "a model worthy of the world's imitation," while Tocqueville and Beaumont found "an incontestable advantage" at Philadelphia, where complete separation interdicted "the fatal influence of the wicked upon each other." Discussion turned on whether isolation was a salutary means of inducing "moral and religious reflection" or a species of psychological torture likely to drive inmates insane.

Beyond this point of tactics, domestic and foreign observers alike hailed American penitentiaries for approaching felons as redeemable citizens instead of hopeless reprobates fit only to be killed, tortured, or locked away. Prison discipline rested on a sincere if stern faith in the chance of rehabilitating even the worst offender. Basil Hall remarked that Americans devoted much effort and expense to "the most hardened, the least educated, and the most unprincipled men in the country"—people who "in England would be got rid of altogether" by banishment or execution. Instead, Hall saw the American convict learning "habits of industry," temperance, obedience, "order, cleanliness, and punctuality, all new and agreeable to him." Silence and separation, combined with religious instruction, encouraged contemplation and repentance. Prison labor inculcated useful skills and work habits while defraying the high cost of confinement.

In short, the whole thrust was not just to punish, nor even to maintain good order within the walls, but to school the inmate for useful life outside. If the system was strenuous, rescuing men from the depths of depravity demanded no less. What struck observers most forcibly about American prisons was not the severity of their discipline but the ambitious end it served. Tocqueville and Beaumont noted skeptically that philanthropists saw penitentiaries as a "remedy for all the evils of society." Their American translator, Francis Lieber, viewed criminality as a disease to be cured, and the substitution of "moral power" for "physical force" in its treatment as an epoch in human advance.

If adult malefactors could be saved, then surely so could children. In 1825 New York opened the nation's first House of Refuge for juveniles. Boston and Philadelphia followed by 1828. Separate institutions for youth grew from the desire to shield novice offenders from the contagion of hardened felons. The House of Refuge was more and less than a children's penitentiary. It took in orphans and vagrants as well as delinquents, and put them under a discipline that was, in Tocqueville and Beaumont's words, "a medium between a school and a prison," blending mental and moral instruction with manual labor, and balancing reward for good behavior with strict punishment for misconduct.

New York's House of Refuge was the brainchild of a private charitable foundation, the Society for the Prevention of Pauperism. Like-minded groups in other cities, most notably the Prison Discipline Society of Boston, backed the era's experiments in behavioral reform. They drew leadership and support from prominent ministers, merchants, and manufacturers. Their approach to the problem of crime fused Christian humanitarianism with a hardheaded business realism.

Institutional Uplift

Signs of success with criminals encouraged reformers to expand their sphere of usefulness. From their experience with convicts they extrapolated rules for elevating the citizenry at large. In 1829 the Prison Discipline Society, observing in penitentiaries a "connexion between architecture and morals," recommended separate sleeping rooms as a way to promote "order, seriousness, and purity in large families, male and female boarding schools, and colleges." Prison regimens of work and instruction offered a model for academies, almshouses, and houses of refuge to follow. The rule of "unceasing vigilance" could be "a principle of very extensive application to families, schools, academies, colleges, factories, mechanics' shops."

As they drew lessons from prisons, reformers widened their assault on social ills, promoting orphanages, asylums for the insane (Massachusetts's Worcester State Lunatic Hospital of 1833 set the pattern), almshouses for the indigent, and workhouses for the unemployed. In a well-ordered institution, said Louisiana reformer Edward Livingston, those "able to work, but idle, intemperate, or vicious" could be "corrected by seclusion, sobriety, instruction, and labour." To all these ventures projectors brought an environmentalist approach to character and a faith in the possibility of genuinely curing, not merely containing, distress. As a New York report on poverty urged in 1824, an educated public and vast natural resources, combined with "the spirit of enterprise and habits of industry which so generally pervade our country, the purity of our laws, the excellence of our civil institutions, and our remote situation from European conflicts," meant "that pauperism may, with proper care and attention, be almost wholly eradicated from our soil."

Whatever later generations might come to think of their program, and whatever might become of the institutions they created, the founders' activating impulse was uplifting, not repressive. They aspired beyond the traditional duty of administering charity to the poor and punishment to the unworthy. They wanted literally to re-form people, to fit them for lives of happiness and usefulness by instilling traits of self-control and habits of order. As Joseph Tuckerman, Unitarian minister to the poor of Boston and proponent of almshouses and workhouses, put it, without neglecting "the *temporal wants*" of "suffering fellow creatures, it is yet never to be forgotten by any who can serve them, that the most effectual means by which we may improve their condition is, by *improving their characters*."

The notion that character could be improved, that people could elevate themselves by concerted effort, would eventually lose its exhilarating novelty and become, at least for some, a rhetorical mask for social indifference, an excuse to blame the unfortunate for their misery. But when first put forth, it was fresh and exciting. It inspired energy and activity, not complacency and contempt. Trust in progress lent a liberating, even utopian cast to experiments in human engineering.

Much of the institutional program was hardly questioned in its day. Everyone from evangelists to labor activists agreed that self-discipline was the key to success in a free society. The obsession with the minutia of prison and asylum routine, even with the details of institutional architecture, reflected a wider faith, shared by visionaries from Robert Owen to John Quincy Adams, in the capacity of rational, holistic systems to unleash human potential and catapult Americans to a new plane of happiness and achievement.

A like belief propelled perhaps the most ambitious of the era's ventures in human reconstruction: the effort to turn American Indians into Europeans. Generations of Americans had watched in fascinated horror as tribal cultures crumpled and populations shrank before the whites' inexorable advance. Torn between admiration and contempt for Indian ways, whites also vacillated in assigning blame for the tribes' predicament. Philanthropists deplored the injustice and abuse Indians suffered at white hands. Yet they also held Indians responsible (even while pitying them) for their failure to adapt to new circumstances. This mixture of compassion and censure, acknowledging external causes of distress yet looking to the individual for its remedy, mirrored the stance of institutional reformers, builders of prisons and asylums. Even the most sympathetic observers believed that tribespeople could escape doom only by remaking their characters and conquering the same debilitating traits—idleness, intemperance, improvidence—that bred criminality and dependence among whites.

Efforts to convert Indians to European ways, thus rescuing them from oblivion and salving white consciences over their fate, dated from the earliest days of settlement. In 1819 a fusion of governmental and charitable resources gave them new impetus. Under Thomas L. McKenney, United States Commissioner of Indian Affairs, federal funds built some forty Indian schools for which missionary societies supplied teachers. The venture brought government into collaboration with evangelical cosponsors like the American Board of Commissioners for Foreign Missions, founded by Lyman Beecher and New England Congregationalists in 1810. But enthusiasm for Indian schools transcended denominational and political boundaries. One vigorous proponent, founder of an academy for Choctaw youth in 1825, was Richard M. Johnson of Kentucky, congressional defender of church-state separation and champion of the fight against Sabbatarianism and Sunday mail closings.

The Indian schools sought to retool their pupils in all ways for life in white America. As McKenney said, "their whole character, inside and out; language, and morals, must be changed." A central element in this program, just as in corrective and charitable institutions, was reshaping everyday habits and behaviors. Along with literary and manual skills, teachers imparted the usual prescriptions for industry, temperance, and discipline. Flush with optimism, missionaries to the Cherokees in 1823 reported their progress toward making the Indians "as happy as enlightened and as moral as any part of the United States or any part of the Christian world." Given "a system adequate in extent, and power," McKenney hoped "to civilize the whole (I mean the rising generation, of course) *in a single generation.*"

It is easy to read in all these endeavors, from prisons to Indian schools, a condescension that seems to call in question the sincerity of their purposes. One sees, all too readily, the self-serving posturing of comfortable citizens chiding the unfortunate for their distress and prescribing, as its only cure, a regimen of self-denial they would not dream of imposing on themselves. The truth was otherwise. Those who headed the new experiments in human uplift were indeed well-to-do. But of course, only they had time and funds for such work. Every town had its charities and benevolences, its orphanages, asylums, and relief societies. Donors and volunteers included new families and old; evangelicals and Quakers and Episcopalians and Unitarians; Yankees and southerners; men and women.

Reformers did practice in their households what they preached for others. Their stress on discipline as the essence of character, and character as the key to usefulness and happiness, may have been naive. But it was not hypocritical, and it appeared well grounded in experience. Activists were certainly not inspired (as critics would later charge) by anything as transparent as a desire to tame the turbulent poor for docile industrial labor. Behavioral institutions appeared before factories. If anything, the latter copied the former, as manufacturers sought a well-regulated workplace that, like a school, would impart useful habits of discipline. At any rate few philanthropists were industrialists. What self-interest underlay their work was rather indirect than direct, and more ideological than material. Men and women invested much more effort in trying to cure social ills than it would have taken to shield themselves from their effects. What drove them forward was less an instinct for self-defense than a vision of a good society.

Personal success fostered in many a profound sense of obligation. Philanthropists believed with other Americans that all progress was of a piece. Material and moral elevation were inseparable. Private and public likewise served each other; the nation would advance as its citizens achieved. True service to self then intertwined with service to society. "Happiness and usefulness" were complementary, even identical. By infusing traditional injunctions of charity with an overarching significance, this conviction steered people powerfully toward labors of benevolence. The equation of social purpose with self-fulfillment made doing good, as well as doing well, both a duty and a pleasure.

Practitioners of benevolence sought ways to enable people, not restrain them. Still an undercurrent of urgency, even of fear, propelled their energies. They accepted, often trumpeted, the unprecedented openness of American society that gave opportunity for individual success and social progress. Yet liberty and abundance also invited the blind gratification of immediate desire, fatal to hopes of either private or public good. Citizens needed enlightenment to recognize their true interest, and discipline to pursue it. As both Indians and criminals proved, untrained liberty produced dissipation and debauchery. Spread widely, it threatened social chaos. Lacking external controls, only an internalized mechanism could prevent Americans from squandering their chances and prostrating their futures in an orgy of self-indulgence. The end would be anarchy or a recourse to repression—either way, the forfeiture of American promise. Believing this, philanthropists saw the country's fate riding on their success in teaching the responsible use of liberty. If the prospects for advance were entrancing, the consequences of failure were frightful.

Self-Improvement

The activities of philanthropists merged and overlapped with those of other citizens. Strategies for bettering character enlisted patricians dispensing charity, evangelicals striving for Christ's earthly kingdom, entrepreneurs angling to get ahead, and wage-laborers grasping for independence. Agendas collided at some points, but joined at others. Though defining it with varying stringency, nearly all shunned intemperance as fatal to self-control. In everyone's eye, self-discipline was the crucial catalyst of improvement—the key to reaching responsible citizenship, financial security, social respectability, mental and moral fulfillment, and thus true happiness.

To assist in their drive for mastery, citizens turned to what was becoming a distinctively American form of organization—the voluntary society. In 1827 Ralph Waldo Emerson listed among the *"Peculiarities of the present Age"* (along with religious reform, paper money, joint stock companies, and the ascendancy of "the first person singular") the "disposition among men of *associating* themselves to promote any purpose. (Millions of societies.)" Alexis de Tocqueville observed Americans organizing for all ends, from building a road to enacting a political program. What especially struck him were "the intellectual and moral associations of America"—associations for forging and sustaining character.

In 1828 the village of Utica, New York, population eight thousand, boasted forty-one "Benevolent and Charitable Institutions." The number rose in the 1830s as older societies were joined by evangelical Bible, tract, temperance, and missionary groups; a self-helping Maternal Association for mothers; a Female Moral Reform Society to combat licentiousness; and a Young Men's Association, Literary Club, and Workingmen's Association devoted to self-improvement and mutual aid. "The truth is that we are *society mad,*" a Cincinnati editor observed in 1830, and proceeded to list fifty of them in the city. Besides religious and charitable groups, Cincinnatians supported fraternal lodges, literary and debating clubs, and mutual support societies, some organized along craft and ethnic lines and others open to all.

Lyceums and mechanics' institutes joined the thirst for self-improvement with the craving for knowledge and science. In October 1826 Josiah Holbrook, Yale-trained son of a Connecticut farmer, published a plan for "Associations of Adults for Mutual Education" in the new *American Journal of Education*. Holbrook proposed a network of societies "to diffuse rational and useful information through the community" through lectures, libraries, and discussions, thus "raising the moral and intellectual taste of our countrymen" and combating "that monster, intemperance." A month later Holbrook founded the first branch of his American Lyceum in Millbury, Massachusetts.

In 1828 a Boston lyceum began with great fanfare. Daniel Webster headed its first list of speakers. Soon fifteen societies were at work in Boston alone, and the movement was racing across the country. At its peak in the mid-1830s it embraced perhaps three thousand local groups, fifteen state organizations, and an annual national convention. Groups with names like the Young Men's Mutual Improvement Society, Young Men's Mercantile Library Association, Ladies Institute and Lyceum, and Union Literary and Debating Society held discussions, maintained libraries, and sponsored lectures on everything from natural and human history to travel and the arts. Ralph Waldo Emerson spoke on science, biography, and literature, and a young Abraham Lincoln on "The Perpetuation of Our Political Institutions." Mechanics' institutes paralleled the lyceums' edifying labors, focusing more closely on matters scientific and technological.

Beyond their overt mission of spreading "personal, social, political, intellectual and moral improvement," lyceums and other uplifting associations served an important socializing role. Engaging in such endeavors denoted civic leadership and satisfied cravings for status and recognition. Clubs and societies offered diversion, company, and moral support to mill girls, shop clerks, and other single youth away from home.

Benevolent, charitable, and self-improvement societies especially provided a public function for women. Rising incomes and newly available store goods allowed many wives and daughters to reduce their household chores. Yet law and custom still barred women from pursuing professional or business careers or entering politics. Volunteer work was their logical, indeed nearly their only, outlet.

Prevailing notions of female personality encouraged women's benevolent and charitable work even as they closed off alternatives. Woman's character was presumably ruled by emotion; man's by intellect. Women reigned in affairs of the heart as men did in those of the head. Not in itself new, this idea of a nurturing female temperament received new emphasis in a burgeoning literature that prescribed the route to happiness and usefulness for both sexes. For women, that route lay in exercising their maternal and domestic faculties. As the *Ladies Museum* declared in 1825, "Man shines abroad—woman at home. Man talks to convince—woman to persuade and please. Man has a rugged heart—woman a soft and tender one. Man prevents misery—woman relieves it."

While such phrasings warned women away from the rough-and-tumble world of business and politics, they invited them into the realm of organized benevolence, where feminine traits of sympathy and charity could find extension outside the home. Women's own choices tended to bear out the presumption of an innate female disposition toward good works. For years they had outnumbered men among the religious faithful. Now women filled the working ranks of benevolences, charities, and evangelical groups. Many new uplifting societies were exclusively female.

While it provided paths of usefulness for individual men and women, association also lent structure and cohesion to communities undergoing rapid turnover. Americans were a mobile people. The overall westward shifting of the population masked an almost pervasive transience. The ethos of progress encouraged the ambitious and the frustrated to leave home and try somewhere else. In the face of this flux, volunteer groups, including churches and later political parties, secured stability by quickly assimilating newcomers into a set of like-minded acquaintances. In growing towns, associations were the very building-blocks of community. They furnished members with a ready identity, while affiliation with state and national organizations furthered the feeling of participating in a wider and greater cause.

But if association served to connect Americans to one another, it also served to divide them. While sharing aims of improvement and uplift, groups offered varied definitions of the good society and strategies for achieving it. Their programs at once overlapped, competed, and clashed. The proliferation of societies, like that of churches, encouraged citizens to make very public, and in some measure exclusive, choices of affinities and goals. In selecting associates and avowing purposes, Americans exposed and deepened social fault-lines and helped to carve new ones. As people became more organized, they became more separated.

Some associations reflected existing social boundaries. The most impenetrable barrier in America, North and South, was race. Shut out from white society, free black people from Boston to Charleston fashioned a network of churches and charities that paralleled and mirrored their white counterparts. Black Philadelphians organized Masonic lodges, an Angola Society, the Sons of Africa, Daughters of Ethiopia, Daughters of Samaria, musical and literary groups, and African Episcopal, Methodist, Baptist, and Presbyterian churches. By 1830 the city's 14,600 blacks sustained more than forty benevolent societies and a dozen churches.

In the 1820s fifty thousand Irish emigrated to the United States, and in the 1830s two hundred thousand more. Already branded as outsiders by their prevailing poverty, illiteracy, and Catholic faith, the Irish rallied their spirits and fanned Protestant suspicions by clustering in an insular set of associations around their clans and the Catholic Church.

At the opposite end of the scale, especially within the clutch of families of inherited wealth and truly aristocratic pretensions, organizing took on an exclusionary tone. Professions of openness and equality notwithstanding, the activities of groups like New York's Society for the Encouragement of Faithful Domestic Servants, founded in 1825, or the elite clubs of Boston and Philadelphia did more to highlight social divisions than to hide them.

The greatest range of associational choices faced men and women whose station remained least settled, neither fixed at the bottom by color or creed nor held at the top by wealth and status. Evangelists of a half-dozen denominations trolled for their souls, along with communitarians and utopians, moral crusaders, social critics, health faddists, and self-help groups of all kinds. Association reflected, and guided, choices in politics, religion, affinity, and outlook. In effect, it determined identity. Artisans and wage-earners announced their view of workplace relations by joining in solidarity with their employers or setting up against them. Women channeled their energies through organizations purveying various mixes of charity, piety, and reform. Charleston, South Carolina, offered benevolent Christians a choice of Episcopal, Unitarian, Methodist, and nondenominational Bible, tract, missionary, education, and temperance societies. Men craving conviviality could select from the South Carolina Society, Hibernian Society, St. Andrew's Society, and German Friendly Society—none of which, despite their names, enforced ethnic criteria for membership.

The upshot of all this joining and organizing was a citizenry both newly mobilized and newly differentiated. The fracturing of society was highly visible, marked in the noisy activity of competing groups and even in public ceremony. City fire companies organized by occupation, neighborhood, and ethnicity raced each other to the flames and fought each other in the streets. Community growth brought fragmentation along with association. On July 4, 1820, residents of Steubenville, Ohio, met at the courthouse square to hear the Declaration of Independence and partake of a public dinner. Ten years later, when the town had doubled in size, this communal ritual was but a memory. Various groups staged separate events.

Organization put a public seal on emerging cleavages of status, persuasion, and belief. Still, a common impulse buoyed all the debate societies and young men's clubs, lyceums and mechanics' institutes, sororities and fraternities, charities and church groups. Americans of all backgrounds embraced Benjamin Franklin's idea of self-improvement as the way to happiness and usefulness, key to personal uplift and collective well-being.

Schools

Hope of a better world focused Americans' attention on the rising generation. Children took on a new importance, not merely as bearers of name and tradition, but as the means of projecting improvement into the future. Educate them correctly, exhorted George B. Emerson in 1831, "and you will give a permanent impulse to the onward movement of the race, which it can never lose. Each individual begins his progress from a higher level, and, with equal exertion, will bequeath a richer inheritance of knowledge and wisdom to his successors." As parents prepared their offspring to achieve beyond themselves, the two main means of shaping their characters for the task—the school and the family—assumed a sudden prominence in public discourse.

The principle of universal schooling, at least for white males, had rarely been questioned in republican America. But lack of means, compounded by localism, sectarian rivalry, and resistance to taxation, had foiled the hopes of Thomas Jefferson and Benjamin Rush for comprehensive state systems. Communities and charities shouldered the task of teaching. While sufficient to sustain literacy, their efforts evinced little sign of system or higher purpose. Poorly funded, haphazardly organized, with classes undifferentiated by grade or skill level and indifferently taught, American schools were hardly fit to serve as instruments of national uplift.

In 1818 the Englishman Joseph Lancaster came to America to promote his monitorial plan of teaching. Under Lancaster's system older students drilled younger pupils, permitting simultaneous instruction of hundreds of children at different levels under a single master. Lancaster's method created a sensation. Many schools adopted it, while publicists called it "a branch of that wonderful providence which is to usher in the millennial day."

Another European influence entered the country through Robert Owen and his coadjutor William Maclure. Both men had acquired a new pedagogical approach from the Swiss educators Johann Pestalozzi and Philipp von Fellenberg. Maclure sponsored three French Pestalozzian teachers in America—Joseph Neef, Marie Fretageot, and William S. Phiquepal—and in 1825 brought them with him to New Harmony. While Owen launched his communitarian venture, Maclure's teachers began an experiment in social rebirth through education.

At New Harmony children were to develop their faculties and acquire practical knowledge by learning experientially at their own pace. Usefulness would govern curriculum, as students imbibed mathematics, mechanical science, geography, and natural history through instruments, apparatus, models, and specimens. Memorization, instruction in dead languages, and punishment were forsworn. Maclure saw his system as a blueprint for remaking society. Convinced by "experience that the inequality of knowledge is the source of all the evils that torment humanity," he envisioned education for everyone, not just the privileged who could afford it. Combining manual labor with practical training would make his schools self-supporting.

In 1826 this program was bold indeed. Free universal schooling existed nowhere. Most teachers still leaned on drill and discipline to pound lessons into their students' heads, and higher learning was still chained to the classics. Even at the most progressive schools, like the academy George Bancroft and Joseph Cogswell established in Northampton, Massachusetts, in 1823, the curriculum centered on Latin and Greek.

Though they outlasted Owen's community, Maclure's New Harmony schools led a brief and turbulent existence. Only a School of Industry, centered around a printing press, survived into the 1830s. Still, the writings of Maclure, of Neef, of William Russell (who began publishing the *American Journal of Education* in 1826), and of Archibald D. Murphey (who proposed a state school system in North Carolina as early as 1817) gave growing currency to Pestalozzian theories.

The infusion of Lancastrian and Pestalozzian ideas fed a widening taste for pedagogical experiment. New schools of all sorts appeared—infant schools, charity schools, manual labor schools, Sunday schools, specialized academies of every kind and description. Ideas for educating the young were as myriad as projects for the improvement of the self. Discussion of educational issues—curriculum and teaching methods; the proper balance of mental, moral, and physical training; the merits of Pestalozzian induction versus Lancastrian recitation; strategies for reaching the deaf and blind; instruction for blacks and females; and means of training and supplying teachers—filled the columns of newspapers and journals.

Lyceum speakers, clerics, philanthropists, and politicians spread the gospel of education. Schools figured in projects for social regeneration put forth by everyone from labor activists to evangelists to communitarians. Even Thomas Cooper, president of the University of South Carolina, took time from denouncing Yankee tariff oppression in 1826 to urge, as "the first duty of a republic," primary instruction for "every class of the people," plus public universities to teach the "higher grades of science and literature" that "constitute the indispensible basis of all national power, national wealth, prosperity, reputation, and happiness."

Whatever their special premises, pedagogical schemes shared the goal of fusing moral with mental improvement, forging students' character while training their intellect. New Harmony freethinkers and Boston Unitarians experimented with noncoercive means of leading youngsters to "a love of moral effort and self-control." As Jacob Abbott told the American Institute of Instruction in 1831, the student who acquired a "taste for moral improvement," who learned to discover "new pleasure in the voluntary discharge of duty,—in meeting and resisting temptation,—in receiving proofs of confidence and showing himself worthy of the trust," was on the way to a life of happiness and usefulness.

As with other forms of uplift, pedagogical experiment pointed simultaneously toward diversity and conformity. Schools based on new approaches and philosophies launched in every direction, while educators searching for the one best formula devised ideal curricula and diagrammed model classrooms. Benevolent reformers, Workingmen, and lyceum activists endorsed inclusive free public instruction as the proper republican mode. Despite resistance to taxation and central control, the drive for state systems gathered steam. Massachusetts, where the first public high schools appeared in the 1820s, led the way. The creation of a state Board of Education in 1837, the appointment of crusader Horace Mann to head it, and his inauguration of the first state teacher-training school marked the road toward universal, standardized public education.

Schooling had once been a means of raising boundaries between the few who could afford it and the many who could not. Now, at least in aspiration, it became an instrument for breaking them down. Leading citizens went beyond conceding education as a necessary expedient in a country where nearly every white man had the vote, to embracing it as an element of social justice. Edward Everett exulted in 1831:

Our system of free schools has opened a straight way from the threshold of every abode, however humble, in the village or in the city, to the high places of usefulness, influence, and honor. And it is left for each, by the cultivation of every talent; by watching, with an eagle's eye, for every chance of improvement; by bounding forward, like a greyhound, at the most distant glimpse of honorable opportunity; by grappling, as with hooks of steel, to the prize, when it is won; by redeeming time, defying temptation, and scorning sensual pleasure, to make himself useful, honored, and happy.

Though the principle was easier enunciated than implemented, the rationale for universal instruction was complete. Americans had forged that link between education, opportunity, and progress which has remained a staple of democratic rhetoric ever since.

Families

Everyone knew that schools alone could not do the job of producing better Americans. Reformers, philanthropists, and educators all looked to the home as the real crucible of character. "The business of parents is to develope each individual character so as to produce the greatest amount of usefulness and happiness," admonished Lydia Maria Child in her 1831 treatise, *The Mother's Book*. Studies of criminals and deviants showed them to be the offspring of intemperate, negligent, or absent parents. The Boston Prison Discipline Society reported that for all the success of their "invaluable experiments on man," correctional institutions only underscored *"the importance of family government"* in steering children right in the first place.

Within the home, the task of moral governance fell mainly on the mother. The same assumptions about female temperament that relegated women to the domestic realm (and its public extension through charity and benevolence) charged them with special responsibility, not just for answering children's physical needs, but for shaping their character. It was woman's "higher destiny," George B. Emerson told the American Institute of Instruction in 1831, "to be a mother, and to form the heart, the character and the mind of her children." "Mothers," announced the Reverend John S. C. Abbott in 1833, "have as powerful an influence over the welfare of future generations as all other earthly causes combined." Francis Lieber detected a "worthless mother" or a "slothful and intemperate wife" behind every man gone wrong.

In manuals like Lydia Maria Child's *Mother's Book* and *The American Frugal Housewife* and journals like the *Ladies Magazine* and *Godey's Lady's Book*, women learned to achieve happiness and usefulness within the home by managing resources properly and maintaining a healthful and attractive environment. They also, and especially, received instruction on the importance and the means of implanting moral fiber and its essence, self-discipline, in their children.

These guides marked a departure in articulating wifely duties. Partitioning household labor according to sex was not new. Neither were admonitions, especially from clergy, to women to know and keep their place. Women's writers now reached a wider audience, though still perhaps not as wide as they hoped. Authors assumed too readily that every woman could devote full time to home and children. But their real innovation was to take a conventional idea of woman's duty, one that had always been linked to presumptions of female weakness and subordination, and elevate it to an autonomous social and moral mission. The new women's literature made wives and mothers partners in the great project of national uplift. Domestic economy and family governance became the means, not merely of sustenance, but of advance. Writers approached the home as an institution capable of perfection, and household management as yet another improving science.

While advice books and magazines apotheosized the home as an incubator of character, others rethought the family in more radical ways. By the early 1830s Bronson Alcott, one of the coterie of romantic seceders from New England Unitarianism known as Transcendentalists, was immersed in child-raising experiments that took ideas of childhood innocence and parental nurture to a perfectionist extreme. The link between the marriage bond and Christianity, and the way that prevailing rules of property and exchange supported a sex-based division of labor, also made the family a point of attack for those who dreamed of rebuilding American mores and institutions from the bottom up.

This was why Robert Owen's "Declaration of Mental Independence" joined marriage with private property and religion in a demonic trinity of evils responsible for all human misery. In the United States, as in Britain, the common law of marriage subsumed a wife's legal identity under that of her husband, gave him control of property and children, and made divorce on any grounds but abandonment or extreme cruelty next to impossible. Owen charged that these rules ruined an affectionate relationship by polluting it with selfish economic motives and compulsions. Religious superstition cloaked the sordid transaction in "mysterious forms and ceremonies" to bind the parties for life. Owen wanted marriage to be what the "law of nature" meant it to be: a consensual act between two parties "equal in wealth, education and condition," based on "natural feelings and affections" and dissoluble at will. Only a free and fair union could conduce to true happiness.

Owen's promise to overhaul marriage and place men and women on equal footing came no closer to realization than his other plans for New Harmony. But a few disciples carried his precepts into practice. In New York in 1830 his son Robert Dale Owen published *Moral Physiology*, a manual on the forbidden subject of birth control. Two years later, when young Owen wed Mary Jane Robinson, he renounced his marital rights as "barbarous relics of a feudal, despotic system, soon destined, in the onward course of improvement, to be wholly swept away."

Frances Wright ventured further. At Nashoba in Tennessee residents touted and practiced nonmarital and interracial sex, to the great horror of some of the community's well-wishers. After its collapse and until her return to Europe in 1830, Wright continued to preach her version of the egalitarian gospel. On the lecture circuit and in the pages of the *Free Enquirer* in New York she championed *"the universal improvement of our human condition"* by means of "a system of RATIONAL AND NATIONAL REPUBLICAN EDUCATION" without distinction of sex. Wright assailed conventional religion and the inequities, including sexual, that it sanctioned. Until women assumed an equal place in society, "human improvement must advance but feebly. It is in vain that we would circumscribe the power of one half of our race, and that half by far the most important and influential. . . . Let women stand where they may in the scale of improvement, their position decides that of the race."

Wright's speeches drew enthusiasts, curiosity seekers, and hecklers. As much as her bold doctrines, her very presence as a woman on the lecture platform defied custom, arousing both admiration and disgust. She became a pariah, albeit a fascinating one. Press and polite society excoriated her. Conceding her eloquence and originality, New York diarist Philip Hone fumed all the more at Wright's attempt "to break down the moral and religious ties which bind mankind together, and to bring into disrepute the institutions which have been revered by all good men."

Frances Wright linked conventions of sexual morality and female propriety with the teachings of religion, and damned them all as instruments of oppression. Christians drew the same connections to an opposite conclusion: church, home, and family were means not of female degradation, but of exaltation. In his Cincinnati debate with Robert Owen, Alexander Campbell argued precisely this point. Christianity had raised women from "ignorance, bondage, and obscurity" to a position of shared and equal responsibility with men. It gave women the influence they "possess, and ought to possess, in forming the character of man" through "the discipline and education" of children. Catharine Beecher, eldest of Lyman Beecher's precocious offspring and an intellect of growing influence in her own right, agreed. "It is Christianity that has given to woman her true place in society"—a place secured by her wielding of "kindly, generous, peaceful and benevolent" influences within "the domestic and social circle." Beecher found Frances Wright's exhibitions "intolerably offensive and disgusting." In throwing off woman's "appropriate character" of modesty, delicacy, refinement, gentleness, purity, and dependence, Wright had abandoned everything of femininity but the mere "shape of a woman."

Conceiving female character in ostensibly opposite ways, Wright and Beecher held more in common than either realized. Wright sought to eradicate distinctions of social role based on sex, Beecher to enshrine them. Yet both viewed woman's assumption of her true place as the hinge on which rested all hope of human advance. Both targeted education as the means of equipping American women to fulfill their mission of raising the character of the nation and the world.

Some men agreed with them. In 1824 William Maclure exclaimed that a "higher order of famil [female] education" enabling women "to fill all places of honor and profit that their physical force will permit them to occupy would be the greatest possible improvement in Society." It would double "the mental force of the great mass of mankind" and enlist "the other half of the creation in the gloriouse work of civilisation." Experiments in female schooling figured in the pedagogical innovations of the 1820s. In 1819 Emma Hart Willard secured the backing of New York's Governor De Witt Clinton in her plea for state-funded women's higher education. Rebuffed by the legislature, she founded the pathbreaking Troy Female Seminary in 1821. Two years later Catharine Beecher established another seminary in Hartford, Connecticut.

Willard and Beecher premised their schools explicitly on sexual "difference of character and duties." Woman's nature was separate from man's, but her social mission was even more critical. "The cultivation and development of the immortal mind" was "her especial and delightful duty." It was up to women, "in the single relation of mothers," to guide the development of the rising generation and thus "elevate the whole character of the community." Willard and Beecher repudiated the old-style female boarding school, which trained its well-to-do pupils in social graces and "frivolous acquirements." Their academies offered instruction in mathematics, history, morals, and philosophy, along with scientific home management. They aimed to fit women for usefulness, not adornment.

That usefulness, though radiating from woman's maternal office, was not to be confined within the home. The goal of the female seminary was to prepare teachers as well as mothers. "It is to *mothers*, and to *teachers*, that the world is to look for the character which is to be enstamped on each succeeding generation," Beecher argued. Formal teacher training would raise "the *formation of the minds of children*" from a species of low-paid drudgery to "*a profession*" promising "honour, influence, and emolument." Setting females over classrooms would entrust the shaping of young characters to those endowed by nature for it, while opening an avenue of service to women "necessarily debarred" from other occupations and "now nearly useless to society." Besides, young single women without dependents to support would work cheap. Beecher envisioned an army of thirty thousand female teachers spreading over the land, propelled more by moral and patriotic zeal than hope of gain.

Beecher and Willard conceived the home less as a shelter and refuge from the world than as a seat of power. There, women could "watch the formation of their [children's] characters with unceasing vigilance." From there, via the schoolroom, they would project their sway over the character of the nation as a whole. If the source of feminine influence was domestic, its reach was universal. Ultimately women, not men, would control America's destiny.

Women

Depending on who wielded it, the idea of a distinct female mission could fasten extreme limits or almost no limits on women's public activity. It could chain them to the care of husband and children or spring them out upon the world. By confining their operations to the home and its immediate extension in the classroom, Catharine Beecher and Emma Hart Willard fit their belief in women's transcendent influence within existing conventions of feminine propriety. They did not, like Frances Wright, challenge the assumption that most arenas of public life were fit only for men. But if women were truly the annointed guardians of character, then in theory there were few realms of endeavour that might not profit from their aid—from education, religion, and benevolence even to electoral politics. Expediently but somewhat arbitrarily, Beecher, Willard, and most of their compatriots avoided opprobrium by accepting, even championing, their disbarment from political activity. But the very rationale they invoked to draw that line would justify a few women in crossing it.

Not surprisingly, it was the issue of slavery, which posed such a stark affront to white Americans' other comfortable notions, that also challenged this one. Slavery entangled impulses of religion, benevolence, and charity with politics in ways that made them impossible to separate.

Though men organized and led the American Anti-Slavery Society, women predominated in the abolitionist rank and file, as they did in church congregations and benevolent groups. After failing to convert slaveholders by direct appeal, abolitionists turned their hopes to Washington. In 1836 they showered Congress with petitions urging it to abolish slavery in the national capital and to make no more slave states. Most of the circulators and signers were women. Critics North and South reproved their intrusion into the masculine realm of politics and government. Much of the censure came from people hostile to abolition in any form. But the question of women's role brought discord even into antislavery ranks. Controversy especially centered on the activities of the Grimké sisters, Sarah and Angelina.

The Grimkés arrived at their reform commitment by way of a religious pilgrimage unusual only in that their road to antislavery began in South Carolina. Born to a Charleston family prominent in politics and benevolence (a brother was active in peace and temperance movements), the sisters left home and their parents' Episcopalianism to become Presbyterians and then Quakers in Philadelphia. Their quest for a spiritual mission finally found an object in abolitionism. In 1835 Angelina joined the Philadelphia Female Anti-Slavery Society and started to write for William Lloyd Garrison's *Liberator*. A year later they began speaking in public.

Angelina Grimké's *Appeal to the Christian Women of the South* and Sarah's *An Epistle to the Clergy of the Southern States,* both published in 1836, planted their case against slavery on ground of religion and femininity. Cramming her pages with scriptural exegesis, Angelina begged southern "Sisters in Christ" to wield all their womanly influence against slavery. "I know you do not make the laws, but I know also that *you are the wives and mothers, the sisters and daughters of those who do;* and if you really suppose *you* can do nothing to overthrow slavery, you are greatly mistaken." Women could pray; they could teach and succor their slaves; above all, they could persuade by voice and pen. Precisely because women had no stake in politics, their disinterested *"moral suasion"* against slavery, shining forth in the purity of Christian truth and righteousness, would prove "irresistible." Slavery was doomed to perish, Grimké warned, "by moral power or physical force, and it is for *you*," southern women, to choose between them.

Predictably the Grimkés' appearance in print and at the lectern drew condemnation from slavery's defenders—but not only from them. The Congregational clergy of Massachusetts censured their "unnatural" abandonment of "the mild, dependent, softening influence of woman," a "source of mighty power" if used rightly in "unobtrusive and private" ways. And Catharine Beecher, whose Hartford academy Angelina Grimké had nearly attended, addressed to her an *Essay on Slavery and Abolitionism, with reference to the duty of American females.* Assailing abolitionists for their inflammatory tactics, Beecher especially reproved women who sacrificed the moral advantages of appearing "dependent and defenceless" to contend with men on men's own ground.

"The investigation of the rights of the slave has led me to a better understanding of my own," wrote Angelina Grimké in response. Starting from Christian premises akin to Catharine Beecher's, the Grimkés had reached a position close to Frances Wright's. "Men and women were CREATED EQUAL; they are both moral and accountable beings, and whatever is *right* for man to do, is *right for* woman." In May 1837 the first Anti-Slavery Convention of American Women, meeting in New York City, approved Angelina Grimké's motion that "as certain rights and duties are common to all moral beings, the time has come for woman to move in that sphere which Providence has assigned her, and no longer remain satisfied in the circumscribed limits with which corrupt custom and a perverted application of Scripture has encircled her." Sarah Grimké's *Letters on the Equality of the Sexes and the Condition of Woman* charged that notions of sexual supremacy and subordination, "creating a distinction which God never made," had spawned "an infinity of evils" and robbed women of the means to perform their Christian mission.

Out of the crusade against slavery was thus born, quite unexpectedly, a crusade for women's rights. As abolition had cleaved the ranks of evangelical Christians, so the "woman question" divided abolitionists. The Grimké controversy foreshadowed the fate of the American Anti-Slavery Society. Soon it would shatter into snarling fragments over the place of women in the movement and other questions of tactics.

No matter where it ended, all reasoning on women's role and women's rights began with the same premise: Americans had it in their power to raise themselves to new heights of happiness and usefulness. It was women's special duty to find and occupy their appointed place, whatever it might be, in the great scheme of national uplift. That same faith in the mutability of American character and American society powered efforts in behavioral tutelage, self-improvement, education, and family government. In their drive to elevate themselves, as in other realms of progressive endeavor, Americans shared an exhilirating sense of possibilities. But again, a nearly universal inspiration gave birth to divisive consequences. As Americans defined their ends and fashioned means to meet them, they uncovered unexpected differences with one another. The urge to improve produced unforeseen and difficult choices.

The Politics of Democracy

If it be true, that the gifts of mind and heart are universally diffused, if the sentiment of truth, justice, love, and
beauty exists in every one, then it follows, as a necessary
consequence, that the common judgment in taste, politics, and religion, is the highest authority on earth, and
the nearest possible approach to an infallible decision. . . .
The world can advance only through the culture of the
moral and intellectual powers of the people. To accomplish this end by means of the people themselves, is the
highest purpose of government. . . . The duty of America
is to secure the culture and the happiness of the masses by
their reliance on themselves.   —George Bancroft, 1835

Let the Banks perish! Let the monopolists be swept from
the board! Let the whole brood of privileged money-
changers give place to the hardy offsprings of commercial freedom, who ask for no protection but equal laws,
and no exemption from the shocks of boundless competition. . . . Now is the time for the complete emancipation
of trade from legislative thralldom. . . .

The same enterprise which freights the ocean with our
products, which breaks our rivers into a thousand eddies
with the revolving wheels of steamboats, which perme-
ates the land with canals, and binds state to state in the
iron embrace of railroads, would be abundantly able to
perform the humble functions of banker, without the aid
of legislative favour, or protection. Enterprise would build
up, and competition would regulate, a better system of
banks than legislation ever can devise. . . .

Let us now test the experiment of freedom.
                        —William Leggett, 1837

Jackson in the White House

Andrew Jackson began his presidency in March 1829 amid a vast uncertainty. His health was fragile, and the death of his wife Rachel days after the election had devastated him. His plans and policies were a mystery. What opponents had said in the campaign was true: Jackson had little experience of statecraft, and no one could be sure he knew what he was doing. His first official act, the selection of a cabinet, was unnerving even to his friends. Past presidents had surrounded themselves with eminent statesmen. The cabinets of James Monroe and John Quincy Adams had featured men of presidential caliber. Jackson filled his with nonentities. Secretary of State Martin Van Buren of New York was the only name of distinction.

Jackson's personal favorite in the cabinet, Secretary of War John Henry Eaton of Tennessee, an old friend and campaign biographer, made things worse by touching off a Washington social scandal. Two months before the inauguration he wed Peggy O'Neill Timberlake, a young widow of loose reputation. Her first husband, a naval officer, had died mysteriously abroad, reportedly by suicide in despair over Peggy's wanderings. Half Jackson's cabinet conspicuously snubbed Mrs. Eaton. To Jackson's mortification, so did his nephew and niece, who were serving the president as private secretary and White House hostess. Still in mourning himself, Jackson likened the gossip swirling around Peggy Eaton to old slanders that had dogged his beloved Rachel and, he believed, hastened her death. Jackson made it a point of honor to uphold feminine virtue and his wife's memory by defending Mrs. Eaton. His obsession with vindicating her split his administration before it fairly began.

Jackson's secondary appointments were even more disquieting than his cabinet. Many were partisan newspaper editors—John Quincy Adams called them "electioneering skunks"—of dubious character. Against all advice, Jackson named adventurer Samuel Swartwout to head the New York customhouse, where the federal government collected half its revenue. Swartwout later absconded with more than a million dollars. Even more shocking was the appointment of Henry Lee (Robert E. Lee's elder half-brother) to a diplomatic post. Lee was a scribbling sycophant who had outraged proper Virginians by impregnating his wife's sister. A congressman gasped at Jackson's choices:

Lee — — — — — — !!
Eaton—with Mrs Timberlake

> Berrien [attorney general], who married a vulgar woman for her money &
>   always after used her, as a child bearing machine only 'till she died.
> Branch [Navy secretary]—Oh Lord! O h L o r d

It took Jackson two years to cleanse his cabinet and shake loose of
the paralyzing Eaton scandal. But in the meantime he set out, remarkably
straightforwardly under the circumstances, to carve out a line of administration policy.

Jackson and the American System

The most urgent question facing Jackson was the fate of the American System. Friends of the tariff and internal improvements, Jacksonians
among them, expected the new president to sustain the policy. Most southerners demanded its overthrow. South Carolina, once a bastion of economic nationalism, had by now swung to the opposite extreme. Just as
Jackson was elected in 1828, the state legislature published an *Exposition
and Protest* against the "unconstitutional, oppressive, and unjust" protective tariff. Secretly authored by Vice President John C. Calhoun, the
exposition argued the right of a sovereign state to declare null and void
any federal law that the state deemed unconstitutional. Calhoun conceived
nullification as a peaceable check upon the national government's abuse
of its powers. But his doctrine invited naked state defiance of federal authority, leading perhaps to secession (the withdrawal of the state from the
Union) and even civil war.

To complicate matters, a new controversy over federal land policy had
emerged in the 1828 campaign. Americans regarded the vast, seemingly
illimitable, stretches of western domain as a kind of national birthright,
an assurance of propertied independence for all citizens. But just as with
the tariff and internal improvements, this unifying vision had fragmented
during the 1820s into sectional variants. Residents of western states and
territories saw the lands as most valuable for the population they could
attract. They wanted the government to lower its asking price from $1.25
per acre, or even give the land away, to spur emigration and hasten the
transfer of idle public property to productive private hands.

Few people in the older states thought westward migration needed more
encouragement than it already received. The present land price, when
added to federal action to remove the Indians, guard the settlements, and
open communications, furnished incentive enough. Beyond that, eastern

politicians eyed the proceeds from land sales as a means to pay the federal debt and perhaps to fund schools, internal improvements, and other good works. From this point of view it was less important to unload the lands quickly than to get a decent return for them. John Quincy Adams preferred to husband the domain as a capital resource, a national endowment for perpetual improvement. Western Jacksonians made Adams's policy a point of attack in the 1828 campaign. They expected the new president to take their side.

A Senate debate that erupted soon after Congress convened in late 1829 dramatized the choices and the dangers lurking ahead. It began over land policy, with Jacksonian Thomas Hart Benton of Missouri accusing self-ish Yankees of trying "to check the growth, and to injure the prosperity of the West" by upholding current prices. Robert Hayne of South Carolina chimed in to espouse nullification and denounce the protective tariff, a measure of "grievous oppression" that would "soon involve the whole South in irretrievable ruin." Benton and Hayne intimated that South and West might combine for cheap land and a lower tariff. Daniel Webster of Massachusetts rose to break the project up. In a stirring speech Webster repelled the attacks on New England, defended the tariff and internal improvements, savaged nullification, and closed with a ringing hosanna to "Liberty *and* Union, now and forever, one and inseparable!"

Webster's peroration warmed patriotic hearts. But the overall tone of the debate was anything but reassuring to friends of harmony and union. Together the combatants vented an extraordinary accumulation of sectional ill will. Recriminations flew between East and West, North and South, free state and slave state. The Webster-Hayne debate exposed a bitter irony. The competitive scramble among regions to secure developmental resources of population and capital was visibly threatening to tear the country apart. Architects of the tariff and internal improvements had expected to submerge local interests and jealousies in the grand march of national progress. The reverse was happening. Instead of extinguishing sectionalism, the American System was breeding it.

Andrew Jackson, as ardent a nationalist as anyone in the country, held no truck with South Carolina doctrines. He thought it unpatriotic, even treasonable, to rank state interests above the welfare of the country as a whole. At a political dinner in 1830 he pronounced his ban on nullification by staring at Calhoun and toasting, "Our federal Union: *It must be preserved.*"

Yet Jackson was reconsidering his own assumptions. Previously he had touted the tariff and internal improvements as tools of national defense and prosperity. "It is time we should become a little more *Americanized,*" he urged in an 1824 campaign letter that nearly equated protectionism with patriotism. But his observations of the Adams administration shook Jackson's faith in Congress's ability to allocate resources honestly and evenhandedly. In place of high-minded statesmanship he saw only electioneering and horse-trading. Convinced that government had fallen into corruption and profligacy, Jackson was determined to restore its purity by returning to principles of economy and simplicity. He began with no plan in mind. Moving with events, he altered his stance frequently to suit circumstances. But over the four years of his first term, advancing by degrees, working sometimes with Congress and sometimes against it, he proceeded to dismantle the American System.

First to fall were internal improvements. A bill to purchase stock in Kentucky's Maysville Road company reached Jackson's desk in his first congressional session in 1830. It encapsulated all his misgivings, political and constitutional, about the policy. The road ran within a single state, and Henry Clay's home state at that. The bill pledged public funds to a private undertaking, and by precedent opened the door to unlimited expenditure on projects of all sorts—"a scramble for appropriations that have no relation to any general system of improvement, and whose good effects must of necessity be very limited." Jackson vetoed the bill, followed by three others. In a follow-up message he urged Congress to "establish some fixed general principle" for internal improvement that would "afford the least ground for sectional discontent." The vetoes halted direct subsidies and land grants for roads and canals.

Jackson clung longer to the tariff. He preached moderation and the reduction of unnecessary rates. But still he held to the principle of levying duties for protection even if the income was needed for no other purpose, a position anathema to southerners. Where both sides in the American System debate had linked tariff receipts to internal improvement spending, Jackson sought to disengage the two. He accepted a permanent revenue surplus as a likely consequence of protection. "As long as the encouragement of domestic manufactures is directed to national ends it shall receive from me a temperate but steady support," he avowed in the Maysville Road veto. "There is no necessary connection between it and the system of appropriations." In lieu of congressional spending, Jackson proposed distributing surplus federal funds to the states. This compromise satisfied neither road and canal men, who wanted direct aid, nor southerners, who feared it would put off tariff reduction forever.

So far Jackson stood midway between friends and foes of the American System. Events soon compelled a further retreat. By 1831 nullification was rumbling in South Carolina and the national debt was nearly paid off. With a revenue surplus looming, Jackson quietly pulled back from protection, calling for "a reduction of our revenue to the wants of the Government" and relief from all "unnecessary taxation."

Jackson's turn against the tariff was in part a tactical move to undercut southern hotheads by quashing their main grievance. But it also bespoke his growing distrust of government. Jackson, no less than John Quincy Adams, was an enthusiast of national achievement. His messages gloried in the country's situation and prospects—"the extent of its territory, its increasing and happy population, its advance in arts which render life agreeable, and the sciences which elevate the mind!" The United States was the nursery of education, the asylum of the oppressed, the very "picture of happiness and honor." But Jackson traced these results less to sound leadership than to a sound citizenry. Ultimately he looked to the people rather than the government to provide the mainsprings of progress. As he announced in 1830, "the obvious and increasing improvement of all classes of our fellow-citizens in intelligence and in public and private virtue," proved "the great truth that the resources of the nation beyond those required for immediate and necessary purposes of Government can nowhere be so well deposited as in the pockets of the people."

Viewing union itself as the one prerequisite of American destiny, Jackson at bottom cared more for sectional conciliation than for any course of developmental policy. He also suspected, probably correctly, that in their excitement the tariff combatants were overstating both its benefit to manufacturers and its harm to southern planters. His detachment from the issue gave Jackson a useful freedom to maneuver.

In 1832 the awaited crisis of federal authority erupted in the South. Congress lowered some tariff rates in July, but without relinquishing protection. Concluding that hope of further relief was "irrevocably gone," South Carolinians rushed toward confrontation. In November a state convention adopted an Ordinance of Nullification pronouncing the tariff unconstitutional, "null, void, and no law," and forbidding the collection of duties within the state. Jackson, true to his nationalism, answered with a proclamation affirming the supremacy of the federal government and the constitutionality of the tariff. Nullification, he warned, meant substantive disunion, and "disunion by armed force is *treason*."

South Carolina's defiance and Jackson's determination appeared to presage civil war. But behind their public belligerence the parties left leeway for an accommodation they both preferred: a further amelioration of the tariff. In the Senate Henry Clay, looking to save what he could of protection, and John C. Calhoun, desperate to avoid bloodshed at home, united on a compromise. Their bill passed Congress and received Jackson's signature in March 1833. It provided a gradual lowering of rates over the next nine years. The anomalous alliance of Clay and Calhoun, who had taken opposite stances on the American System but were both hated enemies of Jackson, forecast a new political combination against the president. Jackson, ironically, would have welcomed even greater tariff concessions. Still, he accepted the result with equanimity. The tariff issue was stilled, and the Union preserved.

Less obviously, the Compromise of 1833 also resolved the last of the sectional economic issues, the public lands. Road and canal proponents had answered Jackson's internal improvement vetoes by turning to the proceeds from land sales as an alternate source of funds. In 1832 Henry Clay produced a bill to distribute federal land revenues to the states for internal improvement, schools, and colonization of free blacks. While it surrendered central control over the spending, Clay's bill was an effort to salvage something of the grand Adams policy of national improvement by national means. By vesting every state with a stake in the land fund, it was also meant to thwart western calls to reduce prices or surrender the lands outright to the states where they lay.

Jackson countered by embracing the western position. "The speedy settlement of these lands constitutes the true interest of the Republic," he announced in December 1832. To quell sectional jealousies and give "every American citizen of enterprise the opportunity of securing an independent freehold," Jackson advised Congress to cut prices to a minimum and "abandon the idea of raising a future revenue out of the public lands."

Jackson's new land policy melded with his broader theme of releasing developmental resources from the government to the people. Still, Congress passed Clay's distribution bill together with the tariff of 1833, as part of what Clay and Calhoun hoped would be a general sectional pacification. Jackson pocket-vetoed it. For the rest of his presidency and some years after, Jackson's and Clay's land proposals stymied each other, leaving the existing system to continue by default.

Jackson's Philosophy

The defusing of sectional crisis in 1833 marked the end of a distinct phase in federal relations. The tariff issue, touchstone of controversy for a decade, was silenced. Later the contentious triad of tariff, internal improvement, and land policies would revive, but never with the same urgency or in the same sectional garb. Though legislators continued to fight over the distribution of federal largesse, the American System as John Quincy Adams and Henry Clay had once conceived it—a master plan of development toward a series of defined national objectives—was stricken beyond recovery.

Adams's dream of a "permanent and regular system" of development "by National means and National energies" had not only failed. It was becoming irrelevant. Adams had essentially underrated the country's capacities. As late as 1837, seemingly blind to the canals and railroads multiplying on every hand, he was still bewailing the "limping gait" of internal improvement by state and private means. By the time Andrew Jackson laid the axe to the American System, the development of manufactures, the opening of transportation routes, and the settling of the West had already escaped from federal control. The spread of resources and the seizure of initiative by citizens and local governments made central direction not only unnecessary but pointless.

That was just as Andrew Jackson wanted it. Jackson's aspirations were, in their own way, as expansive as Adams's. But where Adams premised his plans on concentrating developmental energies, Jackson based his on their release. At the root of both men's political economy was their faith in the progressive potential of a republican polity. Adams thought the voluntary efforts of a free and enlightened citizenry, harnessed through the agency of government, could vault the United States past all rivals in the race for economic, intellectual, and moral improvement. Jackson, by contrast, came to see the operations of authority as crippling, not enlivening, the talents of the people. In his view republican government would prove its worth not by corralling the participation of citizens, but—for the first time in history— by standing well out of their way. Beginning with similar convictions and looking toward much the same future, Adams and Jackson reached opposite conceptions of the federal role in realizing it. Adams believed that only public power, properly employed, could fulfill the people's capacities. Jackson saw federal agency not as nurturing energies and morals, but sapping them. Adams wanted to guide Americans to progress. Jackson expected them to find their own way.

Central to Jackson's distrust of government was his suspicion, confirmed by observation of the American System under Adams, that its promotional powers never had been and never could be deployed fairly. The well-born, well-connected, and well-to-do would always be able to bend general measures to serve their interests. Hence no matter how high-minded the intent, government's exercise of distributive functions was inevitably unequal and unjust. Instead of fostering enterprise and a spirit of independence, public patronage bred privilege, dependence, and corruption.

Better, then, to abjure developmental powers altogether than to see them subserve, as they always did, the interests of the privileged against the unprivileged, the few against the many. "The World is Governed Too Much," proclaimed the Washington *Globe,* Jackson's journalistic mouthpiece. Government's "true strength," said Jackson in 1832, "consists in leaving individuals and States as much as possible to themselves." It was best to surrender all interference in the affairs of business, and confine government to the bare protection of lives and property and of national honor and interest abroad.

Jackson's call for lower tariffs and land prices, his attack on federal internal improvements, and his enthusiasm, which became nearly an obsession, for paying off the national debt all reflected his urge to disengage the workings of government from the enterprise of the country. So did his personnel policies. Jackson's wholesale replacement of high-ranking federal bureaucrats served some pointed political ends. But it also bespoke his conviction that government employment, if held for long, corrupted those who held it, turning public service into a shield for private gain. "Office is considered as a species of property, and government rather as a means of promoting individual interests than as an instrument created solely for the service of the people," he complained to Congress. Believing that "the duties of all public officers are, or at least admit of being made, so plain and simple that men of intelligence may readily qualify themselves for their performance," Jackson saw frequent turnover as a way to prevent government from becoming "an engine for the support of the few at the expense of the many."

Jackson and the Bank of the United States

The evolution of Jackson's ideas showed most clearly in the issue that came to define the philosophy of his administration—his war against the Bank of the United States.

Under presidents Langdon Cheves and Nicholas Biddle the Bank recouped its power and rebuilt its image in the decade after the Panic of 1819. By Jackson's inaugural it had become an institution of enormous weight, the only truly national financial entity in the country. Its branches scattered through the states, its millions in capital, and its unique public duties and privileges towered the Bank over the state banks with whom it did business and sometimes competed. The Bank wielded more financial leverage than the national government itself. Indeed, in some measure it governed the government—managing its funds, paying its debts, and providing its currency. Deploying their powers discreetly and with careful political neutrality, Cheves and Biddle succeeded in raising the Bank from public disgrace to a position of unquestioned integrity and acknowledged indispensability. One could not touch the Bank without shaking the nation's credit and commerce, its very system of value and exchange, to their foundations.

Jackson assailed the Bank almost from the moment he took office. Arousing astonishment and consternation even among his friends, he challenged its legitimacy in his first message to Congress in 1829 and renewed the attack the next two years. The Bank's congressional charter was due to expire in 1836. Jackson's assaults goaded Bank president Biddle into seeking an early renewal in 1832, while Jackson was standing for re-election to a second term. Henry Clay, the opposing presidential candidate, guided a recharter bill through Congress. It passed in July, months before the election. Jackson vetoed it.

Jackson's veto message proclaimed the core of his grievance against the Bank: though performing public functions, it was a privately owned and managed profit-making institution. While defenders pointed to its faithful discharge of duty, Jackson stressed the advantages Bank stockholders reaped from their official connection. The conjoining of public and private purposes was inherently corrupting. "Grants of monopolies and exclusive privileges" prostituted government "to the advancement of the few at the expense of the many." Government could never aid all equally. So its true policy was to stand aside:

It is to be regretted that the rich and powerful too often bend the acts of government to their selfish purposes. Distinctions in society will always exist under every just government. Equality of talents, of education, or of wealth can not be produced by human institutions. In the full enjoyment of the gifts of Heaven and the fruits of superior industry, economy, and virtue, every man is equally entitled to protection by law; but when the laws undertake to add to these natural and just advantages artificial distinctions, to grant titles, gratuities, and exclusive privileges, to make the rich richer and the potent more powerful, the humble members of society— the farmers, mechanics, and laborers—who have neither the time nor the means of securing like favors to themselves, have a right to complain of the injustice of their Government.

Jackson's veto was like no state paper before. Slashing and contentious, it struck some horrified readers as an invitation to class war. Jackson had always deplored sectionalism, disparaging talk of oppression and preaching the harmony of interests. Yet here he seemed to promote a new and uniquely frightening kind of divisiveness. No president had publicly arrayed the many against the few, the poor against the rich. To some, Jackson's reckless stirring of resentments signified the end of republican discourse, the descent of democracy into demagoguery. "It is really a manifesto of anarchy—such as Marat or Robespierre might have issued to the mob of the faubourgh St. Antoine," fumed Nicholas Biddle. Abandoning neutrality, Biddle distributed thousands of copies of the veto, thinking it would aid Henry Clay's presidential bid.

Biddle misjudged. It was true that much of Jackson's argument was contemptible to anyone versed in finance. Jackson railed against British ownership of Bank stock as a threat to national autonomy. But the charter banned foreign stockholders from voting their shares. On any rational ground their investment in the undercapitalized American economy was to be welcomed, not scorned.

But the veto's strength lay in its symbolism, not its logic. Jackson made the Bank of the United States a metaphor for elitist privilege and illicit power in all their forms. It was indeed a manifesto—but of democracy, not of anarchy. The message enthralled dissidents and outsiders in business, politics, and religion. It became a totem for all who chafed under the rule of "aristocracy."

Jackson defeated Clay handily in the 1832 election. The Bank of the United States was the main issue, and Jackson read his victory as a referendum on its fate. Its emergence as an overt political antagonist, "a vast electioneering engine," merely confirmed what he had decided long before:

the Bank was innately illegitimate, irredeemably corrupt. A corporation, endowed with power by the people's representatives to serve their needs, was instead deploying that power, along with the people's money, to perjure the political process and defy their will. Jackson now framed the Bank question as one of the very continuance of republican rule: "whether the people of the United States are to govern through representatives chosen by their unbiased suffrages or whether the money and power of a great corporation are to be secretly exerted to influence their judgment and control their decision."

Though rebuffed in its bid for recharter, the Bank was still alive and still powerful. As soon as the election and the South Carolina nullification crisis passed, Jackson moved to sever all ties between the government and the Bank for the three years left under its present charter. In late 1833 he began shifting federal funds on deposit in the Bank of the United States to state-chartered banks selected, in part, for their friendliness to his administration.

In removing the deposits Jackson defied the counsel of two-thirds of the House of Representatives and nearly all his own cabinet. Coming on top of his frequent vetoes, Jackson's action roused fears of executive tyranny. It was "the most flagrant usurpation of power which has ever been attempted in our country," raged New York merchant Philip Hone. In the mindless street cries of "hatred to the moneyed aristocracy! HURRAH FOR JACKSON! JACKSON FOREVER!" French visitor Michel Chevalier saw signs of an incipient *"reign of terror."* Henry Clay warned that "we are in the midst of a revolution, hitherto bloodless, but rapidly tending toward a total change of the pure republican character of the government, and to the concentration of all power in the hands of one man." At Clay's instigation the United States Senate passed an unprecedented censure on Jackson, declaring he had "assumed upon himself authority and power not conferred by the Constitution and laws, but in derogation of both."

Critics charged Jackson with recklessly endangering the nation's currency and credit. The Bank of the United States was a proven, responsible agent, authorized and regulated by law. The state banks were unsanctioned, untried, and unregulated. Even Jackson deemed their use an "experiment." He put the deposits there because he had nowhere else. Jackson's own logic pointed toward severing public finance from any private institution. He had already proposed a government bank as a branch of the Treasury, with no charter, no stockholders, no power to make loans or hold property, and thus "no means to operate on the hopes, fears, or interests of large masses of the community." But the route to this goal proved long and tortuous. In the interim Jackson made do with state banks.

The removal of deposits prompted Bank president Biddle to retaliate. Still hoping to force a recharter, he curtailed loans, causing a sharp business downturn over the winter of 1833–1834. While the Bank's friends blamed Jackson, the president and his supporters read Biddle's action as further proof of the Bank's unwarrantable power. Failing in Congress, Biddle relented, and the transition to state banking proceeded more smoothly. In 1836 the Bank's federal charter quietly expired, and it converted to a state bank with a Pennsylvania charter. But its demise coincided with an ominous disordering of the currency, now consisting entirely of state-bank notes.

While Jackson warred with the Bank of the United States, state legislatures had busily chartered banks, doubling their number from 1830 to 1835. Now freed from restraint, and with plentiful assets on which to loan in the form of government deposits, state banks issued an abundance of paper. Together the ready currency, rising exports, and momentum from years of prosperity floated a wave of expansion in the mid-1830s. From 1833 to 1836 cotton exports doubled in value. Farmers, planters, and businessmen borrowed to buy land, slaves, and equipment. States and companies embarked on ambitious, loosely financed road and canal projects. Frenzied trading sent the price of city lots and the volume of western land sales to new heights. Fortunes were made and multiplied.

To appearances, the country had never thrived so well. But by 1836 the rise was beginning to spin out of control. Some saw symptoms of a speculative cycle and predicted a bad end. Wage-earners and credit-seeking businessmen felt the pressure of higher prices and interest rates. Doomsayers warned of inflated values caused by "overtrading." Fears of an imminent, perhaps catastrophic collapse gathered over Jackson's last days as president.

The War Against Privilege

That all this came to pass under the administration, and seemingly in response to the policies, of a president who avowed his hatred for banks and speculation and paper money was an irony more noticed by Jackson's critics than by himself. Jackson's fixation on killing the Bank of the

United States at whatever cost inspired hysterical denunciation from his foes. Those who treasured the Bank's stabilizing influence attributed all the monetary gyrations of Jackson's second term—the squeeze of 1833–34, the inflationary spiral that followed, and the devastating panic that finally broke just as he retired in the spring of 1837—to the reckless tampering of this vindictive, foolhardy, power-mad president.

Jackson's adherents disagreed. Seeing the Bank's power as illegitimate, they found his challenge exhilarating. Where opponents condemned his obstinacy, supporters applauded his firmness. To Jackson and his followers, the unsettled finances of the 1830s merely proved the danger of the "money power." In struggling against it they broadened his special grievance against the Bank of the United States into a critique of the existing business system. The attack on the Bank became the vehicle for promulgating an alternative vision of American enterprise.

Jacksonians came to view all chartered corporations, whether state or federal, as creatures of privilege. "They are *not* for the public good—in design or end," complained a typical editorial. "They are for the aggrandizement of the stockholders—for the promotion of the interests of the *few*." Jackson's Farewell Address, published on his retirement from the presidency in 1837, warned of the secret power wielded by "great money corporations" over the real working people of the country, "the planter, the farmer, the mechanic, and the laborer." Jackson now assailed the tariff and internal improvements not as weapons of sectional oppression but as tools of corruption, by which incorporated interests picked the pockets of the people.

Of course the most pernicious corporations were banks. Of all exclusive privileges the most valuable and vicious was the power to issue banknotes. Not by superior industry or virtue but by sheer legislative prerogative—purchased, often as not, by sordid means—bankers endowed their notes with the authority of money. Control of credit and currency gave mastery of the people's earnings and savings, their livelihoods, their very existence to a handful of corruptionists. The power of bankers imperiled more than prosperity. It threatened the moral fiber of the republic.

Jackson saw all banknotes as intrinsically suspect, and note issue itself as little more than legalized fraud. He blamed the instability and underlying worthlessness of paper currency for the business upheavals of the 1830s. "Having of itself no intrinsic value," paper money was "liable to great and sudden fluctuations." Its dips and thrusts, while providing foul profit to insiders, spawned a multitude of evils: ruinous credit contractions, fluctuations in wages, surges of speculation. The remedy for all this was to return to the sound constitutional currency of gold and silver coin. To begin this cure, and to curb speculation in western lands, Jackson late in his term issued a "specie circular" decreeing that only coin would be accepted at federal land offices.

Though his opponents believed otherwise, Jackson was no enemy to commerce or manufacturing. Over and over he sang the praises of American enterprise. He surrounded himself with successful entrepreneurs in business and politics; his foreign policy sought the widest field for American trade. But like many Americans he distinguished between productive, useful activity—"the sober pursuits of honest industry"—and wanton, destructive speculation. The moral line he drew between legitimate and illegitimate business and his identification of the latter with banking fed the distrust of easily acquired wealth that lingered from the Panic of 1819. Like critics from John Taylor to the Workingmen, Jackson posited a two-class society: producers on one side, parasites and papermongers on the other.

Jackson's singular achievement was to join a democratizing economic vision to the populist political tide that first swept him into office. His war on the Bank of the United States let loose a spirited, wide-ranging debate on commerce and credit. In the course of it Jackson and his publicists built a political party and developed a unifying philosophy and program. Calling themselves the Democracy, they denounced "aristocracy" and declaimed against privilege in all its forms. They branded their antagonists as guardians of exclusivity and elitism in business and social relations as well as politics.

Jackson's opponents read his railings against banks and corporations and "the rich" as attacks on property itself. They derided assaults on monopoly and the moneyed aristocracy as arrant demagoguery, and warned of "commercial anarchy" if Democratic nostrums prevailed. In fact, commercial anarchy was very close to what the most consistent and extreme Jacksonian theorists—such as editors William Gouge and William Leggett—wanted. Shouting "the glorious principle of equal rights," they demanded as perfect a freedom in commerce as in politics and religion. They attacked all governmental interventions, whether promotional or regulatory, as instruments of favoritism, shackles on the spirit of enterprise, and interferences with the rule of supply and demand.

Gouge and Leggett talked of throwing open every field of endeavor, including banking and even the coining of money and delivery of mail, to "universal enterprise and competition." Their position was radical, though not in the way opponents perceived. Jacksonians were no levelers. The equality they championed was of initiative. "They are the best friends of property and of men of property who would abolish every unequal and unrighteous means of acquiring it," explained Democrat Theodore Sedgwick. "It is those unequal and unrighteous modes of acquiring it which stimulate the jealousy and arouse the indignation of the less fortunate classes." Democrats did not seek equality of property. Yet they believed that great concentrations of wealth resulted from artificial, not natural, advantages. Banishing special privilege and putting everyone on the same footing of opportunity would produce an economic order both more just and more equal.

Jacksonian ideologues dreamed of a commercial revolution to replace abundance for the few and oppression for the many with competence and independence for all. They espoused a liberty of enterprise that in their minds was the counterpart of liberty of opinion and belief. Their faith in perfect freedom was as simple and intoxicating as John Quincy Adams's faith in perfect guidance. They believed "the operations of nature" would produce an economic order more sound and fair and in the end more prosperous for all than anything policy could devise. Left alone, the natural workings of people's own impulses would magnify true wealth, banish distress, remedy all injustice. Shorn of corrupting government interference, "sound credit will take the place of unsound, and legitimate enterprise the place of wild speculation." Legislation would be purified, "the moral and intellectual character of the people" elevated; and "the operation of the natural and just causes of wealth and poverty," by which riches become "the reward of industry, frugality, skill, prudence, and enterprise; and poverty the punishment of few except the indolent and prodigal," again restored.

As Democrats organized, they carried Jackson's war on monopoly and aristocracy from Washington to the states. They attacked legislative privilege, agitating for the abolition of banks and chartered corporations or, by the same egalitarian logic, for general incorporation laws to throw open the chance of associated enterprise to all comers.

Jacksonian Jurisprudence

In 1835 the Jacksonian revolution reached the United States Supreme Court. Chief Justice John Marshall died, and in his place Jackson appointed Roger Taney of Maryland. As attorney general, Taney, alone among Jackson's cabinet, had urged the removal of federal deposits from the Bank of the United States. As Treasury secretary, he had executed it. Later, while chief justice, he drafted Jackson's political testament, his Farewell Address of 1837. Taney stood closer to the ideological heart of Jacksonianism than anyone save Jackson himself. His first major decision on the Court, in *Charles River Bridge v. Warren Bridge,* embodied the Democracy's version of the creed of progress.

In 1785 the Massachusetts legislature chartered a company to build a toll bridge across the Charles River from Boston to Charlestown. Replacing an unreliable ferry, the bridge opened a vital route to Boston's northern hinterland. Over the years it also yielded a fortune to company stockholders. The charter, extended in 1792, was to run seventy years. But in 1828 complaints of overcrowding and high tolls induced the legislature, on grounds of "public convenience and necessity," to charter a parallel, competing Warren Bridge. Projectors looked for a return in commerce, not tolls. Their charter provided that once expenses were recouped, and in any event after six years, the Warren Bridge would revert to the state and become free.

An adjacent free bridge would make the Charles River stock worthless. Claiming that their franchise was meant to be exclusive and that the new bridge abrogated their rights, the old bridge proprietors sued in state, then federal, court. In the Supreme Court, where the case arrived in 1831, Marshall and his associates found the balance of right and precedent so fine they could not reach consensus. The Dartmouth College case of 1819 established the inviolability of charter rights. But subsequent decisions, including some written by Marshall, had narrowed that ruling. No words in the Charles River charter prohibited a competing bridge. Certainly the charter was not meant to be valueless. Yet the company had already reaped forty years of monopoly profits. Could it claim them for thirty more, at whatever cost and inconvenience to the community?

In 1837 the Court, with Taney now sitting at its head, ruled for the new Warren Bridge. Taney rejected the claim of an implied exclusivity in the old company's charter. In interpreting unstated rights the interest of the community must be weighed with that of the stockholders, and the community's interest was clearly for innovation and competition and against monopoly. "In a country like ours, free, active and enterprising, continually advancing in numbers and wealth, new channels of communication are daily found necessary, both for travel and trade, and are essential to the comfort, convenience and prosperity of the people." Taney warned that reading monopoly rights into charters would pervert the state's power to promote progress into a company's power to stop it. Railroads and canals would come to a halt;

we shall be thrown back to the improvements of the last century, and obliged to stand still until the claims of the old turnpike corporations shall be satisfied, and they shall consent to permit these States to avail themselves of the lights of modern science, and to partake of the benefit of those improvements which are now adding to the wealth and prosperity, and the convenience and comfort, of every other part of the civilized world.

The *Charles River* case marked the demise of the Marshall Court's consensual mode of adjudicating. The majority behind Taney consisted entirely of Jackson appointees. Holdover justice Joseph Story, who dissented vigorously, and Daniel Webster, who had argued the case for the old bridge, were appalled. "A case of grosser injustice, or more oppressive legislation, never existed," Story wailed. Public comment on the case reflected the growing influence of partisanship. Reading Taney's judicial doctrines in light of their fears, Jackson's opponents greeted the decision as signifying the end of property rights, and the end of the world. Democrats hailed it as a triumph of popular justice over monopoly and "aristocracy."

Behind the rhetoric the case revealed as much commonality as distance between Jacksonians and their foes. There was no question here of the sanctity of property, which Taney as much as anyone believed must be "sacredly guarded," nor of the duty to provide an encouraging environment for development. Taney could never outdo Story himself in championing commerce and enterprise. At issue was not whether there should be progress, but how to procure it. On one side was the old policy of inviting innovation by safeguarding investors' privileges and prerogatives; on the other, the new idea that to stimulate improvement one should throw the field open and leave the energies of entrepreneurs and the workings of competition to do the rest. Which way did community benefit lie? Did adventurers deserve reward, or merely a chance at success? Were goals best defined by law, or by the law of supply and demand? Like John Quincy Adams and Andrew Jackson, the Court faced a future that could be either directed or directionless, structured or chaotic. On one side were order, safety, and, said Jacksonians, "aristocracy." On the other side were democratic disorder and risk. Led by Taney, the Court leaned to the latter.

Jackson and the Evangelicals

The Democracy's attack on authority broadened from politics and commerce to morals and religion. Here, as in the Bank War, Jackson and his party developed a principle out of what started as personal predilections. Jackson began his presidency as no foe of Christian crusaders. Though not a church member he was a deeply religious man, made more so by the death of his devout wife. Despite his violent past some champions of public morality, like the Reverend Ezra Stiles Ely, author of the call for a "Christian party in politics," actually expected more by way of example and encouragement from the Presbyterian Jackson than from Unitarian John Quincy Adams.

The Eaton affair early in his administration helped turn Jackson against self-anointed guardians of Christian virtue. Two Presbyterian divines, Reverend John N. Campbell of Jackson's Washington church and Ely himself in Philadelphia, led the drive to oust Peggy Eaton from Washington society and her husband John from Jackson's confidence. They spread tales of Mrs. Eaton's promiscuity and dared to invoke the authority of Jackson's sainted Rachel for their veracity. Jackson was furious at the unchristian "defamation and slander" that tarnished Peggy's reputation and his own wife's memory. At an emergency cabinet meeting he shouted his pastor down, then quit Campbell's church in disgust. The attempt to coerce him left Jackson deeply embittered at the arrogance and hypocrisy of meddling clerics.

It also buttressed a sense of personal grievance he had long nursed against the standards and exemplars of cosmopolitan culture. Despite his urbane manners and acquired wealth, Jackson's background was rough-and-tumble. He had fought duels and brawls. He spoke no foreign languages, had never been abroad. His parents were poor and unlearned. Sophisticates like John Quincy Adams and Nicholas Biddle ridiculed Jackson's thin schooling and bad grammar. Moralists scorned his reckless past and the hazy legality of his marriage to Rachel, who when they wed was estranged, but not divorced, from a previous husband. Jackson knew all this and resented it. A congressional effort in 1819 to censure his campaign against Spanish Florida and his exclusion from the presidency in 1824 fed his anger at the political establishment. Jackson saw his election in 1828 as a triumph of the plain people over the aristocrats. He came to Washington believing that a clique of insiders had leagued themselves against him and the common citizens of the country.

Feeling himself an outsider and a challenger, Jackson cast himself as the champion of such. His sense of alienation from the best circles lent force to his denunciations of privilege. It underlay his purge of federal officeholders, whom he believed had conspired against his election. In the Bank War it fed his rage at Nicholas Biddle as an emblem of perfumed arrogance. The wielding of clerical influence against Peggy Eaton prompted Jackson to add paraders of Christian righteousness to his growing list of adversaries.

Jackson and the Indians

The debate over Indian policy cemented Jackson's view. Emerging as the great moral issue of his administration, it arrayed him openly against the weight of organized Christian benevolence. When Jackson took office federal Indian relations were snarled with historical and legal contradictions, reflecting white Americans' ambivalent feelings toward the original inhabitants of the soil. Officially the tribes were treated both as sovereign nationalities and as dependent peoples. They were encouraged both to assimilate into white society and to remove westward out of its way. Whites alternately welcomed and mourned the dwindling of Indian numbers and the disintegration of tribal integrity. Accepting without question the superiority of their own civilization and the inevitability of its advance, they remained unsure whether the fate decreed to the Indians by the inexorable law of progress was absorption or extinction.

The anomalies and confusions of federal Indian policy fostered conflicting expectations, pulling state, federal, and tribal governments toward confrontation with each other. In the 1820s the last large landholding tribes east of the Mississippi, the Cherokees, Creeks, Chickasaws, and Choctaws of Georgia, Alabama, and Mississippi, dug in their heels against removal to the west or submission to state authority. Pointing to their progress in acculturation and to the government's treaty guarantees, they called for federal protection against the incursions of white trespassers on their land and of southern states upon their sovereignty.

The Adams administration backed the tribes while trying to break the knot by negotiating terms for their removal. Its efforts failed, and the states prepared to take over tribal lands and impose their law on the Indians by force if necessary. A direct clash of federal and state power was forestalled only by southern whites' expectation that the new president, unlike the old, would take their side.

They were correct. Jackson introduced no new precepts but a distinct shift of emphasis. Seeing Indians as children in need of governance, he cast himself as a stern but solicitous father. This patronizing stance suited precedent as well as Jackson's temperament. But he also brought to Indian relations an urgency no previous president had shared. Jackson's memory of wars against Indians allied with the Spanish and British, his hunger for expansion, and his own residence in the southwest all led him to feel the grievance of stymied state governments and land-hungry frontiersmen more than the plight of threatened tribes. Jackson found the idea of an Indian sovereignty within state bounds unacceptable. In his first message to Congress he repudiated it outright. Jackson's predecessors, though believing Indian removal inevitable, had let time and circumstance control its pace. Jackson was eager to force the issue. And while he observed the custom of treating with the Indians as if they were separate nations, he would not let it stand in his way.

To speed the Indians' departure Jackson asked Congress to set aside land west of the Mississippi, beyond any state or territory, where the tribes could live as they chose and gradually acquire the arts of civilization in safe quarantine from its abuses. Congress approved the removal bill in May 1830. It was the only major legislation passed at Jackson's behest during his presidency.

Indian removal was so important to Jackson that he conducted the first negotiations in person. Wielding promises of a secure homeland and generous aid on one side, and the threat of abandonment to state authority on the other, he essentially compelled the tribes to submit. Having no real choice, the Choctaws and Chickasaws soon signed removal treaties. The Creeks gave in later and less willingly.

The Cherokees refused altogether. When the state of Georgia seized Cherokee lands and dissolved tribal authority by extending its laws over their territory, the Indians turned to the Supreme Court. In *Cherokee Nation v. Georgia* (1831), Chief Justice Marshall admitted the essential justice of their case. The Cherokees were a nation, with rights of territory confirmed by treaty. But since they were a "dependent domestic nation" instead of a foreign nation, the Court lacked jurisdiction under the Constitution to enforce those rights against Georgia.

Marshall's opinion faced, without resolving, the essential contradiction in the Indians' status: they were simultaneously a separate sovereignty and wards of the United States in a state of "pupilage." A following case, *Worcester v. Georgia* (1832), went further toward judicial protection for the beleaguered Cherokees. Here the Court did strike down a Georgia law regulating passage into the Indian country. "The Cherokee Nation," said Marshall, "is a distinct community" under federal protection "in which the laws of Georgia can have no force."

But this vindication did nothing to solve the Cherokees' predicament. With Jackson's connivance Georgia circumvented the ruling, while both state and federal governments kept pressuring the Indians to leave. Exploiting divisions within the tribe, Jackson signed a removal treaty with a minority faction in 1835. Under this facade of consent the Georgia Cherokees were finally removed, some by armed force.

Jackson was not blind to the moral dimension of the removal issue. The Indians' plight, he told Congress, made "a most powerful appeal to our sympathies," and the way the country treated them would reflect profoundly on "our national character." Jackson believed that removal, even against their wishes, was as necessary to Indian survival as it was to the states' advance "in population, wealth, and power." Tribes that had earlier stood in the path of expanding civilization had not assimilated but disintegrated. Whole Indian peoples had already disappeared without trace. Escorting those who remained to a refuge out of harm's way was humanitarian and more: it was the only real alternative to their destruction. Removal, said Jackson, would preserve the tribes' integrity while buying time for them to "cast off their savage habits and become an interesting, civilized, and Christian community."

Following a policy "not only liberal, but generous," and one pursued in broad measure by his predecessors and indeed all Americans since colonial times, Jackson thought he had "a right to expect the cooperation of Congress and of all good and disinterested men." He did not get it. The removal bill of 1830 inaugurated a searching debate that continued unabated to the end of Jackson's presidency and beyond. More bluntly than any issue of the day save slavery, Indian removal forced Americans to question the meaning of progress.

Apostles of Christian benevolence spearheaded the opposition to Jackson's policies. The American Board of Commissioners for Foreign Missions, the Tappan brothers, and William Lloyd Garrison all rallied behind the Indians. So did missionaries in the field. (It was Georgia's arrest and imprisonment of two missionaries that brought the *Worcester* case before the Supreme Court.) In Congress Senator Theodore Frelinghuysen of New Jersey, prominent in Bible, tract, temperance, and Sunday School causes, led the opponents of the removal bill of 1830.

Critics agreed with Jackson that Indian removal presented a litmus test of American righteousness, and on that ground they condemned it. They saw Jackson's rationalizations as a sophistic cover for naked aggression. Jackson's bribing and browbeating Indians into surrendering their rights and territory made a mockery of negotiation; the treaties he procured by such means disgraced national faith and honor. The fate of the Cherokees proved the hypocrisy of his hopes for Indian civilization. The tribe that had progressed farthest in acculturation to white ways—even to the use of the white legal system—incurred Jackson's deepest enmity and in the end endured the most egregious suffering.

Jackson's drive to remove the Indians quickly and cheaply provided a cover for brutality and chicanery. The transgressions of civil and military officials, settlers, and speculators climaxed in the notorious Creek land frauds under Jackson and the Cherokee "trail of tears" under his successor Martin Van Buren. None of the outrages surprised removal's critics. Jackson himself neither justified nor seemingly noticed the abuse. His messages, touting the "spirit of enlarged liberality" behind removal, implicitly dismissed its flaws as inconsequential. Opponents did not think so. To them the atrocities and depredations were inseparable from the policy's basic injustice and revealing of its fundamental immorality.

At heart Indian removal raised troubling questions of means and ends. Senator John Forsyth of Georgia accused the Cherokees' defenders of trying to "arrest the progress" of his state. They in turn condemned removal as no progress at all, but a regression to barbarism. Seemingly this encounter set interest against principle. Yet Forsyth and Jackson, no less than Frelinghuysen and the missionaries, believed in the unity of material and moral advance. Prosperity and character were linked. A corrupt nation could not flourish. Yet which way lay true justice? Jackson challenged removal's critics to offer an alternative. Taking "a comprehensive view of the general interests of the human race," would they really trade an "extensive republic, studded with cities, towns, and prosperous farms, embellished with all the improvements which art can devise or industry execute, occupied by more than 12,000,000 happy people, and filled with all the blessings of liberty, civilization, and religion" for "a country covered with forests and ranged by a few thousand savages"? If not—and to Jackson the question answered itself—then the opponents of removal were the true hypocrites, enjoying the fruits of progress while shunning acceptance of its costs.

To Jackson this was the key to the issue. As he saw it, removal was a necessary adjunct of progress—as much in the Georgia of his day as in

Massachusetts two hundred years before—and those who failed to perceive or refused to admit this were either fools or knaves. Over and over Jackson compared his benevolent policy to the exterminationist record of early New England, now the home of his deepest critics. In the peculiar constituency of the antiremoval alliance—comprising chiefs and chief justices, paragons of piety and partisans of the card-playing Henry Clay—Jackson saw only political expediency and deep-dyed duplicity. Resistance to his Indian policy confirmed in his mind what the Eaton affair had first suggested: that the union of religion and politics was fatal to the integrity of both.

Jackson and his followers shaped his budding anticlericalism into a principled avowal of the separation of church and state. Richard M. Johnson of Kentucky became a Democratic hero, and later vice president under Van Buren, by his ringing defense of religious freedom against the Sabbatarian campaign to close the Sunday mails. When the Senate, in the midst of a cholera epidemic in 1832, debated asking the president to name a day of fasting and prayer, Jackson prepared a scathing veto. Renouncing a practice begun by Washington and continued by John Adams and James Madison, Jackson declared such proclamations an infringement on constitutional religious liberty.

Party publicists picked up the theme. William Leggett trumpeted *"perfect free trade in religion."* In 1835 the Democrats in national convention lectured abolitionists that "whenever religion leaves its proper home, the heart, to join in the noise and strife of the affairs of State, it is out of its province, and ever sullies its purity." By the end of his presidency, the estrangement between partisans of Andrew Jackson and those who looked for government to procure a more Christian nation was nearly complete.

Jackson's Legacy

In 1837 Henry Clay complained in the Senate that Jackson had "swept over the government, during the last eight years, like a tropical tornado." Indeed he had. Starting almost from nowhere, with ill-formed views and a vaguely defined following, Jackson had almost single-handedly reordered the political landscape. He had disabled the American System and helped quell the threatening controversies over tariffs, internal improvement, and public lands. He had killed the Bank of the United States and destroyed the system of national finance over which it presided. He had cut the government off from those who would shape its policies to elevate Americans' Christian character.

Beyond all this, Jackson developed and propagated an approach to government that melded his policies and his followers from disparate parts into coherent wholes. Jackson's political precepts were rooted in American tradition. The Jeffersonian echoes in his attack on expensive and intrusive government established a historical context and legitimacy for his views. But the Jacksonian assault on all forms of privilege, its libertarian thrust in commerce and morals as well as politics, drew as much on the novel ideas of Owenites and Workingmen as on precedent. The synthesis Jackson fused, in its totality, was no throwback. Like Jefferson's own thought in its day, it was self-consciously progressive, forward-looking, rooted in old verities but fixing its hopes on the future. In this it was much like the American System, whose policies it challenged at every point. Against one vision of improvement Jackson counterposed another, equally comprehensive, equally controversial.

Jackson's last, unintentional accomplishment as president was to provoke a union of the opposition. His outspoken leadership, like that of Adams before him, rallied the administration's foes as well as its friends. By the end of Jackson's stormy eight years his myriad antagonists, some old, some new, some champions of the American System and others its erstwhile enemies, were congealing into a new political party. In 1834 Henry Clay christened them Whigs, in remembrance of Revolutionary fighters against royal tyranny. Soon they would be as well organized and fully committed as Jackson's Democrats. From then on the debate over America's future would be largely channeled into, and in the end submerged within, the turbulent stream of party strife.

Descent into Discord

> It is easy to see the end. By the necessary course of
> events, if left to themselves, we must become, finally, two
> people. . . . Abolition and the Union cannot co-exist.
> —John C. Calhoun, 1837

Democrats and Whigs

The bifurcation of American politics began under John Quincy Adams,
when foes of his policies and friends of his disappointed rivals for the presidency combined behind Andrew Jackson. It proceeded through Jackson's
election in 1828 and re-election in 1832, through the Indian removal, American System, and Bank controversies. Still, midway through Jackson's presidency, political organization remained amorphous and alignments fluid.
As prominent a figure as Daniel Webster toyed with changing sides as late
as 1833, while northern Antimasons and southern nullifiers long resisted
throwing in their lot with either Jackson or the Adams-Clay men.

As the two major groupings were slow to cohere into parties, they were
equally so to take names. The appellation of Democrats for Jackson's followers gained currency slowly, not winning exclusive usage until late in the
1830s. Many anti-Jacksonians skirted the Whig label for years after Henry
Clay coined it in 1834. In 1832 Jackson confronted two challengers for the
presidency, Clay and the Antimason William Wirt, and in 1836 his Democratic heir Martin Van Buren faced three. Only in 1840, when the logic of
the electoral system and the craving to unseat Van Buren finally united his
opponents behind the Whig candidacy of William Henry Harrison, did a

system of politics premised on the enduring rivalry of two national parties prevail.

The original anti-Jacksonians were the Adams and Clay group, who for a time called themselves National Republicans. This core of opposition received periodic infusions of disaffected Jackson men, starting with those who had credulously backed him and the American System in 1828. The most important accretions came in the wake of the nullification crisis. Jackson's strident nationalism affronted southern-rights extremists in and out of South Carolina. In Congress Clay and Calhoun made common cause against Jackson in 1833 and continued it through the Bank War.

Once Jackson retired, the issue of "executive tyranny," which had joined Clay and Calhoun, lost its force. Calhoun and his following returned to the Democrats, their natural home. But many southerners stayed with the Whigs. In the South, Jackson's success in displacing sectional issues with the banking question worked in the end to his party's disadvantage. The tariff settlement of 1833 and the Bank War procured a renewed southern constituency for the American System. Slaveholding politicians could again proclaim the merits of a national economic program without seeming to truckle to Yankee oppression. Stripped of sectional connotations, the idea of promoting balanced development through modest aid to manufactures and transportation found ready southern support. So did a national bank. Planters who borrowed for land and improvements and vended their crops on an international market suffered greatly from monetary instability. The roller coaster of the 1830s induced merchants and planter-entrepreneurs to long for the days when a national bank dampened currency fluctuations and smoothed overseas exchange.

Loyalty to a fellow southerner and slaveholder restrained rebellion as long as Jackson occupied the White House. But Jackson's choice of the New Yorker Van Buren to succeed him in 1836 brought wholesale defections from the southern Democracy. Whig inroads extended deep into the ranks of original Jacksonians. Tennessee turned against Van Buren in the 1836 election, then went Whig in the next three, even against local son James K. Polk in 1844. The three southerners in Jackson's first cabinet, including the favorite John Eaton for whom he had risked so much, all wound up as Whigs.

In the North too, political competition sprouted in place of one-party dominance. The Ohio valley and the middle states from New York to Maryland were electoral battlegrounds as early as 1824. New England joined them by stages. After twice losing all six states to Adams, Jackson carried

Maine and New Hampshire in 1832. Van Buren added Rhode Island and Connecticut in 1836.

Though far from consolidated—the Whigs still had no national convention, candidate, or platform in 1836—a two-party system was becoming visible by the end of Jackson's presidency. Whigs everywhere espoused improvement under the fostering care of government. Chastened by experience, they promoted a somewhat diluted version of the original American System. They favored a less aggressive tariff, and they endorsed Henry Clay's plan of distributing land revenues to the states for internal improvement, schools, and black colonization in place of direct federal spending. Whigs wrestled with ideas for a fiscal agent that would regulate currency and credit, yet be less powerful and obnoxious than the old Bank of the United States.

Whig policy embraced moral and intellectual as well as economic advance. Whigs championed state school systems and a more humane and just approach to Indian removal. They looked kindly on works of Christian benevolence and uplift, and they lent cautious sanction to the improvement of morals through Sabbatarian and temperance legislation. Where Democrats advocated throwing off restraint, Whigs stressed principles of system and discipline. Without these they believed no progress was possible in character, and without that, no progress at all.

Whigs repelled Democratic accusations of exclusivity and class bias in their program. Social advance benefited everyone, and the tools of success, especially education, were (or would be, if Whigs had their way) open to all. Their theme of elevation through self-improvement spoke to aspirations of citizens in all parts of the country and in every stratum of society. Still, the Whig ethos did hold special meaning for people who sat in seats of authority, whether in business, government, or the traditional church. Beneficiaries and custodians of social order, they feared the chaos so recklessly endorsed—or so it seemed to them—by Jacksonians. It was natural for those holding secure positions within the status quo to appreciate its virtues, to loathe disruption, and to see continuity and regularity as tools of progress rather than obstacles to it. The directors of the Lowell mills, who carried control to the point of obsession, were fervent Whigs.

With its stress on order and discipline, Whiggery carried a certain aura of moral superiority, of caste if not class. The raucous scenes at Jackson assemblages (beginning with a near-riot at his inauguration), the scruffy antecedents and clamoring ambition of leading Democrats, the unbridled and unprincipled greed for which the party seemed to stand—all these affronted people who prized decorum and decency and valued good breeding and good manners. Ralph Waldo Emerson was no apologist for conformity or hierarchy. He trumpeted the transcendent independence of the self-reliant individual as boldly as any Jacksonian. "The root & seed of democracy," he affirmed, "is the doctrine Judge for yourself. Reverence thyself." "Yet seemeth it to me," he also mused, "that we shall all feel dirty if Jackson is reelected." The "unmixed malignity, the withering selfishness, the impudent vulgarity" at Democratic gatherings filled the polite Emerson with disgust. Under "ANIMALS" in his notebook he noted, "the favorite word & emblem of the Jackson Party is a Hog."

The association of Whiggery with respectability reinforced its appeal to self-styled leaders of society, from opulent planters to mill owners, merchant princes, and mainline Protestant clergy. Their presence in Whig ranks lent credence to the perennial Democratic cry of "aristocracy." Whigs repudiated the term. Denying the presence of classes in egalitarian America, they ascribed eminence to individual merit. The chance for self-improvement was there for everyone to seize. The attainments of those at the head of society should be emulated, not condemned.

Andrew Jackson and his followers, for their part, yielded to no one in their hope of betterment. But they saw existing disparities in wealth and status as the products of privilege, not talent. Democrats charged that Whig programs and institutions would buttress social barriers, not break them down. What Whigs called avenues for advancement, Democrats saw as threats to independence.

Democratic assaults on "aristocracy" resonated powerfully among those who saw their pursuit of happiness blocked and their liberty abridged by wielders of power and prestige. Jacksonian anti-authoritarianism drew together a collection of self-conscious outsiders. Labor activists and communitarians assimilated its attack on privilege to their critique of class oppression. Tariff opponents like South Carolina's Thomas Cooper, intellectual heir of John Taylor, linked it with their demand for free trade. Religious dissenters, from freethinkers and Universalists at one end to Catholic immigrants at the other, cheered Jackson's battle against benevolent Protestantism's claim to moral monopoly. Farmers and tradespeople and entrepreneurs, proud to make their way without help or favor and wanting only to be left alone, rebelled at the expense of the Whig development program and the attempted dictation of Whig aristocrats.

Democrats cast themselves as simple folk. They not only confessed their rusticity, they wore it as a badge of honor. They were the plain honest people, "the planter, the farmer, the mechanic, and the laborer" of Jackson's Farewell Address—"uncorrupted and incorruptible," "the bone and sinew of the country; men who love liberty and desire nothing but equal rights and equal laws" and who "know that their success depends upon their own industry and economy." Sturdy and self-reliant, they saw themselves locked in struggle against a phalanx of wealth, power, and influence. They accused legislatures and courts of succumbing to elite pressure and making laws that buttressed inequality and subverted justice. They thought to curb government's abuse by stripping away much of its power. They would overthrow the guardians of privilege and invite every white man to pass unhindered and unaided.

Essentially Whigs and Democrats presented competing, yet overlapping, prescriptions for progress. Whigs emphasized self-discipline and celebrated the harmony of interests. Democrats praised self-determination and condemned "aristocracy." One party trumpeted the benefits of system, the other of liberty. One preached cooperation, the other self-reliance. Each saw a different obstacle blocking the way to advancement. Whigs hoped to correct characters, Democrats to correct circumstances.

The parties' opposing orientations thus incorporated themes that had run through the various debates over the direction of American development. Whigs and Democrats were enough alike in their aspirations to each attract broad followings, yet sufficiently distinct in rhetoric and policy to inspire passionate attachments. Each party claimed to embody basic American beliefs and traditions. Each program featured a spectrum of familiar ideas, reconfigured into an essentially new whole and cemented with a unifying rationale.

Party Politics

In the 1830s party organization spread across the country, assimilating local factions and absorbing citizens into newfound national alliances. Preempting the political field, Democrats and Whigs compelled voters and office seekers to choose between them. Though swayed by background and circumstance, the decision where to cast one's loyalty was never automatic. Some found it difficult and even painful, as choosing forced them to relinquish some hopes for the chance of achieving others. As the two parties shaped their philosophies and fixed their approach to a broad range of issues, they prompted a complex process of consensus-building. Men pondered their priorities and sought out allies with whom they could agree on enough of importance to work together. Joining a party, like joining a church or society, became an act of self-discovery and self-definition. It linked men across boundaries of occupation, residence, and faith while dividing neighbors, friends, and families.

After 1837 the building of parties sped forward under the press of hard times. In the spring, just as Van Buren succeeded Jackson as president, a fall in cotton prices and withdrawal of English credit sparked a wave of mercantile failures that signaled the end of expansion. In May banks suspended specie payment. Unemployment spread through the towns; property values plummeted, and western land sales fell off from record heights to almost nothing. The next year brought hope of recovery, but a new shock in 1839 sent the country spiraling into the longest, deepest depression Americans had yet seen.

The Panic of 1837 revived the soul-searching that had followed the collapse of 1819. Reproach fell on bankers, traders, legislators, reckless debtors, usurious creditors, hard-hearted employers, improvident wage-earners, greedy merchants, and luxury-loving consumers. Again Americans tried to locate a villain and extract a lesson by drawing the line between laudable enterprise and evil speculation. Again they warred over remedies: an expansion of banking and credit to counter the shrinkage of prices and wages, or a remorseless contraction to wring out false values and bring trade down to a sound and substantial basis. State legislatures again debated stay laws and relief schemes.

Once again the explanations and prescriptions exposed, without doing much to clarify, an ambivalence in Americans' feelings about wealth and acquisitiveness. Those who yesterday had celebrated enterprise, innovation, and opportunity now decried speculation, adventurism, and greed. But this time the search for solutions was framed within the dialogue of political parties. The crisis fortified the coalescing Whigs and Democrats by centering attention on the reasons they gave for the depression and the means they offered for its cure.

Led by President Van Buren, Democrats censured the "redundancy of credit" and "spirit of reckless speculation" that led to hyperactive trading, excessive debt, and "the rapid growth among all classes . . . of luxurious habits founded too often on merely fancied wealth, and detrimental alike to the industry, the resources, and the morals of the people." At the root of all these "destructive consequences," of course, lay paper money. It was the bankers with their corporate and commercial allies, dangling the "temptations of sudden and unsubstantial wealth" before the citizenry, who had lured Americans from the slow but sure "rewards of virtue, industry, and prudence."

The catastrophe wrought upon state governments by the panic confirmed, in Democratic eyes, the evils of paper finance and the "certain dangers of blending private interests with the operations of public business." While prosperity reigned in mid-decade, states had begun mammoth transportation projects, borrowing millions, mainly from European investors, for canals, railroads, turnpikes, and river improvements. By 1840 most construction had stopped, leaving half-finished, sometimes worthless works and ruined public credit. A few states were left nearly bankrupt. Others taxed themselves back into solvency.

The expansion of banking also came back to haunt the states. Paper circulation rose by half between 1830 and 1834, then again by 1837. Growth was fastest in the southwest, where Indian removal opened up rich new land. Hopes of cotton fortunes fueled a wave of buying and a bottomless thirst for money. Mississippi had one bank in 1830 and eighteen by 1837, with a thirteenfold increase in capital. Some legislatures did not stop at chartering. Hoping to stimulate development and share in its fruits, states bought bank stock with public funds and underwrote banking operations with public credit. Some joint banking ventures were linked to improvement projects. Several western banks were wholly state owned.

Instead of profits, depression brought irrecoupable losses. Bank failures spread, accompanied as in 1819 by revelations of malfeasance and fraud. Most devastating—and to Democrats, gratifying—was the collapse of the old Bank of the United States, which continued as a Pennsylvania state bank after its federal charter expired in 1836. Still the largest bank in the country, it staggered into increasing disrepute and in 1841 finally closed its doors, the victim of Nicholas Biddle's hubris and a doomed effort to sustain falling cotton prices.

Scandal and bankruptcy incited a new revulsion against bankers and financiers. Reaction was most acute where the failure of state-owned or state-financed banks saddled citizens with burdensome new taxes in the midst of depression. In Mississippi feeling ran so high that the legislature repudiated its own bonds and sacrificed the state's credit and reputation rather than rescue its banks.

Not all these consequences were yet visible when President Van Buren convened a special session of Congress to deal with the crisis in September 1837. But enough was clear for him to point the Democratic moral: any connection between the functions of government and the business of banking was fundamentally wrong. Government should withdraw and leave "private interest, enterprise, and competition, without the aid of legislative grants or regulations by law," to restore prosperity. Resurrecting Jackson's old plan, Van Buren proposed that the United States Treasury manage federal funds in complete separation from the banks.

An "independent National Treasury" or "divorce of bank and state" became the rallying point of the Van Buren administration. Again following Jackson, Van Buren urged that the federal government spurn all banknotes for its operations and collect and disburse only coin. Democrats in the states demanded revocation or restriction of bank charters, repudiation of banknote money, and return to the stable constitutional currency of gold and silver.

The Democrats' cry for "hard money" played powerfully on popular anger against the banks. But as Whigs hastened to point out, it promised no end to the depression. Instead it was likely to make things worse. Business was already painfully contracting. Slack work and falling wages forced families into poverty. Tight credit made it impossible to repay debts. A specie currency, said Whigs, would make scarce money still scarcer, for there was not enough gold and silver in the country to replace banknotes in circulation. The Democrats' solution would not alleviate, but sharpen, the people's distress.

Van Buren believed the supply of specie was adequate. But he also made it a point of principle not to consider short-term consequences. The people, he lectured Congress, should look to themselves for rescue:

Those who look to the action of this Government for specific aid to the citizen to relieve embarrassments arising from losses by revulsions in commerce and credit lose sight of the ends for which it was created and the powers with which it is clothed. . . . It was not intended to confer special favors on individuals or on any classes of them, to create systems of agriculture, manufactures, or trade, or to engage in them either separately or in connection with individual citizens or organized associations.

Government meddling in business, especially in banking, had invariably done harm. The best it could do now to "promote the real and permanent welfare" of the citizens was to leave them to themselves. In 1839, with conditions worsening, Van Buren reiterated the theme: "relief is not to be found in expedients." Only by returning to "strict economy and frugality," forsaking indulgence and extravagance for "republican simplicity and economical habits," could Americans find "effectual relief, security for the future, and an enduring prosperity."

Van Buren's homilies were in strict accord with Jacksonian philosophy. But changing circumstances had reversed their meaning. It was one thing to invite the people to thrive on their own, another to tell them to suffer on their own. When Jackson amidst prosperity proclaimed that government should leave people alone, he seemed to show regard for their welfare. When Van Buren said the same thing, it looked like callous unconcern. Hard times tested Democratic fidelity to the principle of governmental abnegation. Van Buren passed with distinction. But many of his auditors did not want a lecture on self-reliance. They wanted help.

Whigs promised to give it to them. Van Buren's seeming indifference to distress—what Henry Clay called his "cold and heartless insensibility to the sufferings of a bleeding people"—gave Whigs a chance to shed the onus of "aristocracy" for a new identity as the party of prosperity. "We are all," said Clay, "bound up and interwoven together, united in fortune and destiny, and all, all entitled to the protecting care of a parental government." The old developmental program of tariff, transportation, and public works was reborn as a cure for depression. Stripping off its grand connotations of planning and control, Whigs refurbished the American System as a simple growth package to stimulate recovery.

They also championed banking and credit against the Democrats' call for hard money. Whigs ripped Jackson for wrecking prosperity in his war against the banks. Now they charged Van Buren with fostering an invidious distinction between the people's money and the government's. Under his independent treasury and hard-money system, the government would require specie for its needs—specie that, instead of being employed as of old through a national bank to underwrite commerce and a sound currency, would be hoarded away useless in federal vaults until doled out exclusively to recipients of administration patronage. "A hard-money government and a paper-money people!" cried Clay. "A government, an official corps—the servants of the people—glittering in gold, and the people themselves, their masters, buried in ruin, and surrounded with rags."

With this flourish Whigs flung the charge of aristocracy back in Democratic faces. "A young, growing, and enterprising people" needed good currency, and it was the government's duty to give it to them. Coin was too scarce and clumsy to serve the country's needs. Reversion to specie would set growth back centuries. Gold and silver were rich men's treasures, while credit was "the friend of indigent merit." Nicholas Biddle explained that paper money was the people's money:

> What laboring people want is labor, work, constant employment. How can they get it? In building shops and building houses; in coal mines; in making roads and canals; and how are all these carried on except by credit in the shape of loans from banks. . . . If there was nothing but gold and silver in the country, the banks would be limited to what could be paid by gold and silver, and the owners of gold and silver would be the only persons who could employ workmen; so that all men who had nothing but their industry to depend on could have no chance of getting up in the world. It is the banks who give them credit to enable them to rise. . . . Gold and silver are for the rich—safe banknotes are the democracy of currency.

Democrats and Whigs marshaled upon the battle lines of the "specie system" versus the "credit system" for the 1840 presidential contest. The campaign completed the reconstitution of American politics, as the two parties absorbed the last independents under their mantles. Whigs held their first national convention and chose William Henry Harrison of Ohio to challenge Van Buren. A final detachment of old Jacksonians, aghast at Democratic hard-money ideas, broke off to join them. Wielding new resources of discipline and enthusiasm, the two sides put on an all-out, razzle-dazzle campaign topped by the Whigs' portrayal of Harrison as a simple log-cabin farmer and Van Buren as an effete aristocrat. Voters turned out in record numbers, and Harrison defeated Van Buren. The enthronement of a two-party system was complete.

The Reassessment of Character

The emergence of national parties with tentacles extending into states and localities marked, in one sense, the blossoming of America's democratic promise. With party fanfare pulling four of five eligible voters to the polls, more men took part in politics than ever before. But the routinization of party strife spelled the death of another compelling vision, of national harmony and unity in the march of progress. In enlisting with parties, bowing to their discipline, and warring on their behalf, Americans implicitly accepted the presence of enduring, implacable divisions within the citizenry. Whig and Democratic prescriptions for the future were in some degree exclusive. Everyone had to choose between them. America's favored circumstance, it now became plain, would bring no release from old-world contention and error. If the party was right, then many of the people were wrong.

Democrats quelled this disturbing reflection by excluding their opponents from the ranks of the real people. In their minds the Democratic party *was* the people; all else was "aristocracy." The two parties were "as opposite as day and night," announced William Leggett in 1834. "The one party is for a popular government; the other for an aristocracy." Andrew Jackson sounded the theme with his warnings to "the people" against the "money power."

With their holistic program and their abhorrence of conflict between classes or interests, Whigs shied from such combative language. Denying any real ground for social antagonisms, Whig rhetoric promoted inclusion, not division. With as much certitude as Democrats, Whigs avowed that they represented, if not the numerical whole of the population, at least its preponderance of brains, talent, industry, and morals. A Whig paper asked what Democrats meant by "aristocracy," and answered: "a majority of the virtuous and intelligent part of the community, . . . those who are too intelligent to be imposed upon and too independent to succumb to demagogues."

Still, no matter how rationalized or denied, the cleavage of the electorate essentially undercut Americans' confidence in their uniqueness. The unitary road to progress had divided. No matter how fervently each party clung to its principles, it was hopeless to pretend that either could command universal assent. The broad, easy march to the future was gone. Americans would have to be pushed and dragged toward their destiny.

Other events of the same years jeopardized Americans' hope of escape from the historical fate of humanity. Depression brought the kind of suffering that new-world abundance and enterprise were supposed to prevent. Tales of want and woe filled the news. The press reported massive unemployment and its consequences—homelessness, indigency, cold, hunger, even starvation—among the working population. In New York City there were bread riots.

Americans had endured privation in the past, but this was different. Deepening past 1840, the downturn lasted much longer than that of 1819. Centered in the towns, the distress was more visible and, at least to appearances, more acute than before. Even more disturbing than the immediate scene of suffering was the question of responsibility. Previous setbacks could be readily traced to external causes—war, diplomatic crisis, or shift in international trade. But no easy foreign villain appeared to explain this panic. Instead Americans blamed themselves, and each other.

In hindsight the expansion that led up to the panic seemed bloated, delusive, false. Even in 1836 Albert Gallatin, Treasury secretary for thirteen years under presidents Jefferson and Madison, had questioned the value of headlong growth. "The apparent prosperity and the progress of cultivation, population, commerce, and improvement are beyond expectation," he observed. "But it seems to me as if general demoralization was the consequence; I doubt whether general happiness is increased; and I would have preferred a gradual, slower, and more secure progress." Five years later, with the country sunk in depression, Gallatin repeated his lament: "We have rioted in liberty and revel in luxury." The "thirst of gold" had undermined "the moral feeling and habits of the whole community."

Others shared Gallatin's perception of a deterioration in character. Watching the "emphatic & universal calamity" in 1837, Ralph Waldo Emerson concluded "the present generation is bankrupt of principles & hope, as of property." Emerson found one gain in the wreckage: that it disabused him of dreams of broad human progress. "Society has played out its last stake; it is checkmated. . . . Behold the boasted world has come to nothing." Henceforth, Emerson vowed, he would look not to the mass—"the winding procession of humanity"—but to the individual, the "Soul erect and Unconquered still." In solitary transcendence, not social elevation, he now placed his hope for man.

In 1838 James Fenimore Cooper returned to the theme of American character he had explored a decade earlier in *Notions of the Americans*. But his new exposition, *The American Democrat*, took the form not of panegyric but of indictment. Ten years abroad and at home had darkened Cooper's tones. Where he once had lauded Americans' honesty and sturdy good sense, now he censured their love of demagoguery and flattery, their poverty of culture, taste, and manners, the fickleness and ignorance of their public opinion, their subservience to "vicious influences" of ambition, fraud, corruption, envy, and prejudice. In place of candor Cooper saw only cant; instead of enterprise, mere rapacity.

The speculative excesses, the chicanery and sharp dealing that attended the rush for riches in the "flush times" before the panic became the stuff of legend, the reproach of sermons, the butt of jokes. A witness of the Mississippi land mania of 1836 caustically recalled the scene:

In the fulness of time the new era had set in—the era of the second great experiment of independence: the experiment, namely, of credit without capital, and enterprise without honesty. The Age of Brass had succeeded the Arcadian period when men got rich by saving a part of their earnings, and lived at their own cost and in ignorance of the new plan of making fortunes on the profits of what they owed. . . . Money, got without work, by those unaccustomed to it, turned the heads of its possessors, and they spent it with a recklessness like that with which they gained it. The pursuits of industry neglected, riot and coarse debauchery filled up the vacant hours.

The cyclone of expansion and collapse wrought a lasting change in Americans' self-image. It dealt a telling blow to presumptions of a refined national character. Americans would continue to celebrate what Gallatin called their "marvellous energy" and "improvements of stupendous magnitude," their endless inventiveness and abundant resources. But looking back on what now seemed a passage of delusion and folly, a "reign of humbug, and wholesale insanity," they were less ready to claim a patriotic exemption from human foibles and failings. After the panic Americans assessed themselves with less reverence and more skepticism. The sharper, the trickster, the huckster, the braggart joined the honest farmer and sober man of business in the country's cultural pantheon. Poor Richard made room for Simon Suggs and Aristabulus Bragg.

The Constriction of Choices

Hard times encouraged Americans to take a less heady view of their prospects. They faced the future with narrowed horizons—still broad, but no longer boundless. The idea of an oncoming epiphany, of great things in the offing, seemed less plausible in an environment of stringency and want. The depression dulled visions and enthusiasms and dampened social tinkering.

Endeavors of all kinds felt the pinch. Internal improvements halted. Lyceums declined, and the national American Lyceum folded in 1839. Falling wages and employment wiped out trade societies. Experimentation in ways of organizing society was momentarily stilled. It revived, but never recaptured the same hope of easy change. When canals and steamboats and Lowell and New Harmony and business corporations and labor associations were all new and untried, it seemed that all things were possible. Citizens felt it in their power to build as they pleased, to work an imminent transformation for good. That sense of freedom was passing.

In 1837 Arthur Tappan and Company went bankrupt. The flow of funds to evangelical and philanthropic enterprise slowed to a trickle. Benevolent agencies curtailed or suspended operation. Campaigns for reform and uplift survived, but with lowered vitality and reduced expectations. Americans still cherished dreams of improvement, but they felt less sure of reaching the millennium any time soon.

Strengthening the parties while straitening other paths of activity, the depression helped funnel Americans' social energies into party politics. By 1840 partisan debate had engrossed public discourse. Autonomous political groupings withered away or were submerged in the two national organizations. Antimasons disbanded. New York City regular Democrats absorbed the ideologically fertile Equal Rights or "locofoco" faction, heirs to the Workingmen, with whom Tammany Hall had flirted and feuded for years. Reformers and crusaders found new careers in party ranks. Ely Moore, pioneer labor spokesman in Congress and first president of both the General Trades' Union of New York and the National Trades' Union, settled in as a Democratic functionary with a customhouse job from Van Buren. Robert Dale Owen traded his daring ideas on schooling, sex, and marriage for a Democratic seat in the Indiana legislature and in Congress.

When Frances Wright returned to America and resumed lecturing in 1836, she sidelined her old causes and focused her fire on the Bank of the United States. Wright's latest formula for reform was not sexual equality or universal education, but Martin Van Buren and the Independent Treasury. Even so, and although she avoided criticizing slavery and attacked the abolitionists, Wright encountered hostility and violence beyond anything previous. Her presence on the platform was nearly enough to incite riot. A decade earlier, when Wright and Robert Owen burst on the scene, audiences listened tolerantly, if not approvingly, to the most radical and far-reaching schemes for overhauling society. Now they shouted them down.

Leeway for divergence in thought and behavior shrank as ideas and plans hardened over time into dogmas and formulas. Schools, prisons, and asylums designed to remake society settled into sustaining it. Imperceptibly reformers muted their aspirations from eradicating evils to ameliorating them. In 1830 a confidence that "we could *prove to the world,* to the very most skeptical and cavilling, that characters can *be made over*" fired Catharine Beecher's plans for female education. Time and trial sapped such expectations. By the 1840s the idea of a distinct feminine character was transmuting from an instrument of change to a bulwark of stasis, from a way to arm women for uplift to a rationale for confining them in the circle of home and family. Subtly the notion of special female attributes shifted from a source of transformative power to a justification for fixing sexual boundaries. The disengaging of daily tasks of family maintenance and public charity from hopes of national rebirth reduced women's transcendent mission to a mere domestic function.

Slavery and Sectional Cleavage

More than anything else, the intractable slavery question served to expose the growing brittleness in American society and to erode confidence in the nation's hopeful destiny. Fenimore Cooper registered the change. In 1828 he saw a sentiment against slavery "silently working its way throughout the whole of this nation," especially the South. Peaceful emancipation, followed by colonization, would surely come. "Unless the christian world recedes, its final success is inevitable." Ten years later Cooper's optimism had vanished. He still foresaw slavery's end, but only at the cost of "inextinguishable hatred" between the races. "The struggle that will follow, will necessarily be a war of extermination. The evil day may be delayed, but can scarcely be averted."

When Cooper first wrote, leading southerners still openly condemned slavery. Distinguished statesmen, including Thomas Jefferson, had welcomed Frances Wright and her plans for an emancipationist colony in the heart of the cotton kingdom. In 1831, in the wake of the Nat Turner revolt, Jefferson's grandson initiated a searching debate on slavery's future in the Virginia House of Delegates. After fully airing the merits and dangers of continued bondage, emancipation, and colonization, legislators rejected a motion that action against slavery would be "expedient" by only seventy-three to fifty-eight.

But southern response to abolitionist postal and petition campaigns in the mid-1830s showed that latitude for public debate was closing. In 1835 the American Anti-Slavery Society mailed thousands of abolition tracts directly to southern clergy, officials, and prominent citizens. Many were never delivered, intercepted by alert postmasters or, as in Charleston, South Carolina, by angry mobs. Meetings demanded the suppression, by violence if necessary, of outside efforts to subvert the peace of slaveholding society. Aroused citizens dealt summary justice to insubordinate slaves and suspected abolition sympathizers. Southern legislatures made it a felony, punishable even by death, to distribute antislavery literature. They insisted that free states cooperate in suppressing "incendiary" activities and publications.

The next year the war of abolitionist agitation and slaveholding repression carried over into Congress. South Carolinians John C. Calhoun in the Senate and James Henry Hammond in the House of Representatives met the flood of petitions for abolition in the District of Columbia by demanding a halt to all congressional discussion of slavery. Neither house went this far, but both adopted the first of a series of annual "gag rules" designed to ensure the stifling of antislavery petitions.

The gags passed Congress by heavy majorities. Neither Whigs nor Democrats, North or South, welcomed the eruption of slavery into national politics. Partisans saw the issue as an annoying distraction that steered attention from crucial questions of commerce and credit and inspired dangerous sectional cleavages. Dwelling on slavery was inimical to the task of building up national party coalitions and constituencies.

Presidents Jackson and Van Buren did all they could to squelch the subject. Jackson and Postmaster General Amos Kendall sanctioned the interception of abolitionist mailings by state and local officials. Jackson recommended federal suppression of "incendiary publications" and damned agitators' "unconstitutional and wicked attempts" to incite slave insurrection and "produce all the horrors of a servile war." His Farewell Address warned of the disunionist consequences of sectional fanaticism. In his inaugural the same day, the new president Van Buren tried to head off discussion by announcing his "inflexible and uncompromising" opposition to emancipation in the District of Columbia. Whig leader Henry Clay too denounced abolitionists.

In the short run these efforts at political containment succeeded. The bulk of white voters still preferred not to confront the slavery dilemma. Northern politicians of both parties shunned the abolitionists while southerners excoriated them. Southern Whigs and Democrats tried to tar each other as untrustworthy guardians of slaveholding safety. But this competition did not impede, on either side, the cementing of partisan alliances with northerners. The construction of national parties proceeded irrespective of the slavery question.

Abolition itself suffered a loss of institutional drive after the petition campaign. Shorn of funds after the Panic of 1837, demoralized by lack of success, and rent by internal controversy, the American Anti-Slavery Society fractured in 1840 into two groups. One, based in Boston, was led by Garrison; the other, quartered in New York, by Lewis Tappan. Neither was as effective as the old organization. Leadership in antislavery, as in other causes, passed to those who thought mainly in political terms, who dreamed not so much of converting slaveholders as of beating them at the

polls. After experimenting with means of influencing Whigs and Democrats, the politicos founded their own Liberty Party in 1839, and the next
year offered the first antislavery presidential candidate, former Alabama
slaveholder James G. Birney.

Birney got seven thousand votes out of more than two million cast.
His puny showing and the excitement generated by Whig and Democratic
campaigns seemed to signify the final ascendancy of partisanship over sectionalism. But appearances deceived. Abolition, like other millennial enthusiasms, languished after 1837. But the underlying divisions between free
North and slave South remained unhealed. While politics brought them
visibly together, the two sections were quietly but decisively growing apart.

As early as 1830 in his Senate debate with Daniel Webster, South Carolina's Robert Hayne turned the defense of slavery into an attack on the very
ethos of improvement. It was the "spirit of False Philanthropy," said Hayne,
that produced "golden dreams of national greatness and prosperity," and
"filled the land with thousands of wild and visionary projects, which can
have no effect but to waste the energies and dissipate the resources of the
country." Demanding a gag rule six years later, James Henry Hammond
went further. He repudiated democracy, reform, and experiment. Abolitionists, said Hammond, charge slaveholders with aristocracy. "In this they
are right. I accept the terms. *It is a government of the best.* . . . Slavery
does indeed create an aristocracy—an aristocracy of talents, of virtues, of
generosity and courage."

"Many in the South once believed," John C. Calhoun recalled in 1838,
that slavery was "a moral and political evil." But "that folly and delusion are gone; we see it now in its true light, and regard it as the most
safe and stable basis for free institutions in the world." No clash of ide-
ologies and interests, no social antagonisms threatened "the harmony, the
union, and stability" of slave society. The plantation subsumed and reconciled all parties within "a little community, with the master at its head."
Because plantation society was corporal and hierarchical instead of atom-
istic and individualistic, it was stationary and conservative. Because of that,
it was good.

Here was an argument that would have astonished Thomas Jefferson.
The Declaration of Independence was nonsense. Equality was a delusion.
Aristocracy was a boast, not an epithet; and slavery was not an incubus
on progress but, in Hammond's words, the foundation for "the highest
toned, the purest, best organization of society that has ever existed on the
face of the earth." Slaveholding society did not need to aspire to perfection

because it had already reached it. Unrest and innovation and debate in the North were marks not of vitality, but of disease.

As yet this kind of frank reactionism was still unusual. Calhoun and Hammond spoke for an extreme of opinion in the South's most extreme state. But the defense of slavery was warping other southerners too toward repudiating the larger vision of progress they once shared with the North. Southern evangelicals had eagerly pursued temperance and moral uplift. But the abolitionist taint of reform Christianity threatened their influence with slaveholding neighbors and parishioners. Clerics salvaged their status and their mission by disclaiming antislavery sentiments and disassociating with antislavery northerners. In 1835 southern presbyteries, Methodist conferences, and Baptist associations answered the American Anti-Slavery Society's postal campaign by branding abolitionists as interlopers and false Christians. Once critics of slavery, southern evangelicals became its apologists. They threw their energy into improving its Christian character by enlightening masters and instructing slaves. From rebels and shakers, they became bolsters of the slaveholding status quo.

Before long the gap grew too wide to bridge. Even while northerners and southerners joined politically they began to separate spiritually. In 1837 national Presbyterianism purged its northern reform wing over issues that included abolitionism. The question of ministerial slaveholding fractured Baptists and Methodists. Even nonabolitionist northern clerics refused to sanction slavery by elevating slaveholders to national church office. After years of friction southern Methodists in 1844 and Baptists in 1845 broke off to form their own organizations. The United States might have national political parties, but in its three largest denominations it no longer had national churches.

Toward Civil War

Imbedding themselves deeper in northern and southern society, opposing social principles lacked only a point of political friction to set the two sections at odds. The Texas question, arising in the mid–1830s, revealed how deeply visions of national destiny had cleaved along both sectional and partisan lines and how far territorial acquisition had gone from being a cement of union to a corrosive.

Americans North and South had once welcomed expansion as an unalloyed good. The nearly effortless advance of their sway across the continent seemed but another sign of the country's favored destiny. In 1818 the

United States agreed with Britain to extend the Canadian border westward to the Rockies and share the Oregon country beyond. In a treaty with Spain a year later, negotiated by Secretary of State John Quincy Adams, Americans acquired Florida and a southwestern boundary running all the way to the Pacific. Hailed as triumphs, both pacts were unanimously ratified.

The treaty line of 1819 left Texas as part of Spanish Mexico. After Mexico won its independence presidents Adams and Jackson both tried to buy the province. Mexico would not sell, but it did for a time welcome Americans into the Texas territory. In 1835 American settlers, mainly southern emigrants, revolted against Mexican rule. The next year they defeated the Mexican armies, declared independence, and in 1837 petitioned for annexation to the United States.

Ten years earlier Texas would have been welcomed into the Union. But slavery and partisanship together had dissolved the consensus for expansion. Whig senator Daniel Webster and John Quincy Adams, now a Massachusetts congressman and antislavery spokesman, joined abolitionists in charging a plot to expand slave territory. Wary of embroilment with Mexico and sectional disruption in his own Democratic party, President Van Buren spurned annexation. Texas remained, for the time, independent.

Beyond its particulars in Texas, the question of expansion came to exemplify the differences in Democratic and Whig conceptions of progress, showing how far the two parties had diverged. Democrats cheered new territory, whether won by absorption, purchase, or outright conquest, as proof and product of the superiority of American civilization. The wider the field for liberty and enterprise, the better. By extending its reach over adjacent lands and peoples, the United States was but enlarging the area of freedom.

Whigs were more cautious. They wanted to integrate the republic, not distend it. Their hopes for a more moral, harmonious, and refined society called for connecting Americans instead of dispersing them. They came to think of the frontier as the seat not of freedom but of license, where civilization unraveled and wantonness and irreligion reigned. To Whigs, war and conquest, like forced Indian removal, spelled betrayal and corruption of true progress, since both sacrificed America's aspiration for virtue in the thirst for sordid gain. In Whig eyes territorial craving exposed the moral canker at the heart of the Democratic creed.

Implicit in each party's germinal ethos, these attitudes came to the fore in the 1840s, when the annexation of Texas led finally to war against Mexico and territorial conquest in the southwest and California. But the expansion issue, framed in terms of party, lurked even more ominously because of its interpenetration with the question of slavery. Abolitionism, despite its political rebuff, had succeeded in imbedding the fate of slavery into the heart of Americans' divergent expectations and aspirations for the future. By 1846, when war with Mexico began, the United States could no longer acquire new territory without provoking citizens to ask immediately if it should be slave or free.

That question implicated the character and destiny not just of the West, but of the nation. Dividing Americans North and South, it also set principles that all held sacred against each other in a hopeless tangle: liberty against property, democracy against freedom, nationality against autonomy. As the slavery controversy grew in the 1850s, it channeled social discourse into sectional justifications and recriminations and concentrated political debate on the sole point of whether slavery should be, in Abraham Lincoln's words, "placed where the public mind shall rest in the belief that it is in the course of ultimate extinction." By 1860 a majority of citizens, North and South, had come to see the promise of their future, and the goodness of their society, turning on the fate of slavery. With Lincoln's election as president, an answer could no longer be postponed. Ahead lay civil war.

The slavery controversy, like others in the decades after 1815, was driven by a concern for the future. Americans strained to see themselves not as they had been, but as they might become. They believed they were a special people, blessed with special advantages and appointed to a special destiny. In the full flush of youthful nationhood it seemed, wonderfully, that all things were possible. Time and events foreclosed some opportunities and opened others, settled old questions and raised new ones. Overall, American society has perhaps never again seemed as flexible, as open to visions of change and improvement and regeneration, as it did at the Jubilee. Yet the hope of a better tomorrow has never died.

Bibliographical Essay

To review the historical literature on Jacksonian America would take a book in itself. My purpose is more confined: to indicate the published works that have especially helped to shape my understanding of the period. Most of these fall in two distinct categories: contemporary documents available in modern editions, and recent works of historical scholarship. The best way to approach any era is through the words of the people who lived it. For that reason, and because the prevailing thrust in some realms of current scholarship seems to me to obscure Jacksonian realities more than reveal them, this work draws heavily on primary materials. Still, the writing of history compels the practitioner to an interior dialogue not only with sources, but with predecessors. Even where it departs from theirs, my view of the Jackson years has been informed and clarified by the work of other investigators.

Works marked with an asterisk (*) contain bibliographic essays that offer a more thorough guide to the literature on their respective subjects. Many of the works listed herein are informative on an array of topics. To avoid repetition, I usually cite a work only at the first point of importance in the text. For publications with two dates listed, the second date indicates a revised or reprinted edition.

General Works

Arthur M. Schlesinger, Jr., *The Age of Jackson* (1945), remains, after half a century, the starting point for scholarly debate on Jacksonian America. Partisan in judgment and selective in coverage, Schlesinger still attempted what few since have dared: an overarching, integrative synthesis of the era as a whole. Edward Pessen, *Jacksonian America: Society, Personality, and*

Politics* (1978), highly critical of Jackson and his times, emphasizes what Schlesinger left out. Robert H. Wiebe, *The Opening of American Society: From the Adoption of the Constitution to the Eve of Disunion* (1984), offers a sweeping overview of national evolution that includes this period. Charles Sellers, *The Market Revolution: Jacksonian America, 1815–1846* * (1991), bids to replace Schlesinger as a master narrative. Though bold in conception and brilliant in detail, its central thesis—that Jackson and his party embodied agrarian democracy's last stand against bourgeois capitalism—seems to me untenable.

Alice Felt Tyler, *Freedom's Ferment: Phases of American Social History from the Colonial Period to the Outbreak of the Civil War* (1944), recounts endeavors in social experiment and reform. Though dated, her treatment stresses the "exuberance and optimism" that many later scholars have missed. Ronald G. Walters, *American Reformers, 1815–1860* * (1978), is an excellent brief synthesis.

Several anthologies offer samplings of contemporary writings: Edwin C. Rozwenc, ed., *Ideology and Power in the Age of Jackson* (1964); Clement Eaton, ed., *The Leaven of Democracy: The Growth of the Democratic Spirit in the Time of Jackson* (1963); Edward Pessen, ed., *Jacksonian Panorama* (1976); and David Brion Davis, ed., *Antebellum American Culture: An Interpretive Anthology* (1978).

The most prescient and oft-quoted contemporary observer of Jacksonian society was Alexis de Tocqueville, whose *Democracy in America* has been endlessly reprinted, excerpted, and abridged. The standard modern text is the Phillips Bradley translation (1945), shortened to one volume by Thomas Bender (1981). Other foreign travelers' accounts in modern editions include Frances Trollope, *Domestic Manners of the Americans* (1949); Harriet Martineau, *Society in America* (1962), and *Retrospect of Western Travel* (1968); Basil Hall, *Travels in North America* (1965); Michel Chevalier, *Society, Manners, and Politics in the United States* (1961); and, from a slightly later visitor, Charles Dickens, *American Notes for General Circulation* (1985). *The Diary of Philip Hone, 1828–1851*, ed. Allan Nevins (1927), contains many pungent observations.

Chapter One: The Year of Jubilee

On the American scene at the Jubilee, see Fred Somkin, *Unquiet Eagle: Memory and Desire in the Idea of American Freedom, 1815–1860* (1967); Arthur Alphonse Ekirch, Jr., *The Idea of Progress in America, 1815–1860*

(1944); Anne C. Loveland, *Emblem of Liberty: The Image of Lafayette in the American Mind* (1971); and Marian Klamkin, *The Return of Lafayette, 1824–1825* (1975).

My conception of the Revolutionary legacy has been influenced by Joyce Appleby, *Capitalism and a New Social Order: The Republican Vision of the 1790s* (1984), and *Liberalism and Republicanism in the Historical Imagination* (1992); Gordon S. Wood, *The Radicalism of the American Revolution* (1991); and especially by the writings of Thomas Jefferson. The best compilation is the Library of America *Writings*, ed. Merrill D. Peterson (1984).

Ralph Waldo Emerson's journals and James Fenimore Cooper's *Notions of the Americans* and *The American Democrat* are available in modern editions. For Webster's orations at Bunker Hill and Faneuil Hall, see *The Writings and Speeches of Daniel Webster* (1903), vol. 1.

Chapter Two: The Spirit of Improvement

George Rogers Taylor, *The Transportation Revolution, 1815–1860* * (1951), and Paul W. Gates, *The Farmer's Age: Agriculture, 1815–1860* * (1960), provide classic overviews of Jacksonian economic change. Carter Goodrich, ed., *The Government and the Economy, 1763–1861* (1967), is a collection of important documents.

On novelties in transportation, see Ronald E. Shaw, *Erie Water West: A History of the Erie Canal, 1792–1854* (1966), and *Canals for a Nation: The Canal Era in the United States, 1790–1860* * (1990); Carter Goodrich, ed., *Canals and American Economic Development* (1961); Harry N. Scheiber, *Ohio Canal Era: A Case Study of Government and the Economy, 1820–1861* (1968; 1987); James D. Dilts, *The Great Road: The Building of the Baltimore and Ohio, the Nation's First Railroad, 1828–1853* (1993); Robert Greenhalgh Albion, *The Rise of New York Port, 1815–1860* (1939; 1984); and Louis C. Hunter, *Steamboats on the Western Rivers: An Economic and Technological History* (1949).

On urban rivalry and town promotion, see James Weston Livingood, *The Philadelphia-Baltimore Trade Rivalry, 1780–1860* (1947); Richard C. Wade, *The Urban Frontier: Pioneer Life in Early Pittsburgh, Cincinnati, Lexington, Louisville, and St. Louis* (1959); John W. Reps, *Town Planning in Frontier America* (1969); and Daniel Aaron, *Cincinnati: Queen City of the West, 1819–1838* (1992). Timothy Flint, *Recollections of the Last Ten Years in the Valley of the Mississippi*, has been reprinted (1968).

Thomas C. Cochran, *Frontiers of Change: Early Industrialism in America* (1981), and Brooke Hindle and Steven Lubar, *Engines of Change: The American Industrial Revolution, 1790–1860** (1986), analyze developments in manufacturing and technology. John F. Kasson, *Civilizing the Machine: Technology and Republican Values in America, 1776–1900* (1976), explores their ideological context.

Anthony F. C. Wallace, *Rockdale: The Growth of an American Village in the Early Industrial Revolution* (1978), a marvelous community study with far-reaching implications, places industry in its social and cultural setting. So do Barbara M. Tucker, *Samuel Slater and the Origins of the American Textile Industry, 1790–1860* (1984); Merrit Roe Smith, *Harpers Ferry Armory and the New Technology: The Challenge of Change* (1977); and Judith A. McGaw, *Most Wonderful Machine: Mechanization and Social Change in Berkshire Paper Making, 1801–1885* (1987). The standard treatment of the Boston Manufacturing Company is Caroline F. Ware, *The Early New England Cotton Manufacture: A Study in Industrial Beginnings* (1931).

Chapter Three: The Law of Enterprise

The following have especially informed my understanding of the changing Jacksonian legal environment: James Willard Hurst, *Law and the Conditions of Freedom in the Nineteenth-Century United States* (1956); Morton J. Horwitz, *The Transformation of American Law, 1780–1860* (1977); William E. Nelson, *Americanization of the Common Law: The Impact of Legal Change on Massachusetts Society, 1760–1830* (1975); Peter J. Coleman, *Debtors and Creditors in America: Insolvency, Imprisonment for Debt, and Bankruptcy, 1607–1900* (1974); and R. Kent Newmyer, *Supreme Court Justice Joseph Story: Statesman of the Old Republic* (1985).

Oscar Handlin and Mary Flug Handlin, *Commonwealth: A Study of the Role of Government in the American Economy: Massachusetts, 1774–1861* (1947; 1969); Louis Hartz, *Economic Policy and Democratic Thought: Pennsylvania, 1776–1860* (1948); and Milton Sydney Heath, *Constructive Liberalism: The Role of the State in Economic Development in Georgia to 1860* (1954), reveal the state's role in promoting innovation.

Ralph C. H. Catterall, *The Second Bank of the United States* (1902), is still standard. Bray Hammond's vastly instructive and provoking *Banks and Politics in America from the Revolution to the Civil War* (1957), sparkles with wit and insight. No work explores the multisided crisis of

1819 in full depth. Murray N. Rothbard, *The Panic of 1819: Reactions and Policies* (1962), recounts recovery measures in the states, while Malcolm J. Rohrbough, *The Land Office Business: The Settlement and Administration of American Public Lands, 1789–1837* (1968), details the panic's impact on the federal land system. George Dangerfield, *The Awakening of American Nationalism** (1965), a general history of the United States from 1815 to 1828, paints a broader picture.

G. Edward White, *The Marshall Court and Cultural Change, 1815–1835* (1991), is the premier work on the Court and its constitutional jurisprudence despite White's overreliance on the concept of "republicanism." Francis N. Stites, *Private Interest and Public Gain: The Dartmouth College Case, 1819* (1972), and Maurice G. Baxter, *Daniel Webster and The Supreme Court* (1966), are also useful. Justice Marshall's opinions are gathered in Joseph P. Cotton, Jr., ed., *The Constitutional Decisions of John Marshall* (1905), and have been often reprinted and excerpted. Gerald Gunther, ed., *John Marshall's Defense of* McCulloch v. Maryland (1969), includes the decision and subsequent newspaper exchanges between Marshall and his Virginia critics.

Chapter Four: The Statecraft of Progress

The speeches and public papers, correspondence, and other literary remains of major American statesmen are now appearing in comprehensive multivolume editions. *The Papers of Daniel Webster, The Papers of Henry Clay,* and *The Papers of John C. Calhoun* are complete or nearly so. The Jefferson, Madison, Adams family, and Jackson editions are less far along. Until editions in progress supersede them, Charles Francis Adams's twelve-volume abridgement of his father's diary, *Memoirs of John Quincy Adams* (1874–77), and John Spencer Bassett's seven-volume *Correspondence of Andrew Jackson* (1926–35), remain indispensable. The standard source for presidential messages is James D. Richardson, ed., *A Compilation of the Messages and Papers of the Presidents* (1896–99).

The Library of America Jefferson *Writings* (1981) has a rich selection of his correspondence. John Taylor, *Arator* (1818; 1977), and *Tyranny Unmasked* (1822; 1992), have recently been republished.

On sectional maneuvering in Congress in the Monroe and Adams years, Frederick Jackson Turner, *Rise of the New West, 1819–1829* (1907), is still informative, as is Edward D. Stanwood, *American Tariff Controversies in the Nineteenth Century* (1904). Shaw Livermore, Jr., *The Twilight of*

Federalism: The Disintegration of the Federalist Party, 1815–1830 (1972); Glover Moore, *The Missouri Controversy, 1819–1821* (1953); and P. J. Staudenraus, *The African Colonization Movement, 1819–1865* (1961), are standard monographs. Charles S. Sydnor, *The Development of Southern Sectionalism, 1819–1848* (1948), traces the retreat from postwar nationalism. Herman V. Ames, ed., *State Documents on Federal Relations: The States and the United States* (1906), collects important legislative declarations on the tariff, slavery, banking, and other issues.

Chilton Williamson, *American Suffrage from Property to Democracy, 1760–1860* (1960), details the opening of the franchise. Merrill D. Peterson, ed., *Democracy, Liberty, and Property: The State Constitutional Conventions of the 1820s* (1966), records debates and proceedings in three important states.

On presidential elections of this era, see volume 1 of Arthur M. Schlesinger, Jr., ed., *History of American Presidential Elections* (1971), and, on the 1828 campaign, Robert V. Remini, *The Election of Andrew Jackson* (1963). Mary W. M. Hargreaves, *The Presidency of John Quincy Adams** (1985), gives a comprehensive account.

Chapter Five: The Realm of Reason

The essential work on Owenism in America is Arthur Bestor, *Backwoods Utopias: The Sectarian Origins and the Owenite Phase of Communitarian Socialism in America, 1663–1829** (1970). George B. Lockwood, *The New Harmony Movement* (1905; 1970), and Anne Taylor, *Visions of Harmony: A Study in Nineteenth-Century Millenarianism* (1987), tell the New Harmony story. William Maclure is best approached through Josephine Mirabella Elliott, ed., *Partnership for Posterity: The Correspondence of William Maclure and Marie Duclos Fretageot, 1820–1833* (1994). Patricia Tyson Stroud, *Thomas Say: New World Naturalist* (1992), covers scientific life at New Harmony. On Nashoba see Celia Morris, *Fanny Wright: Rebel in America* (1984). Carl J. Guarneri, *The Utopian Alternative: Fourierism in Nineteenth-Century America* (1991), analyzes the chief successor to Owenite communitarianism.

John C. Greene, *American Science in the Age of Jefferson* (1984), and George H. Daniels, *American Science in the Age of Jackson* (1968), introduce the American scientific enterprise. Nathan Reingold, ed., *Science in Nineteenth-Century America: A Documentary History* (1964), conveys some of its flavor. See also Charlotte M. Porter, *The Eagle's Nest: Natural*

History and American Ideas, 1812–1842 (1986), and George P. Merrill, *Contributions to a History of American State Geological and Natural History Surveys* (1920), and *The First One Hundred Years of American Geology* (1924).

Charles Coleman Sellers, *Charles Willson Peale* (1947); Bruce Sinclair, *Philadelphia's Philosopher-Mechanics: A History of the Franklin Institute, 1824–1865* (1974); and Anthony F. C. Wallace, *Rockdale,* cited in Chapter 2, depict the Philadelphia scene.

On organized science see Alexandra Oleson and Sanborn C. Brown, eds., *The Pursuit of Knowledge in the Early American Republic: American Scientific and Learned Societies from Colonial Times to the Civil War* (1976); and on agricultural reform, Tamara Plakins Thornton, *Cultivating Gentlemen: The Meaning of Country Life among the Boston Elite, 1785–1860* (1989), and David F. Allmendinger, Jr., *Ruffin: Family and Reform in the Old South* (1990).

R. Carlyle Buley, *The Old Northwest: Pioneer Period, 1815–1840* (1950), is an encyclopedic cultural portrait. A useful document source is Henry D. Shapiro and Zane L. Miller, eds., *Physician to the West: Selected Writings of Daniel Drake on Science and Society* (1970). For the language controversy, see Kenneth Cmiel, *Democratic Eloquence: The Fight over Popular Speech in Nineteenth-Century America* (1990).

Chapter Six: The Kingdom of Christ

Jon Butler, *Awash in a Sea of Faith: Christianizing the American People* (1990), and Nathan O. Hatch, *The Democratization of American Christianity* (1989), trace the path to what Butler calls "the antebellum spiritual hothouse." Curtis D. Johnson, *Redeeming America: Evangelicals and the Road to Civil War* * (1993), surveys antebellum evangelicalism as a whole, while Charles C. Cole, Jr., *The Social Ideas of the Northern Evangelists, 1826–1860* (1954); Donald G. Mathews, *Religion in the Old South* (1977); and Anne C. Loveland, *Southern Evangelicals and the Social Order* (1980), assess its sectional components. To really sense the urgency that gripped religious crusaders, one should approach them first hand. *The Autobiography of Lyman Beecher,* ed. Barbara M. Cross (1961), though not really an autobiography, is essential.

Whitney R. Cross, *The Burned-over District: The Social and Intellectual History of Enthusiastic Religion in Western New York, 1800–1850* (1950), is a classic that explores the context and consequences of revivalism. On its leading apostle, see Keith J. Hardman, *Charles Grandison Finney, 1792–1875: Revivalist and Reformer* (1987), *Memoirs of Rev. Charles G. Finney* (1876), and Finney's *Lectures on Revivals of Religion,* ed. William G. McLoughlin (1960).

Clifford S. Griffin, *Their Brothers' Keepers: Moral Stewardship in the United States, 1800–1865* (1960), and Charles I. Foster, *An Errand of Mercy: The Evangelical United Front, 1790–1837* (1960), describe benevolent Christianity. Bertram Wyatt-Brown, *Lewis Tappan and the Evangelical War against Slavery* (1969), is a model study of a central figure.

William Cooper Howells, *Recollections of Life in Ohio from 1813 to 1840* (1963), recounts his spiritual quest. On temperance reform, see W. J. Rorabaugh, *The Alcoholic Republic: An American Tradition* (1979), and Ian Tyrell, *Sobering Up: From Temperance to Prohibition in Antebellum America, 1800–1860* (1979).

Historians have analyzed abolitionists abundantly, even excessively. James Brewer Stewart, *Holy Warriors: The Abolitionists and American Slavery** (1976), is a good introduction. Gilbert Hobbs Barnes, *The Antislavery Impulse* (1933; 1964), focuses on the formative years. Leonard L. Richards, *"Gentlemen of Property and Standing": Anti-Abolition Mobs in Jacksonian America* (1970), probes the sources of anti-abolitionism.

Reading abolitionist writings is a must. Especially revealing is Gilbert H. Barnes and Dwight L. Dumond, eds., *Letters of Theodore Dwight Weld, Angelina Grimké Weld, and Sarah Grimké, 1822–1844* (1934). See also Larry Ceplair, ed., *The Public Years of Sarah and Angelina Grimké: Selected Writings, 1835–1839* (1989); Charles M. Wiltse, ed., *David Walker's Appeal* (1965); and the various editions of William Lloyd Garrison's writings.

Chapter Seven: The Republic of Labor

W. J. Rorabaugh, *The Craft Apprentice: From Franklin to the Machine Age in America* (1986), and Bruce Laurie, *Artisans into Workers: Labor in Nineteenth-Century America** (1989), survey broad changes in work and workplace relations. Clarence H. Danhof, *Change in Agriculture: The Northern United States, 1820–1860* (1969), traces parallel developments on the farm.

Robert F. Dalzell, Jr., *Enterprising Elite: The Boston Associates and the World They Made* (1987), and Ronald Story, *Harvard and the Boston Upper Class: The Forging of an Aristocracy, 1800–1870* (1980), explore the social aspirations of the Boston entrepreneurs. Thomas Dublin, *Women at Work: The Transformation of Work and Community in Lowell, Massachusetts, 1826–1860* (1979) illuminates the world of Lowell's labor force.

Scholarship on Jacksonian social history bears the heavy imprint of theory and ideology. Some current work stresses elements of stasis and traditionalism in early American rural communities, and hence the disruption wrought by the injection of competitive market values into the precommercial village economy. Exactly when this wrenching "transition to capitalism" happened, if indeed it did, is a subject of much debate. Jonathan Prude, *The Coming of Industrial Order: Town and Factory Life in Rural Massachusetts, 1810–1860* (1983), and Christopher Clark, *The Roots of Rural Capitalism: Western Massachusetts, 1780–1860* (1990), focus on the Jackson years. Winifred Barr Rothenberg, *From Market-Places to a Market Economy: The Transformation of Rural Massachusetts, 1750–1850* (1992), offers a refreshing dissent. Allan Kulikoff, *The Agrarian Origins of American Capitalism* (1992), reviews the controversy.

A parallel thrust in labor history paints urban wage-earners as defending autonomy, dignity, community, and republican equality against the onslaught of capitalists wielding evangelical religion as a disciplinary tool. Exemplifying this approach are Sean Wilentz, *Chants Democratic: New York City and the Rise of the American Working Class, 1788–1850* (1984); Alan Dawley, *Class and Community: The Industrial Revolution in Lynn* (1976); and Bruce Laurie, *Working People of Philadelphia, 1800–1850* (1980). Paul E. Johnson, *A Shopkeeper's Millennium: Society and Revivals in Rochester, New York, 1815–1837* (1978), relates revival religion and "Whig repression" to "nascent industrial capitalism," though conceding that "the revival was not a capitalist plot."

These scholars unearth "artisan republicanism" in the same places where William A. Sullivan, *The Industrial Worker in Pennsylvania* (1955), saw progenitors of modern trade unionism; Edward Pessen, *Most Uncommon Jacksonians: The Radical Leaders of the Early Labor Movement* (1967), spied nascent socialism; and Walter Hugins, *Jacksonian Democracy and the Working Class: A Study of the New York Workingmen's Movement, 1829–1837* (1960), found democratizing entrepreneurialism. Teresa Anne Murphy, *Ten Hours' Labor: Religion, Reform, and Gender in Early New England* (1992), and David A. Zonderman, *Aspirations and Anxieties: New England Workers and the Mechanized Factory System, 1815–1850* (1992), discover more variety and complexity in wage-earners' response to factories, employers, coworkers, and evangelists.

In the face of this plethora of views, the documents in volumes 4–6 of John R. Commons et al., eds., *A Documentary History of American Industrial Society* (1910), remain essential.

Paul Conkin, *Prophets of Prosperity: America's First Political Economists* (1980), analyzes Jacksonian economic thinking. Joseph L. Blau, ed., *Social Theories of Jacksonian Democracy* (1954), samples the writings of laborites and other critics. Frances Wright D'Arusmont's addresses are reprinted in *Life, Letters and Lectures, 1834–1844* (1972).

Chapter Eight: The Elevation of Character

On prisons and institutional reform, see David J. Rothman, *The Discovery of the Asylum: Social Order and Disorder in the New Republic* (1971), and Gerald N. Grob, *Mental Institutions in America: Social Policy to 1875* (1973). Gustave de Beaumont and Alexis de Tocqueville, *On the Penitentiary System in the United States and Its Application in France*, has been reprinted (1964), as have the *Reports of the Prison Discipline Society of Boston* (1972), and Joseph Tuckerman's *On the Elevation of the Poor* (1971). On Indian schools see Bernard W. Sheehan, *Seeds of Extinction: Jeffersonian Philanthropy and the American Indian* (1973), and Herman J. Viola, *Thomas L. McKenney: Architect of America's Early Indian Policy, 1816–1830* (1974).

Stuart M. Blumin, *The Emergence of the Middle Class: Social Experience in the American City, 1760–1900* (1989), surveys the role of voluntary associations in self-definition and group formation. Among many case studies detailing the process are Mary Ryan, *Cradle of the Middle Class: The Family in Oneida County, New York, 1790–1865* (1981); Don Harrison Doyle, *The Social Order of a Frontier Community: Jacksonville, Illinois, 1825–1870* (1983); John Mack Faragher, *Sugar Creek: Life on the Illinois Prairie* (1986); William H. Pease and Jane H. Pease, *The Web of Progress: Private Values and Public Styles in Boston and Charleston, 1828–1843* (1985), and *Ladies, Women, and Wenches: Choice and Constraint in Antebellum Charleston and Boston* (1990); Edward Pessen, *Riches, Class, and Power: America before the Civil War* (1973; 1990); Gary B. Nash, *Forging Freedom: The Formation of Philadelphia's Black Community, 1720–1840* (1988); Jay P. Dolan, *The Immigrant Church: New York's Irish and German Catholics, 1815–1865* (1975); and Suzanne Lebsock, *The Free Women of Petersburg: Status and Culture in a Southern Town, 1784–1860* (1984).

On female benevolence and its objects, see Lori D. Ginzberg, *Women and the Work of Benevolence: Morality, Politics, and Class in the Nineteenth-Century United States* (1990); Nancy A. Hewitt, *Women's Activism and Social Change: Rochester, New York, 1822–1872* (1984); Carroll Smith Rosenberg, *Religion and the Rise of the American City: The New York City Mission Movement, 1812–1870* (1971); and Christine Stansell, *City of Women: Sex and Class in New York, 1789–1860* (1986).

Carl F. Kaestle, *Pillars of the Republic: Common Schools and American Society, 1780–1860* (1983), describes the movement toward universal education. See also Carl Bode, *The American Lyceum: Town Meeting of the Mind* (1968), and Anne M. Boylan, *Sunday School: The Formation of an American Institution, 1790–1880* (1988). Document collections on schools and women's role in education include Rush Welter, ed., *American Writings on Popular Education: The Nineteenth Century* (1971); Aileen S. Kraditor, ed., *Up from the Pedestal: Selected Writings in the History of American Feminism* (1968); and Willystine Goodsell, *Pioneers of Women's Education in the United States* (1931).

Kathryn Kish Sklar, *Catharine Beecher: A Study in American Domesticity* (1976), is a model study with wide implications. Jeanne Boydston, Mary Kelley, and Anne Margolis, eds., *The Limits of Sisterhood: The Beecher Sisters on Women's Rights and Woman's Sphere* (1988), presents selected documents.

Jack Larkin, *The Reshaping of Everyday Life* (1988), surveys Jacksonian social change. Barbara Welter, *Dimity Convictions: The American Woman in the Nineteenth Century* (1976); Nancy F. Cott, *The Bonds of Womanhood: "Woman's Sphere" in New England, 1780–1835* (1977); and Jeanne Boydston, *Home and Work: Housework, Wages, and the Ideology of Labor in the Early Republic* (1990), address emerging conceptions of middle-class women's role. Lydia Maria Child, *The Mother's Book* (1831), and *The American Frugal Housewife* (1833), have been reprinted.

Chapter Nine: The Politics of Democracy

Harry L. Watson, *Liberty and Power: The Politics of Jacksonian America** (1990), synthesizes recent scholarship around themes of "republicanism" and the "market revolution." On Jackson's administration see Donald B. Cole, *The Presidency of Andrew Jackson** (1993), and Richard B. Latner, *The Presidency of Andrew Jackson: White House Politics, 1829–1837* (1979). James Parton, *The Presidency of Andrew Jackson,* ed. Robert V. Remini (1967), part of a three-volume biography originally published in 1860, is still enlightening.

Daniel Feller, *The Public Lands in Jacksonian Politics* (1984), unravels congressional maneuvering over the American System. William W. Freehling, *Prelude to Civil War: The Nullification Crisis in South Carolina, 1816–1836* (1966), is a standard account. See also Richard E. Ellis, *The Union at Risk: Jacksonian Democracy, States' Rights, and the Nullification Crisis* (1987), and William W. Freehling, ed., *The Nullification Era: A Documentary Record* (1967). Ross M. Lence, ed., *Union and Liberty: The Political Philosophy of John C. Calhoun* (1992), a volume of writings and speeches, includes the South Carolina *Exposition and Protest* of 1828.

Robert V. Remini, *Andrew Jackson and the Bank War: A Study in the Growth of Presidential Power** (1967), summarizes the struggle, which also forms the centerpiece of Schlesinger's *Age of Jackson* and Sellers's *Market Revolution,* cited in "General Works," and Hammond's *Banks and Politics in America,* cited in Chapter 3. John M. McFaul, *The Politics of Jacksonian Finance* (1972), scrutinizes the Bank War's later stages, and Peter Temin, *The Jacksonian Economy* (1969), reinterprets its consequences. William Gerald Shade, *Banks or No Banks: The Money Issue in Western Politics, 1832–1865* (1972), and James Roger Sharp, *The Jacksonians versus the Banks: Politics in the States after the Panic of 1837* (1970), pursue the controversy in the states. William M. Gouge, *A Short History of Paper Money and Banking* (1833; 1968) and William Leggett, *Democratick Editorials: Essays in Jacksonian Political Economy,* ed. Lawrence H. White (1984), exemplify radical Jacksonianism.

Stanley I. Kutler, *Privilege and Creative Destruction: The Charles River Bridge Case* (1971), is a standard account.

Indian removal as a political issue has yet to be fully studied. Ronald N. Satz, *American Indian Policy in the Jacksonian Era* (1975), is most helpful. Anthony F. C. Wallace, *The Long, Bitter Trail: Andrew Jackson and the Indians** (1993), is a brief account. Michael Paul Rogin, *Fathers and Children: Andrew Jackson and the Subjugation of the American Indian* (1975), offers a wildly provocative psycho-marxist analysis of Jackson and his rapacious democracy. Robert V. Remini, *The Legacy of Andrew Jackson: Essays on Democracy, Indian Removal, and Slavery* (1988), dissents from the usual condemnation.

Chapter Ten: Descent into Discord

The classic account of Jacksonian party organization is Richard P. McCormick, *The Second American Party System: Party Formation in the*

Jacksonian Era (1966). Studies exploring the parties' origins and constituencies in states and localities include Lee Benson, *The Concept of Jacksonian Democracy: New York as a Test Case* (1961); Amy Bridges, *A City in the Republic: Antebellum New York and the Origins of Machine Politics* (1984); Donald B. Cole, *Jacksonian Democracy in New Hampshire, 1800–1851* (1970); Ronald P. Formisano, *The Birth of Mass Political Parties: Michigan, 1827–1861* (1971), and *The Transformation of Political Culture: Massachusetts Parties, 1790s–1840s* (1983); J. Mills Thornton III, *Politics and Power in a Slave Society: Alabama, 1800–1860* (1978); Marc W. Kruman, *Parties and Politics in North Carolina, 1836–1865* (1983); Thomas E. Jeffrey, *State Parties and National Politics: North Carolina, 1815–1861* (1989); and Harry L. Watson, *Jacksonian Politics and Community Conflict: The Emergence of the Second American Party System in Cumberland County, North Carolina* (1981).

Studies of ideological, attitudinal, and psychological bases for party politics include Marvin Meyers, *The Jacksonian Persuasion: Politics and Belief* (1960); Daniel Walker Howe, *The Political Culture of the American Whigs* (1979); Major L. Wilson, *Space, Time, and Freedom: The Quest for Nationality and the Irrepressible Conflict, 1815–1861* (1974); Rush Welter, *The Mind of America, 1820–1860* (1975); John Ashworth, *"Agrarians" and "Aristocrats": Party Political Ideology in the United States, 1837–1846* (1983); and Lawrence Frederick Kohl, *The Politics of Individualism: Parties and the American Character in the Jacksonian Era* (1989).

The Panic of 1837, like that of 1819, remains curiously understudied. No work fully confronts its impact on society and culture. Reginald Charles McGrane, *The Panic of 1837: Some Financial Problems of the Jacksonian Era* (1924), is still useful. Major L. Wilson, *The Presidency of Martin Van Buren** (1984), details the administration's response.

Alison Goodyear Freehling, *Drift toward Dissolution: The Virginia Slavery Debate of 1831–1832* (1982), and William W. Freehling, *The Road to Disunion: Secessionists at Bay, 1776–1854* (1990), explore the paralysis of southern antislavery. Eugene D. Genovese, *The Slaveholders' Dilemma: Freedom and Progress in Southern Conservative Thought, 1820–1860* (1992), and Mitchell Snay, *Gospel of Disunion: Religion and Separatism in the Antebellum South* (1993), trace the turn to proslavery ideology. On the emergence of political antislavery see Richard H. Sewell, *Ballots for Freedom: Antislavery Politics in the United States, 1837–1860* (1976).

Index

Abbott, Jacob, 152

Abbott, John S. C., 153

abolitionists: origins and organization, 110–11; reaction against, 112–13, 199–200, 202; ethos of, 113–14; women, 114, 157–59; petition campaign, 158, 200; Democrats reprove, 183; Calhoun on, 185; Wright attacks, 198; parties oppose, 200; in politics, 200–201; legacy, 203–4. *See also* American Anti-Slavery Society

Academy of Natural Sciences of Philadelphia, 77, 80, 85–86

Adams, John: with Lafayette, 2; death of, 3; appoints Marshall, 45; and Jefferson, 55; and science, 84; proclaims fast, 183

Adams, John Quincy: hosts Lafayette, 3; on John Adams's death, 3; elected president, 10-12, 66, 68–69; attends Owen, 11; commences C&O canal, 21; character and aspirations, 53–54, 70–71, 84, 86, 90, 92, 100; on Calhoun, 59; on Missouri crisis, 63; presidential program, 70–72, 82–83, 143, 164, 166–68; defeated, 72–75, 185–86; on Jackson's appointments, 161; land policy, 163; contrasted with Jackson, 165, 167–68, 175, 177–78, 184; Indian policy, 179–80; and Texas, 203

Adventism, 102–3

agricultural societies, 87, 89–90

Alcott, Bronson, 154

American Anti-Slavery Society: founded, 111, 113; postal campaign, 113, 199, 202; women in, 157, 159; fractures, 200

American Bible Society, 101

American Board of Commissioners for Foreign Missions, 100–101, 144, 181

American Colonization Society, 61, 64-65, 110–11

American Democrat (Cooper), 196

American Education Society, 100–101

American Farmer, 89

American Frugal Housewife (Child), 153

American Geological Society, 85

American Home Missionary Society, 100-101

American Institute of Instruction, 152–53

American Journal of Education, 146, 151

American Journal of Science and Arts, 85–86

American Lyceum, 147, 197

American Peace Society, 110

American Philosophical Society, 85

American Revolution: Jubilee commemoration, 1–5; legacy of, 7–8; and slavery, 60, 112; and suffrage, 67; and science, 84; and religion, 92, 97; and yeoman ideal, 122

American Society for the Promotion of Temperance, 109

American Sunday School Union, 100–101

American System: coined by Clay, 54, 66; in 1824 election, 69; in Adams presidency, 71–74, 82–83; Jackson dismantles, 162–68, 183–86; Whigs

American System (*continued*)
support, 186–87, 193
American Tract Society, 101
Antimasons, 102–3, 185, 198
*Appeal to the Christian Women of the
South* (Grimké), 158
*Appeal to the Coloured Citizens of the
World* (Walker), 112
Appleton, Nathan, 119–20
Arator (Taylor), 57
aristocracy: Revolutionary assault on, 7;
judicial, 52, 90–91; Jefferson fears, 56;
Adams accused of, 70, 74; learned, 90–
93; religious, 98; Antimasons attack,
103; laborites attack, 128–32; bank-
ing feared by, 133–34; denied, 135–37;
Democrats charge, 170–71, 174–75,
177, 188–89, 195; Whigs retort, 193,
195; Hammond defends, 201
asylums, 121, 142–45, 198
Atwater, Caleb, 85
Auburn prison, 140–41
Audubon, John James, 84

Bache, Alexander Dallas, 88
Baltimore and Ohio Railroad, 21–22
Bancroft, George, 76, 151, 160
Bank of the United States, Second: chartered, 40, 54–55; in Panic of 1819,
41, 48; Supreme Court and, 48–50;
Jackson vs., 169–74, 178–79, 185–86;
Whigs and, 186–87; folds, 191; Wright
attacks, 198
banking: charters for, 37–38; postwar
expansion, 39–41, 123–24; in Panic of
1819, 41–43, 45, 48; Virginians attack,
56–58; Workingmen attack, 133–34;
defended, 135–36; Democrats attack,
160, 173–75; 1830s expansion, 171–73,
191; in Panic of 1837, 190–91; parties
debate, 190–94
bankrupt laws, 34–35, 43–44, 46–47
Baptists: and colonization, 64; growth of,
96–99; and slavery, 112–13, 202; and
moral reform, 115, 117
Barlow, Joel, 14, 28
Beaumont, Gustave de, 139, 141
Beecher, Catharine, 100, 155–59, 198
Beecher, Lyman: revivalist, 95–102, 106,
115–16; and millennialism, 100; and

benevolent societies, 100–101, 144;
moral reformer, 107–10; and abolition,
114
benevolent societies: religious, 100–101,
108–9; and behavioral institutions,
138–45; mutual improvement, 146–49
Bentham, Jeremy, 11
Benton, Thomas Hart, 163
Berrien, John Macpherson, 162
Biddle, Nicholas: and science, 84, 88; BUS
president, 169–70, 172, 191; scorns
Jackson, 178–79; extols credit, 194
Birney, James G., 112, 201
Boston Associates. *See* Boston Manufac-
turing Company
Boston Athenaeum, 121
Boston Manufacturing Company, 29–30,
37–38, 119–21, 125
botanic medicine, 91
Bowditch, Nathaniel, 84
Branch, John, 162
Brown, Ethan Allen, 19
Browne, Peter A., 88
Bunker Hill monument, 2–5, 9
Byllesby, Langdon, 129

Calhoun, John Caldwell: nationalist, 19,
53–55, 59–60; on Missouri crisis, 63;
presidential candidate, 66, 68, 70; vs.
American System, 72–73; nullifier,
162–63; and 1833 compromise, 166;
proslavery, 185, 200–202; Democrat,
186
Calvinism, retreat from, 96–99
Campbell, Alexander, 102, 104–6, 155
Campbell, John N., 178
canals: Erie, 14–19; Ohio, 19–20; prolif-
eration, 19–20; Pennsylvania, 20–21;
Chesapeake and Ohio, 21–22; Louis-
ville and Portland, 24
Cane Ridge revival, 96
Carey, Henry, 135–37
Carey, Mathew, 88
Carroll, Charles, 21
Cass, Lewis, 85
Catholics, 100, 115, 117, 188
Charles River Bridge v. Warren Bridge,
176–77
Cherokee Indians, 144, 179–82
Cherokee Nation v. Georgia, 180

Chesapeake and Delaware Canal, 71
Chesapeake and Ohio Canal, 21–22, 71–72
Chevalier, Michel, 136, 171
Cheves, Langdon, 169
Chickasaw Indians, 179–80
Child, Lydia Maria, 153
Choctaw Indians, 144, 179–80
Christianity. *See* religion
Christians (denomination), 97
Church of Jesus Christ. *See* Mormons
Clay, Henry: and Lafayette, 2, 4; nationalist, 53–54, 66, 167; colonizationist, 61, 66, 81; on Missouri crisis, 63; in 1824 campaign, 66, 68–69; in Adams administration, 71–75; on manufacturers, 135; and 1833 compromise, 166; and land bill, 166, 187; 1832 candidate, 169–70; vs. Jackson, 171, 183; Whig leader, 184–87, 193; opposes abolition, 200
Clinton, De Witt: canal advocate, 16–17, 19, 77; and science, 84, 87; and female education, 156
Cogswell, Joseph, 151
Colden, Cadwallader, 15
colonization of free blacks: proposed, 61; debated, 63–64, 199; progress of, 64–65; and Nashoba, 81; abolitionists attack, 110–11; in distribution bill, 166, 187
common law: evolution, 33–36; attacked, 90–91, 131; of marriage, 154
Common Sense (Paine), 8, 12
communitarians, 77–83, 104, 184, 188
Compromise of 1833, 166–67
Congregationalists: Connecticut establishment, 93, 98, 108–9; retreat of, 96–97; and benevolent societies, 101, 117; and temperance, 108–9; and Sabbatarianism, 116; and abolition, 158
Constitution, U.S.: Supreme Court interprets, 45–52, 176–77, 180–81
contracts: in common law, 34–36; Supreme Court on, 46–48, 176–77
Cooper, James Fenimore: on Lafayette, 4; on Americans, 6, 196; on Wright, 11; on commerce, 33; on slavery, 199
Cooper, Thomas, 72–73, 151, 188
corporations: evolution of, 36–38; limited

liability, 38–39; Supreme Court protects, 47–50; Virginians attack, 56–58; Workingmen attack, 133–34; Clay defends, 135; Jacksonians attack, 173–75; Supreme Court circumscribes, 176–77
Coxe, Tench, 28
Crawford, William Harris, 61, 66–70
credit. *See* banking
Creek Indians, 179–80
Crèvecoeur, J. Hector St. John de, 8
Crockett, David, 41
Crowinshield, Richard, 46
Crozer, John P., 93
Cumberland Presbyterians, 97
Cumberland Road, 71

Dane, Nathan, 90
Dartmouth College v. Woodward, 47–48, 176
De Kay, James, 83
Declaration of Independence, 3, 21–22; abolitionists invoke, 112; Carolinians repudiate, 201
Democracy in America (Tocqueville), 134
Democrats: oppose aristocracy, 174–75, 177–78; on church and state, 183; oppose abolition, 183, 200–201; vs. Whigs, 184–90, 193–95; response to depression, 190–93; and locofocos, 198; expansionist, 203
Dickens, Charles, 139–40
Disciples of Christ, 97, 102, 117
Disseminator of Useful Knowledge, 87
Drake, Daniel, 85, 91–92
dueling, 108–9
Dwight, Timothy, 93, 96

Eaton, Amos, 87
Eaton, John Henry, 161, 178, 186
Eaton, Margaret Timberlake (Peggy), 161–62, 178–79, 183
education: at New Harmony, 77, 150–51; and science, 83, 87–89; Workingmen demand, 128, 131–32; consensus for, 137; in House of Refuge, 141–42; Indian, 143–44; lyceums, 146–47; ideas and experiments, 150–53; toward universal, 152–53; female, 155–57, 198; in distribution bill, 166; Whigs favor, 187
Edwards, Jonathan, 96

Ely, Ezra Stiles, 116, 178
Emerson, George B., 150, 153
Emerson, Ralph Waldo: hails America, 6; on Western growth, 116; on associations, 146; lyceum speaker, 147; on Jacksonians, 188; on Panic of 1837, 196
Enlightenment: creed of reason, 79–80; and American science, 84, 88–90; and religious skepticism, 92–93, 97
Episcopalians, 64, 96
Epistle to the Clergy of the Southern States (Grimké), 158
Erie Canal: Lafayette and, 2, 4; plans and construction, 14–17, 21; completion, 17–18; effects of, 18–19, 26, 29, 101; as symbol and example, 30–31, 36; and science, 87; and Sabbatarians, 116
Essay on Slavery and Abolitionism (Beecher), 158–59
Evans, Frederick, 129
Evans, George Henry, 129, 131–32, 137
Evans, Oliver, 22, 27
Everett, Edward, 118, 123, 135–37, 152

Federalists: vs. Republicans, 8–9, 28, 98, 108–9; decline, 55, 59, 66–67; Virginians attack, 56–57; and nationalist program, 58; and Missouri crisis, 63
Fellenberg, Philipp von, 150
Finney, Charles Grandison: revivalist, 98–99, 101–2, 106, 109, 115; moral reformer, 107–8; and abolition, 114
Fisk, Theophilus, 129
Fitch, John, 22
Fletcher v. Peck, 47
Flint, Timothy, 26, 30
Florida treaty (1819), 9, 70, 203
Forsyth, John, 182
Franklin, Benjamin: inventor, 27; represents Enlightenment, 79, 84–85, 87–88; and religion, 92, 97; and temperance, 108; artisan, 122; and self-improvement, 149
Franklin Institute, 87–88
Freemasonry. See Masons
Frelinghuysen, Theodore, 181–82
Fretageot, Marie, 77, 150
Fulton, Robert, 22–23, 28, 50

gag rules, 200–201
Gallatin, Albert, 15–16, 196–97

Garrison, William Lloyd: abolitionist, 110–12, 115, 158, 200; attacks colonization, 110–11; and Indian removal, 181
General Trades' Union (New York), 127-28, 198
General Union for the Promotion of the Christian Sabbath, 116
Genius of Universal Emancipation (Lundy), 110
geologic surveys, 87
Gibbons, Thomas, 23
Gibbons v. Ogden, 50
Gouge, William, 174
Graham, Sylvester, 109
Great Britain: railroads in, 21–22; steamboats in, 22–23; manufacturing in, 27, 29; factory life in, 77, 79, 119–20
Great Seal of the United States, 8
Greek independence struggle, 9
Grimké, Angelina, 112–15, 158–59
Grimké, Sarah, 112, 115, 158–59

Hall, Basil, 140–41
Hamilton, Alexander, 27–28, 40
Hammond, James Henry, 200–202
Harmony Society (Rappites), 78
Harrison, William Henry, 185, 194
Harvard College, 2, 89, 97, 121
Hayne, Robert, 60, 163, 201
Heighton, William, 129
Hicks, Elias, 102
Historical & Philosophical Society of Ohio, 85–86
Hodgson, Adam, 6
Holbrook, Josiah, 146–47
Hone, Philip, 155, 171
Hopkinson, Joseph, 43–44
House of Refuge, 141–42
Howells, William Cooper, 103–4

Independence Day: Jubilee celebration, 1, 3–5, 12–13, 31–32; orations, 5, 110, 116, 136; Owen at New Harmony, 11, 92, 95, 154; canal and railroad commencements, 14, 19–21; at Steubenville, 149
Independent Treasury, 171–72, 192–93, 198
Indian removal: and land booms, 39, 191;

controversy, 179–83, 185; Whigs and, 187, 203
Indian schools, 143–44
internal improvements: expectations from, 14–15, 18–19; Gallatin's plan, 15–16; state programs, 19–22, 191; canals vs. railroads, 21–22; steamboats, 22–25; charters for, 36–39, 176–77; in postwar politics, 54–55, 58–60, 65–67; in Adams years, 71–74; economic impact, 122–26, 167; Jackson vetoes, 164–66; and Panic of 1837, 191, 197. See also American System; canals
Irish immigrants, 115, 121, 148–49

Jackson, Andrew: and Lafayette, 2; 1824 candidate, 10, 66–69, 164; on Panic of 1819, 43–44; nationalist, 53, 67, 163–67; colonizationist, 61, 81; as outsider, 68–69, 74, 178–79; 1828 candidate, 70, 72–75; scientists and, 91–92; Mason, 102; begins administration, 161–62; appointments policy, 161–62, 168, 179; and Eaton scandal, 161–62, 178–79; vs. American System, 163–68, 173, 183–84; and 1833 compromise, 166; land policy, 166, 168; vs. BUS, 169–74, 178–79, 183; Farewell Address, 173, 176, 188–89, 200; vs. money power, 173–75, 195; and Taney, 175–76; anti-clericalism, 178–79, 183–84; Indian policy, 179–83; party leader, 184–89; and Van Buren, 192–93; and abolition, 200; and Texas, 203
Jackson, Rachel, 74, 161, 178
Jefferson, Thomas: hosts Lafayette, 2; death of, 3; on progress, 8, 55; and internal improvement, 16–18; on manufacturing, 28, 79; fears commercialism, 55–58, 134; on slavery and colonization, 60–62, 81, 199, 201; on Missouri, 63; and Owen, 78; reason and science, 79, 84–85; and religion, 92; on farmers, 122, 129; school plans, 150; Jackson echoes, 184
Johnson, Richard Mentor, 44, 144, 183
journeymen, 122–29

Kendall, Amos, 43–44, 200
Kent, James, 67, 90
Key, Francis Scott, 61

King, Rufus, 64

labor unions. See trade societies
laborites. See Workingmen
Ladd, William, 110
Lafayette, Marquis de: return to America, 1–5, 10, 102; in Revolution, 8; on Monroe Doctrine, 9; and Wright, 11–12, 80-81
Lafayette, George Washington, 4
Lancaster, Joseph, 150–51
Lane Seminary, 100, 114
language controversy, 92
Latrobe, Benjamin Henry, 27
Lawrence, Abbott, 73
Lee, Henry, 161
Legaré, Hugh Swinton, 5
Leggett, William, 160, 174, 183, 195
Lesueur, Charles Alexandre, 77
Letters on the Equality of the Sexes (Grimké), 159
Lewis and Clark expedition, 84, 88
Liberator (Garrison), 110–12, 158
Liberia, 65
Liberty Party, 201
Lieber, Francis, 139, 141, 153
Lincoln, Abraham, 147, 204
List, Friedrich, 29
Literary and Philosophical Society of New York, 84–85
Livingston, Edward, 142
Livingston, Robert, 50
locofocos, 198
Long, Stephen H., 87–88
Louisville and Portland Canal, 24
Lovejoy, Elijah, 115
Lowell, Francis Cabot, 29, 37, 119–21
Lowell, Massachusetts, 29–31, 119–21, 187, 197
Lowndes, William, 54
Lundy, Benjamin, 110
Luther, Seth, 129–30
Lyceum of Natural History of New York, 83, 85
lyceums, 146–47, 149, 151–52, 197

Maclure, William: joins Owen, 77, 80; sponsors science, 83–87; religious skeptic, 92; at New Lanark, 138–40; school reformer, 150–51, 156
Madison, James: and Lafayette, 21; and

Madison, James (*continud*)
  internal improvement, 16, 54–55, 58;
  nationalist, 40, 54, 59; appoints Story,
  45; colonizationist, 61; and Owen, 78,
  81; proclaims fast, 183
Magdalen Society, 109
Mann, Horace, 152
manufacturing: early efforts, 26–28;
  spread of, 28–30; corporate charters,
  37–39; science and, 87–88; changing
  organization of, 119–26; aristocracy
  charged, 134–35. *See also* tariff
Marshall, John: on internal improvement,
  20; Supreme Court rulings, 45–52, 176,
  180–81; colonizationist, 61; death of,
  175
Martineau, Harriet, 139–40
Masons, 2–3, 5, 102–3, 148
Massachusetts Bank, 38
Massachusetts General Hospital, 89, 121
Massachusetts Society for Promoting
  Agriculture, 89
Mather, Cotton, 107
Maysville Road veto, 164
McCulloch, James W., 49
McCulloch v. Maryland, 48–51
McKenney, Thomas L., 144
McLean Asylum for the Insane, 121
Mechanics' Union of Trade Associations
  (Philadelphia), 126–27
medicine, 89–92
Methodists: and colonization, 64; expan-
  sion, 96–99; and moral reform, 109,
  115, 117; and slavery, 112–13, 202
Mexican War, 203–4
Miller, William, 102
Missouri Compromise, 62–65
Monroe, James: and Lafayette, 1; Monroe
  Doctrine, 9, 70; presidency, 10, 66, 161;
  and Owen, 11; and internal improve-
  ment, 20, 55, 58, 71; colonizationist,
  61, 81; and religion, 97
Moore, Ely, 128, 198
Moral Physiology (Owen), 154
Morgan, William, 102
Mormons, 102–4
Morris, Gouverneur, 15
Mother's Book (Child), 153
Murphey, Archibald D., 151

Nashoba, 80–82, 155, 199

National Republicans, 186
National Trades' Union, 127–28, 198
Neef, Joseph, 77, 150–51
New American Practical Navigator
  (Bowditch), 84
New England Journal of Medicine, 89
New Harmony: plans for, 10–12, 76–80,
  138, 154, 197; science at, 77, 85–88, 92;
  collapse, 80–83, 93, 105; schools,
  150–52
New Harmony Gazette, 92, 129
New Lanark, 10, 77–80, 138–39
New York House of Refuge, 141–42
New York Institution for the Promotion
  of the Arts and Sciences, 85
Niles' Weekly Register (Hezekiah Niles):
  on progress, 9, 24, 30–31; on Panic of
  1819, 43–44; on enterprise, 123
Noah, Mordecai, 17
Notes on the State of Virginia (Jefferson),
  84–85
Notions of the Americans (Cooper), 6,
  196
Noyes, John Humphrey, 81
nullification, 162–63, 165–66, 185–86
Nuttall, Thomas, 84

Oberlin College, 114
Ogden v. Saunders, 47
Ohio Canal, 19–20
*On the Penitentiary System in the United
  States* (Tocqueville), 139, 141
Osborn v. Bank of the United States,
  50–51
Owen, Robert: in Washington, 10–12, 76,
  81–82; declares mental independence,
  11, 92, 95, 154; at New Lanark, 77–78,
  138–40; New Harmony plans, 78–80;
  failure, 80–83; departs, 86; creed of
  progress, 90, 93, 100, 143, 198; debates
  Campbell, 104–6, 155; and education,
  150
Owen, Robert Dale: doubts progress,
  30–31; skeptic, 92; in New York, 129;
  education reformer, 131–32; and sexual
  reform, 154–55; Democrat, 198

packet boats, 26
Paine, Thomas, 8, 12, 28, 92, 97
Panic of 1819, 9, 23–24, 28; causes, 40–

41; reaction and relief, 41–45; effects, 44–45, 56, 59–60; legacy, 45, 134, 174
Panic of 1837: feared, 172; breaks, 173, 190; parties respond, 190–94; prompts soul-searching, 195–97; saps reforms, 197–98, 200–201
Peale, Charles Willson, 88
Peale, Franklin, 88
Pennsylvania Eastern State Penitentiary, 140–41
Pennsylvania Mainline Canal, 20–21
Pestalozzi, Johann, 150–51
Philanthropist ("boatload of knowledge"), 77–78, 86
Phiquepal, William S., 77, 150
Plan of Union, 96
Polk, James K., 186
Presbyterians: and colonization, 64; and revivals, 96–99; and benevolent societies, 101, 117; and temperance, 108; and abolition, 112, 202; and Sabbatarianism, 116
presidential campaigns: of 1800, 8; of 1824, 10–12, 66–70, 186; of 1828, 70–75, 185–86; of 1832, 169–70, 185–87; of 1836, 185–87; of 1840, 185–86, 194; of 1844, 186
Prison Discipline Society (Boston), 141–42, 153
prison reform, 139–45, 198
public lands: relief for purchasers, 43–45; and colonization, 64; canal grants, 72–73, 164; in 1828 campaign, 162–63; in Webster-Hayne debate, 163; Clay's distribution bill, 166, 187; Jackson's policy, 166

Quakers, 102, 140

Rafinesque, Constantine, 84
railroads, 21–22
Randolph, John, 58, 61, 65, 67
Rapp, George, 78
religion: and science, 92–94; colonial legacy, 95–96; revivals, 96–102; philanthropic, 100–101; creedal competition, 102–6; and moral reform, 106–9, 114–17, 144; and abolition, 110–14, 157–59, 202; and self-improvement, 125, 146, 148–49; and sex roles, 154–55, 158–59;

Jackson and, 178–79, 183; and Indian removal, 179, 181–83; Democrats and, 183, 188; Whigs and, 187–88. *See also under names of denominations*
Republicans (political party), 8–9, 28, 66–67, 98
Rigdon, Sidney, 104
Ritchie, Thomas, 58
Roane, Spencer, 58
Ruffin, Edmund, 89
Rumsey, James, 22
Rush, Benjamin, 84, 91, 108, 150
Rush, Richard, 61, 72
Russell, William, 151

Sabbatarians, 116, 144, 183, 187
Say, Thomas, 77, 83, 92
Schoolcraft, Henry Rowe, 85
schools. *See* education
science: Adams commends, 70–71; growth, 77, 83–86; orientation, 86–90; and law, 90–91; and medicine, 91–92; and religion, 92–94
Scotch-Irish immigrants, 96
Sedgwick, Theodore, 175
Shakers, 78, 82, 97, 104, 129
Shreve, Henry Miller, 23–24
Silliman, Benjamin, 84–86, 89–90, 93
Simpson, Stephen, 129, 131–33
Sing Sing prison, 140
Skidmore, Thomas, 129, 131–32
Skinner, John S., 89
Skinner, Thomas, 100
Slater, Samuel, 27, 30
slavery: southern views, 60–62, 64–65, 199–202; in Missouri crisis, 62–63; northern views, 63–64; and approach to Civil War, 202–4. *See also* abolitionists; colonization of free blacks
Smith, Adam, 57
Smith, Joseph, Jr., 102, 104, 106
Society for Establishing Useful Manufactures, 28
Society for the Encouragement of Faithful Domestic Servants, 149
Society for the Prevention of Pauperism, 142
Society for the Promotion of Industry, Frugality, and Temperance, 125
Society of Friends. *See* Quakers

Speakman, John, 80
specie circular, 174
Springfield armory, 28
stay laws, 42, 190
steamboats, 22–25, 50, 87
Stevens, John, 23
Stoddard, Solomon, 96
Story, Joseph: on law and commerce, 34–
    36, 45, 51; on Supreme Court, 45- 48,
    50–51, 177; on law and science, 90
Strickland, William, 88
strikes, 121, 126–28
Sturgis, Josiah, 46
Sturges v. Crowinshield, 46
suffrage expansion, 61, 67–69
Supreme Court: commercial rulings, 45–
    52, 62, 175–77; criticized, 51–52, 58,
    65; Cherokee cases, 180–81. See also
    under case names
Swartwout, Samuel, 161

Tallmadge, James, Jr., 62–63
Taney, Roger, 175–77
Tappan, Arthur: philanthropist, 101, 106,
    109, 115–16, 181; abolitionist, 111–14;
    merchant, 124; bankrupt, 197
Tappan, Benjamin: and Lewis, 20, 106,
    108, 115; scientist, 85–86, 92
Tappan, Lewis: on improvement, 19–
    20; Christian reformer, 101, 106, 108,
    115–16, 181; abolitionist, 111–14, 200;
    merchant, 124
tariff: of 1816, 54–55, 59; planters op-
    pose, 56–60, 65, 162–63; of 1824, 59;
    in 1824 campaign, 66–67; of 1828, 72–
    73; Jackson and, 164–66; of 1832, 165;
    nullified, 165–66; 1833 compromise,
    166–67. See also American System
Taylor, John: agricultural reformer, 57,
    89; planter spokesman, 57–58, 79, 134;
    and slavery, 60–61; Jackson echoes,
    174, 188
temperance, 108–10, 116, 146, 187
Texas controversy, 202–3
Thomson, Samuel, 91
Thoughts on African Colonization (Garri-
    son), 111
Tocqueville, Alexis de: on religion, 95; on
    manufacturing, 134; on prisons, 139,
    141; on associations, 146

Tompkins, Daniel, 1
town promotion and rivalry, 20–22,
    25–26
trade societies, 126–28, 197
Transcendentalists, 154
transportation. See internal improvements
Trimble, Robert, 47
Trolloppe, Frances, 6–7, 25, 104–5
Troost, Gerard, 77
Troy Female Seminary, 5, 156
Tuckerman, Joseph, 143
Turner, Nat, 112, 199
Tyranny Unmasked (Taylor), 57

Unitarians, 97–98,
United States Military Academy, 89
Universalists, 97

Van Buren, Martin: as Jacksonian, 103;
    in cabinet, 161; president, 182–83,
    185–87; response to depression, 190-
    94; defeated, 194; Wright and, 198;
    opposes abolition, 200; and Texas, 203
Verplanck, Gulian, 35
Views of Society and Manners in America
    (Wright), 11

Walker, David, 112
War of 1812, results, 9, 28, 39, 54–55, 70,
    90
Washington, Bushrod, 61
Washington, George: and Lafayette, 2, 4;
    and canals, 21; and religion, 97, 183;
    and Mason, 102
Webster, Daniel: patriotic orator, 3–5, 9;
    Supreme Court litigant, 48, 50–51,
    177; colonizationist, 61; and American
    System, 73; on Jackson's election, 75;
    lyceum speaker, 147; debates Hayne,
    163, 201; and parties, 185; opposes
    Texas, 203
Weld, Theodore Dwight, 114–15
Whigs: formation, 184–86; vs. Demo-
    crats, 186–90, 194–95; respond to de-
    pression, 190, 192–194; and abolition,
    200–201; and expansion, 203
Whitney, Eli, 27
Willard, Emma Hart, 5, 138, 156–57
Wilson, Alexander, 84
Wirt, William, 103, 185

Wolcott, Oliver, 20
women: abolitionist, 114, 157–59; work-
    ing, 120, 122–25; in trade societies,
    127; wives and mothers, 138, 153–57; in
    associations, 146–48; rights and role
    debated, 154–59, 198–99; teachers,
    156–57
Worcester State Lunatic Hospital, 142

Worcester v. Georgia, 180–81
Workingmen, 127–34; Everett on, 136;
    Jacksonians and, 174, 184, 198
Wright, Frances: in America, 11–12; and
    Nashoba, 80–82, 199; as Jacksonian,
    92, 198; as laborite, 118, 129, 137;
    on schools, 131–32, 155; on sexual
    equality, 155–57, 159

BOOKS IN THE SERIES

The Twentieth-Century American City (2d ed.) Jon C. Teaford

American Workers, American Unions (2d ed.) Robert H. Zieger

A House Divided: Sectionalism and Civil War, 1848–1865 Richard H. Sewell

Liberty under Law: The Supreme Court in American Life William M. Wiecek

Winning Is the Only Thing: Sports in America since 1945 Randy Roberts and James Olson

America's Half-Century: United States Foreign Policy in the Cold War (2d ed.) Thomas J. McCormick

American Anti-Communism: Combating the Enemy Within, 1830–1970 Michael J. Heale

The Culture of the Cold War (2d ed.) Stephen J. Whitfield

America's Welfare State: From Roosevelt to Reagan Edward D. Berkowitz

The Debate over Vietnam (2d ed.) David W. Levy

And the Crooked Places Made Straight: The Struggle for Social Change in the 1960s David Chalmers

Medicine in America: A Short History James H. Cassedy

The Republic of Mass Culture: Journalism, Filmmaking, and Broadcasting in America since 1941 James L. Baughman

Uneasy Partners: Big Business in American Politics, 1945–1990 Kim McQuaid

The Best War Ever: America in World War II Michael C. C. Adams

America's Right Turn: From Nixon to Bush William C. Berman

Industrializing America: The Nineteenth Century Walter Licht

Moralists and Modernizers: America's Pre–Civil War Reformers Steven Mintz

The Jacksonian Promise: America, 1815–1840 Daniel Feller

Democracy and Diplomacy: The Impact of Domestic Politics on U.S. Foreign Policy, 1789–1994 Melvin Small

Library of Congress Cataloging-in-Publication Data

Feller, Daniel, 1950–
    The Jacksonian promise : America 1815–1840 / Daniel Feller.
        p.   cm. — (The American moment)
    Includes index.
    ISBN 0-8018-5167-x (h : alk. paper). — ISBN 0-8018-5168-8 (pbk :
alk. paper)
    1. United States—History—1815–1861.   I. Title.   II. Series.
E338.F45   1996
973.5—dc20   95-18528